THE BEST OF RUSSIAN HUMOR

over 1,500 original Russian jokes,
quips, quotes, and anecdotes

Compiled, translated, and edited by **Vladimir Godunok**
Copyedited by **David McCabe**
Illustrated by **Sergei Kovalenko**

Fragments from the *Announcement of the Coronation of the Emperor Nicolas II* by
Ivan Ropet-Petrov (1845-1908)--Russian architect and artist, and a leading expo-
nent of Neo-Russian style--are used in the cover design.

Published by Russian Doll Publishing

Printed in Canada

Canadian Cataloguing in Publication Data

Main entry under title:

The best of Russian Humor

ISBN 0-9685358-0-1

1.Russian wit and humor. I. Godunok, Vladimir, 1968-

PN6210.B47 1999   891.78'02   C99-932001-7

Quantity discounts are available on bulk purchases of this book for reselling, educational purposes, gifts etc. Find out more by contacting the publisher: Russian Doll Publishing, P.O.Box 25384, London, ON, N6C 6B1, Tel: (519)-679-9139, Fax: (519)-679-9009, E-mail: orders@russian-humor.com, or visit us at www.russian-humor.com

Dedicated with love and respect to all creators
of these jokes—the people of Russia and
countries of the former Soviet Union

CONTENTS

FOREWORD

This collection of Russian jokes, quips, one-liners, humorous quotes, and anecdotes is a result of my modest attempt to bring to English-speaking readers some of the most popular tidbits of Russian wit and everyday humor.

Heard on the street, at home, in the workplace, and lately seen on many Russian Web sites, these jokes represent an integral part of Russian folk humor and provide some candid insights into the Russian character.

The short, humorous stories—real or fictitious—known in Russia as *anekdoty* (compare with English "anecdotes") that comprise most of this book are no more than a drop in the ocean of Russian humor. Many stories had to be left out, some because of the heavy dose of context-related commentaries that would have been required for their successful delivery, others because of the language (especially pun-based) differences between Russian and English, differences which would invariably destroy the intended comic effect when translated. As a result, even readers with little or no knowledge of Russian life will find many original jokes that will leave them in stitches.

What is so special about Russian humor? Perhaps it is the richness of the Russian language, a language that boasts a wide literary heritage; or perhaps it's the multi-ethnicity of the Russian society, which is formed by about 150 distinct ethnic groups. Or maybe it's the topsy-turvy nature of Russian history, a history that has created a phenomenon known as "laughter through tears". It is the history that has been characterized by a series of extremes: from unlimited freedom to total serfdom, from the heights of morals to the depths of disgrace, from communism to an ugly form of capitalism. Or could it be that special, unique destiny, that Russians believe their country to have.

Whatever the case, I hope this collection will help readers to find some clues that will help them to better understand the mysterious Russian soul in a witty and humorous way.

Vladimir Godunok

RUSSIANS ABOUT THEMSELVES AND OTHERS

What is good for a Russian may be deadly for a foreigner.
—An old Russian saying

A foreigner walks down a narrow, unpaved, and muddy village street, condemning his decision to visit Russian countryside. What he sees next only confirms his attitude.

A man, who looks very happy, is walking toward him. He is wearing only one boot; his other foot is bare. The foreigner asks him, "Can't you people fix your streets? Look, you've lost your boot!"

"No, I just found it!" the local man answers, beaming broadly.

"Did you have any problems with your English in Canada, Ivan?"

"No, I didn't have any; the Canadians did."

A man wakes up. "Why do I have this strong urge to work?" he wonders to himself. "Well, I'd better take a nap; that should take care of it."

He won't do anything until a roasted rooster gives him a nibble.

—Russian saying

During the Second World War an American, a Frenchman, and a Russian were captured by the Germans and held as prisoners. Before execution the Germans agreed to grant one last wish to each prisoner.

"I want a case of beer," the American said.

"I want a bottle of champagne and a woman," the Frenchman said.

"I want a good kick in the behind," the Russian said.

"What?" the Germans asked in surprise.

"Yes, just kick me in my behind," the Russian repeated.

Keeping their promise, the Germans chose their strongest man. The force of his kick was so powerful that the Russian flew right into the German guards, knocking them off their feet. The Russian immediately grabbed their guns and shot his way out of the German stronghold, taking with him the American and the Frenchman.

"If you're such a good fighter, why did you wait so long, Ivan?" the American and the Frenchman asked the Russian, once they were a safe distance from the Germans. "They could have killed all of us!"

"Well, such is our Russian character," Ivan answered. "We won't think hard until we get a good kick in the behind."

A man who has emigrated to the States returns to visit his old country. His nephew asks the visitor to help him with his English lesson.

"But I don't speak any English," the visitor replies.

"Come on!" The relatives are surprised. "You've lived in America for ten years, and you don't speak English?!"

"Well," the visitor explains, "I've lived on Brighton Beach all that time. I've never gone to America."

Q: How can agricultural crop output be increased in Rus-

sia?

A: They could stop pouring shit on each other and start taking it into the fields.

Searching for some hot material in support of his report on the meager living conditions of ordinary Russians, a foreign journalist walks into a local bar favored by working-class folk. He approaches the drunkest visitor and politely asks for an interview.

"Go ahead!" the drunk says.

"In my country every family has a car," the journalist begins, "What about you? Do you have a car?"

"Ye-e-s-s? I do," the drunk says proudly. "In fact, I might have not one car, but two!"

"It's not possible. How could it be?"

"Well, say I hit you with this mug right now. (Hic.) They will send one car for me and another one for you in no time."

"**D**id you hear Ivan is working again?"
"I knew he'd do anything for money...".

A Russian tourist gets lost in Amsterdam. With no knowledge of Dutch and with only a Russian-English phrasebook, he ends up in a brothel instead of the embassy.

"What would you like, sir?" the damsels ask him.

"I want Russian consul."

"How about a girl?"

"I want Russian consul."

"Maybe a boy?"

"No, I want Russian consul."

"Okay, how much money do you have?"

Q: Back in the USSR, why did they always plan everything except population growth?

A: Because the Soviet government couldn't nationalize the means of production.

An American, a Canadian, and a Russian are the only survivors of a plane crash, somewhere in the Pacific Ocean. They manage to swim to a small island nearby. Lady Luck continues to smile on them—they catch the magical Golden Fish!

"Let me go back into the ocean, good men, and I will grant each one of you three wishes," the Golden Fish says.

So the American asks for a lot of money, a beautiful wife, and a trip back home.

The Canadian asks for a lot of money, a government job, and a trip back home.

The Russian, in his turn, says, "I want an endless fountain of beer on this island. I want the ocean to be full of smoked herring. And I want those two back."

In a country as big as Russia, New Year celebrations start somewhere in the Far East and finish somewhere under the table.

Attending a business conference, a Russian businessman takes a stand at the buffet, where he commences to devour food. Noticing that his American colleague isn't eating at all, the Russian asks, "Why don't you eat, John?"

"Thanks, Ivan, but I'm not hungry."

"Look at this food! It is simply irresistible, and it's free!"

"Doesn't matter; I eat only when I'm hungry," replies John.

"Just like an animal, ha!?"

A Hollywood star was once staying at a Moscow hotel. One night, as she was taking a bath, a man dressed in dirty work overalls walked into her suite without knocking and headed straight for the bathroom. Once there, and without paying the slightest bit of attention to her, he took out his tools and began to work on the pipes next to the bathtub.

"What are you doing here?! Let me get out of here first!" the shocked star complained, still sitting in the tub.

But the man simply continued his work without saying a word.

Flabbergasted, our star continued to stare at the man until the water turned cool. That was the last straw! She climbed out of the tub and, stark naked, stepped between the man and his work.

The man took one short look at the star, shrugged and said, "What, you've never seen a Russian plumber?"

A Russian and an American are talking: "When I'm in a good mood I drive a red car," the American boasts. "When I'm feeling down, I drive a black car. And when I go for a vacation overseas, I always pick a brightly colored car."

"Things are much easier in Russia," answers the Russian. "If you're in a good mood, say after a few too many shots at a bar, they'll give you a ride in a yellow car with a blue stripe (the colors of the Russian police cruiser). If you feel bad, the car will be white with a red stripe. I was abroad only once, and there I drove a tank."

A Russian and a Ukrainian are arguing about whose vodka is better. "Everyone knows Russian vodka is the best in the world," the Russian insists.

"The other day, my wife and I had a liter of *horilka* (Ukrainian vodka)," answers the Ukrainian. "And it went down so smoothly that the next morning we were able to go to a church and recite all the prayers."

"So what?" The Russian is obviously unimpressed.

"Well, considering that we're Jewish...".

One week in a small town:
Monday. Russians fight Ukrainians in a local bar.
Tuesday. Ukrainians fight Russians in the same bar.
Wednesday. Russians fight Ukrainians.
Thursday. Ukrainians fight Russians.
Friday. Russians fight Ukrainians.
Saturday. Moishe, the bar's owner, closes the place for Sabbath.

What nationality was Jesus?
Three proofs that Jesus was Jewish:
1) He went into his father's business.
2) He lived at home until the age of 33.
3) He was sure his mother was a virgin, and his mother was sure he was God.

Three proofs that Jesus was Irish:
1) He never got married.
2) He never held a steady job.
3) His last request was a drink.

Three proofs that Jesus was Puerto Rican:
1) His first name was Jesus.
2) He was always in trouble with the law.
3) His mother didn't know who his father was.

Three proofs that Jesus was Italian:
1) He talked with his hands.
2) He had wine with every meal.
3) He worked in the construction trades.

Three proofs that Jesus was Black:
1) He called everybody Brother.
2) He had no permanent address.
3) Nobody would hire him.

And finally, three proofs that Jesus was Russian:
1) Despite the fact that he was a firm believer, he never attended church.
2) He didn't have any property, but he always had money for wine.
3) Whenever he had some wine with his friends he liked to talk about the purpose of life.

A fly ends up in a pint of beer. Here's what happens next:
An Englishman pays for his beer and leaves the bar disappointed.

A Frenchman calls the waiter and asks for a replacement.

A German spills his beer on the floor and asks for a replacement.

An Italian fishes the fly out and drinks the beer.

A Chinese man first eats the fly, then drinks his beer.

A Bulgarian sips his beer carefully, in such a way as to avoid drinking the fly. Then he calls the waiter, loudly complains about the fly, and leaves without paying.

A Russian drinks his beer in the same manner as the Bulgarian, then calls the waiter and demands a free refill.

A Jewish man orders a soft drink instead, collects all the flies that were picked out from beers by aforementioned patrons, walks over to the Russian, who is drunk by now, and offers to sell him some "nice flies" for a "very reasonable price."

A cannibal tribe captures three shipwrecked men: an Englishman, a Frenchman, and a Russian. The tribe's chieftain, who is craving for the company of civilized men but is also hungry, says to his captives, "Any of you who can tell me a story that I find hard to believe will be spared his life."

"One day," the Englishman begins, "an English gentleman was late for work…".

"An Englishman was late?!" the chieftain exclaims. "Get lost!"

"A French gentleman once refused to make a love to a beautiful lady…", continues the Frenchman.

"Unbelievable!" the chieftain exclaims. "You get lost too!"

The Russian now takes his turn. "Once, a Russian gentleman…".

"That's enough! You can go! A Russian gentleman?! What an unbelievable phrase!"

Q: How does a wife react when her husband finds her in bed with a stranger?

A: A French wife says, "Jean, move aside…Paul, jump in!"

A Ukrainian wife says, "Petro, is that you? Then who is this man?"

Finally, a Russian wife says (while covering her face from

her husband's fists), "Ivan, please, just spare my face. I have to go to work tomorrow!"

Three friends—a Russian, a Jewish man, and a Ukrainian—are making plans for a weekend together. "Let's get together at my place," the Ukrainian says. "My mother has just visited me and she left a lot of great food in the fridge."

"In that case, drinks are on me!" the Russian says. "I'll bring a case of vodka."

"And I'll bring my brother," offers the Jewish man.

A Russian, a Ukrainian, and a Belorussian farmer are invited to attend an official reception. All three farmers find a large nail sticking out from the fine leather chairs they're offered to sit in. Here are their thoughts:

The Russian, throwing the nail out: "Why the hell would they put that nail in my chair?"

The Ukrainian, pulling the nail out and putting it in his pocket: "I'll keep it; this nail will come in handy."

The Belorussian, bracing himself while sitting on the nail during the entire reception: "They must have put it here for a purpose."

A Gypsy man sends his son out to buy him a pack of cigarettes.

"Aren't you going to give me the money, dad?" the son asks.

"Any fool can buy with money, son," the father says.

The son returns, but he gives his father an empty pack of cigarettes. "Where are the cigarettes? This pack is empty!" the father exclaims.

Replies the son: "Well, any fool can smoke the one with cigarettes, father."

According to statistics, the Japanese represent the nation that sits most often on tatami mats; the Americans, on soft coaches;

the Jewish, on suitcases; and Russians, on stone prison benches.

Q: What does a girl say after her first night with a man?

A: After she gets up and lights a cigarette, an English girl says: "I can imagine my mother's face if she saw me smoking."

A French girl says: "What's your name, mon ami?"

A Russian girl says: "Johnny, my dear, let's get married."

Two friends—one Jewish and the other Russian—get together for a few glasses of vodka. All the food they have between them amounts to two pickled cucumbers—one small and one big, brought by the Russian. After their first glass, the Jewish fellow grabs the bigger cucumber for himself and bites a chunk out of it.

"What are you doing?" the Russian exclaims. "Shame on you, Abram. You never think about your friends; you always take the best for yourself."

"Well, Ivan, what would *you* do in this situation if you were me?"

"I would take the small one!" the Russian answers.

"See, I knew that! That's why I left it for you."

A Russian and an American die and they both go to hell. Satan asks them, "Which hell do you prefer, the Russian or American?"

"What's the difference?" the Russian asks.

"In the American hell, you will be forced to eat one bucket of waste every day; in the Russian, two," Satan explains.

The American decides to go to the American hell. The Russian, being a patriot, chooses the Russian hell.

One year later the two men run into one another. "How's life?" the Russian asks.

"Can't complain," the American answers. "I eat one bucket of waste every morning, and then I'm free for the rest of the day. What about you?"

"It couldn't be better!" the Russian explains. "Just like back on earth! They're either late with waste deliveries, or they're having bucket shortages."

An American, a Jewish man, and a Russian each go for an x-ray. The results show the following:

The American has women in his heart, a steak in his stomach, and a Black neighbor in his liver. The Jewish man has his wife in his heart, a chicken in his stomach, and a tax collector in his liver. The Russian has his Motherland in his heart, vodka in his stomach, and his mother-in-law in his liver.

After World War II, during the time of the Japanese economic miracle, a group of Japanese engineers was invited to visit a Soviet factory.

"What did you like about our country?" the Soviet workers asked the Japanese group when their visit was over.

"Your children!" the Japanese said politely.

"What else did you like about our country?"

"Your children," the Japanese replied again, politely.

"Okay, we like our children too. But was there anything else that you liked here?"

"Your children," the Japanese insisted. "We won't comment on anything else you make."

A Frenchman makes a bet with an Englishman that he can get any tourist to jump from the Eiffel tower.

"Okay," the Englishman says, once they've reached the top of the tower. "There's a Yankee. Go right ahead."

The Frenchman then says to the American, "Sir, I just heard a news flash form the States. It says that you're bankrupt." Hearing this news, the American jumps.

"That guy must be an Italian," the Englishman says, pointing to the next man.

"Excuse me, sir," the Frenchman says, approaching the Italian. "I just heard a news flash. It says that you're bankrupt."

"So what?" the Italian responds.

"However," the Frenchman continues, "they also say your wife has been seen with another man."

"Mama mia!" the Italian exclaims, and he jumps from the

tower.

"Okay, but now you're in trouble," the Englishman says, pointing to a man with an arrogant look on his face. "I think that guy's a Russian."

"Excuse me, sir," the Frenchman says, approaching the Russian. "I just learned that you're bankrupt."

"I don't really care," the Russian says. "My whole country is bankrupt."

"And your wife is with another man…".

"I don't care," the Russian says again. "I know she's been cheating."

"But you won't jump from this tower because of it, will you, sir? You won't jump because you know, it is forbidden."

"Forbidden?!" the Russian yells cockily. "Oh yeah?? Just watch me…".

When an Englishman visits his friends, he brings along his dignity.

When a Frenchman visits his friends, he brings along his wife and children.

When a Jewish man visits his friends, he brings along a cake.

When a Russian visits his friends, he brings along his wife.

When an Englishman returns from visiting his friends, he carries his dignity.

When a Frenchman returns from visiting his friends, he carries in his arms a new lover.

When a Jewish man returns from visiting his friends, he carries back his cake.

When a Russian returns from visiting his friends, he is drunk and is being carried by his wife.

And this is what they think to themselves:

The Englishman: "I hope I didn't lose my dignity."

The Frenchman: "I wonder who my wife left with?"

The Jewish man: "Who shall I visit next before this cake turns stale?"

The Russian: "That bastard gave me a black eye. Well, at least I left him with two missing teeth!"

One day Neptune, the god of the sea, decided to have some fun. He stopped an English ship, grabbed its captain off the deck, and said to him, "I have a dozen bottles of vodka. Tell me, how many could you drink in one sitting?"

"One or two," the English captain said.

The sea roared as Neptune continued, holding back his disappointment with the captain. "I have a dozen daughters. Tell me, how many of them could you satisfy in one night?"

"One or two, I guess," the captain replied timidly.

Neptune then got mad at the English captain and sent a deadly storm down on his ship.

Neptune next stopped an American ship. He grabbed its captain off the bridge and asked him the same questions.

"I can drink six bottles of vodka in one sitting," the American captain said. "And I'm pretty sure I can satisfy half of your dozen daughters in one night."

Apparently, that answer didn't make Neptune too happy either. He sank the American ship too.

Disappointed with people in general, Neptune was ready to call it quits and return to the depths of his watery kingdom when, suddenly, out on the horizon, he spotted an old rusty ship, one that was barely seaworthy. This 'ship' happened to be a Russian barge. Neptune grabbed its half-drunk captain and asked him, "I have a dozen bottles of vodka. How many could you drink in one sitting?"

"Thirteen," the Russian captain replied, without any hint of surprise on his mellow face.

"I said I have only twelve bottles."

"Well, when I go to visit my friends, I always bring one bottle with me."

"Sounds good! I have a dozen daughters," Neptune continued, thinking that perhaps he had finally found a decent competitor. "How many of them could you satisfy in one night?"

"Thirteen."

"But I have only twelve…".

"Well, I like you too, old man!"

A growing airline is hiring more pilots to fly its new jet.

Three candidates—a German, an American, and a Russian—show up for an interview. "Are you familiar with this type of jet?" the official who conducts the interview asks the German.

"Yes," he answers, "I've been flying them for the past three years."

"What are your salary requirements?"

"Three thousand dollars."

"Could you tell me how you would spend this money?"

"Well, I'd spend one thousand on my life insurance, another one thousand I would set aside for my retirement, and the third thousand I would give to my wife for our living expenses."

"Thank you sir. We will call you if we hire you."

The American is next. "Are you familiar with this type of jet?" the interviewer asks.

"No," the American replies, "but in the course of my career I have flown many jets. So a few weeks on the simulator should be enough training for me."

"What are your salary requirements?"

"Six thousand dollars."

"Could you tell me how you would spend your salary?"

"Well, I'd spend two thousand on my life insurance, another two thousand I would set aside for my retirement, and the rest I would give to my wife for our living expenses."

"Thank you sir. We will let you know later whether you're hired or not."

The Russian is last. "Are you familiar with this type of jet?" the interviewer asks him.

"Yes," he answers, "I flew in one as a passenger."

"What are your salary requirements?"

"Nine thousand dollars."

The interviewer looks at the Russian surprisingly and, more out of curiosity than anything else, he asks, "Sir, before your interview, we met with a perfectly qualified German pilot, who asked for only three thousand. How did you arrive at this nine thousand dollars?"

"Well, I need to keep three thousand for myself, give another three thousand to the German, so he can fly the plane for me, and the rest—if we have the deal—I will give to you."

Q: Describe a Russian with German punctuality.

A: A person who is consistently late for work by precisely two hours.

LOVE

Definitions of love:

"Love is a disease that can be treated in bed," says a student.

"What kind of disease is it, if nobody wants to be treated for it?" says a doctor. "Love is an art."

"What kind of art is it, if there's no audience?" says an actress. "Love is a science!"

"What kind of science is it, if the worst student can do it, but I can't?" says a professor.

"Love requires a lot of physical strength," says a worker. "That means it's a labor."

"What kind of work is it, if the major member is simply standing up?" says an engineer. "Love must be a process."

"Well, if one gives something to another, it could be a bribe," says a prosecutor.

"Wait a minute," says a lawyer. "If both parties are satisfied, it must be a deal."

"What kind of deal is it," says a businessman, "if you put in more than you take out?"

Love is a secret. If you want to keep it, don't tell anybody about it, even your loved one.

Α friendship is a friendship, but what about libido?

Α woman who thinks that the path to a man's heart lies through his stomach is aiming a little too high.

He was really good at sex. Now the only thing he needed was a partner.

"You're like an ocean…".
"You mean I'm overwhelming and romantic?"
"No, I mean you're nauseating."

"Do you believe in love at first sight?"
"No."
"Then look at me again."

At a dance club, a teenager approaches a woman in her late twenties and says, "Would you like to dance with me?"

She gives him a superior look and answers, "I don't dance with children!"

"I'm sorry, ma'am," he says. "I didn't know you're pregnant!"

Α young man gets acquainted with a young woman at a party. After the party is over, she asks him if he can give her a lift home. He quickly agrees. When they arrive at the dimly lit site of her building, she asks the young man if he could walk her to her apartment's door. He agrees again. In front of her door she asks him if he would like to have a cup of tea with her before he goes home. But as soon as the man hears these words, he swiftly turns around and runs downstairs.

"Where are you going, Sergei?" she cries to the fleeing figure.

"I'll be back in a few minutes," he replies. "Let me get something for the tea at a nearby drugstore!"

"They say you sleep with men, daughter."
"Oh no, father! You can't really get any sleep with them."

Love is like a full-course meal: A woman likes to serve a salad first, then something hot, then the main course, etc. But a man is like a child: He wants to start with dessert. But should a woman let him have his way, a man will quickly lose his appetite.

Don't save on a condom, or you'll lose on an abortion.
—Mikhail Zhvanetsky (a famous Russian comedian)

"I wish I were so beautiful that every man in our village would chase me," a young woman tells her mother.

"Shame on you," her mother says. "Is it not enough that all their wives are chasing you?"

Happiness is when your wife is a beauty. But to be happy this way is also a misery.

A man is picking wild mushrooms in the forest. He noticed an older lady following him around, armed with a rifle, and looking at him suspiciously.

Finally, the man stops and asks her, "Why are you carrying that rifle? Are you hunting here?"

"No, I'm not hunting," the lady said. "This is just in case you would want to sexually assault me."

"Oh my God, madam," the man protests. "I would never do that."

"Well, son," the old lady says, taking her rifle off her shoulder, "I don't think you have a choice now!"

She gave him such a cold look, he got chilblains.

"I just learned that kissing is unhygienic and, as such, it should be avoided."

"Yeah, I learned it the hard way; I lost a couple of teeth and then my job when I kissed my boss's daughter."

Despite all the protests from her parents, Katya kept bringing home her boyfriend. One day the boyfriend ran into her father.

"Who are you?" Katya's father asked him.

"I'm... I'm her brother," he replied.

"Dad, I need twelve more keys for my friends," a teenaged girl tells her father.

"Maybe we should just install a revolving door instead," the father replies.

"I don't want to date a penny-pincher like you anymore!" she says. "Here's your ring, take it back!"

"And where's the box?" he wonders.

Two young women are talking:

"What do you think?" one asks. "What *did* attract women to men before?"

"What do you mean 'before'?"

"Before there were money and cars."

An ad posted in a dating column:

"Young, handsome, well-built, and intelligent man with a yacht and a mansion in Hawaii is seeking a woman."

An excited woman dials the number. "I can't believe you don't have any bad habits!"

"Well," the male voice on another end says, "sometimes I tend to exaggerate."

A rich man can have many women. A poor woman may need to have many men.

Running from a cat, a mouse ends up in a bottle half filled with wine. The mouse frantically tries to get back out, but her efforts are in vain. She's forced to ask the cat for help:

"You won't let me die in here!?"

"Promise me you won't run away," the cat says.

"Yes I promise, Kitty," she says. "Just get me out of here!"

The cat knocks the bottle over, the mouse gets out, and

immediately runs into a small crack in the floor.

"You promised not to run away," the cat whines, visibly disappointed.

"Well, Kitty," she says, "you haven't learned yet that you cannot trust a woman, especially a drunken one."

"Oh, my poor boyfriend!"
"What happened?"
"Nothing, but I mean, he's so poor…".

A man in a subway is ogling a shapely woman sitting across from him, unable to avert his eyes away from her.

Finally the woman says, "Sir, please dress me again. I'm getting off at the next station."

Two young cadets are following a shapely woman as she strolls down the street. They pick up the pace so they can see her face. Once they reach her and their eyes meet, one cadet loudly remarks to his friend, "If she was as beautiful from the front as she is from behind, I'd kiss her!"

The woman turns sharply to the outspoken cadet and says, "Why don't you kiss me in the part you like?"

"Does your husband still love you the same way?"
"Oh, no. Luckily, he's learned something new."

"Hey, babe, what time is it?"
"One hour—one hundred rubles!"

A young man hugs a girl, whispering into her ear, "I feel like I'm in heaven!"

To that she replies, "And I feel like I'm on an overcrowded bus!"

"Aren't my eyes deep blue like the skies, honey?"

"Yeah."

"Aren't my lips red like roses?"

"Yeah."

"I like it so much when you tell me these things, dear!"

She used to be the woman of my dreams until I learned the dreams of my woman.

A shy fellow finally decides to propose to the girl he's been dating for some time, but he decides to do it over the phone:

"Is that you, Katya?" he asks.

"Yes, it's me," the voice on the other end says.

"Would you like to marry me?" he asks.

"Yes, of course I would!" she says excitedly. "But who is this?"

"Stop thinking about it, honey," she says. "I'm not going to let you do it before the wedding."

"In that case," he says, "give me a call after the wedding!"

"Tell me, colonel," she said, "what hobbies did you have in your youth?"

"Women and hunting!" he said.

"What did you hunt for?"

"Women."

"So, Sergei," she says, "you've been around me all night. You must be having some big plans for tonight?"

"Frankly," he says, "I didn't even think about that."

"No?" she cries. "Then why are you wasting my evening like this?"

"Who are these men?" a young fellow asks his girlfriend when he sees an entire wall pasted with pictures of men. "Your ancestors?"

"No," she replies, "your predecessors."

A Georgian farmer walks down the street, spitting every few steps as he repeats the same phrase over and over again:

"How she played badminton! How she played badminton!"

"What's the matter, Gogi?" his friend asks him.

"You see," Gogi says, "yesterday morning when I took my sheep to the mountains, I met a beautiful young woman with a pair of badminton rackets. She was so beautiful I couldn't let her go. So she said, 'Let's play badminton. If you win, I'm yours. If I win, you'll kiss the butt of every sheep you own.' You should see how she played badminton!... How she played badminton!"

Seduced by an artist, a lady gives in and visits him at his studio. When she sees him naked, she bursts into laughter. "Now I know why you told me that miniatures are your specialty!"

"Your have a run in your panty hose," one woman tells another.

"Oh, those damn tanks…".

"What tanks?"

"The little ones on the epaulets."

"I'm dating two men now. One of them is so handsome, intelligent, well-mannered, and kind…".

"Then, what do you need the second one for?"

"The second is straight."

One hundred men and one woman are on a secluded island in the ocean. The woman is being treated like a queen. One man, who had gone to fetch her some wine, drops the jug and spills the wine.

"What's your number?" she asks.

"Fifteen," he says.

"Now it's thirty-five," she says.

On another secluded island, the island's population now consists of one hundred women and one man—who sits on top of a tree, closely watched by the impatient women.

Two young women are talking.

"I'm going to marry a man I fall in love with."

"Me too, if I don't find anything better."

Two elderly women are killing some time, sitting on a

park bench and chatting. "Tell me, Nina," one says, "what do you think my husband is hiding in his pants?"

"Well, it could be money," says the other.

"No…it's the end of love and two bags of memories!"

"Hello, could I speak to Ivan, please?"

"Yes, who's calling, please?"

"This is his girlfriend."

"Which one?"

"Well… that's okay… doesn't really matter anymore…".

Q: Why do girls always look down when guys tell them about their love?

A: To see if it's true.

"Honey," she says, "if you kiss me just one more time, I'll be yours for life!"

"Thanks for the warning," he says.

Q: What do a couple of lovers and a couple of frogs fear most?

A: A stork.

A tourist in Moscow asks a well-endowed woman who's standing near a hotel entrance, "Do you speak English?"

"A little," she says, smiling.

"How little?" he asks.

"Two hundred dollars…".

WOMEN

Better to give birth to a baby once a year than to shave every day.

—An old Russian saying

"Mother, Vasily says that I am a 'beautiful, intelligent, and well-bred girl'. Can I invite him over for dinner?"

"You'd be better not, honey," the mother says. "Let him think that way for as long as possible."

"What happened to you? You've lost so much weight," one woman says to another.

"Well, I'm so depressed after I found out that my husband sees another woman."

"So, why didn't you divorce him?"

"Not yet, I need to lose another 20 pounds."

"Is it possible for a Russian woman to live on her salary?"

"It is, providing she dresses herself on credit and undresses for cash."

During a museum tour the guide explains, "Here you can see the statue of Minerva…".

"Excuse me, madam," a visitor interjects. "Who is that man behind her? Is he her husband?"

"No, Minerva wasn't married: She was the goddess of wisdom."

"We need to get the phone company to check our phone," a woman tells her husband. "Every time I talk with Sonya, we can't understand each other."

"Have you tried talking in turns?"

"Why did you pick that name?" one woman asks another. "Jerk is not a common name for a dog."

"Well, you should see how much attention I get from men when I walk him on the streets!"

Apparently, the reason God created woman after man was that he didn't want any advice from her.

A woman is explaining the kind of man she wants at a dating service:

"He has to be polite, he has to have various interests, he has to know how to have a good conversation, he has to know what's going on around the world, and he has to never interrupt me."

"You don't need a man, madam, you need a TV!"

"Okay, okay," a tired husband tells his wife after a long argument. "Let it be the way you want…".

"Now it's too late," she says. "I just changed my mind."

"Hi," he says and hands her a nice bouquet of flowers and a box of chocolates. "This is for you, honey!"

"Who is it from?" she asks.

Two women are overheard talking:

"I've heard," one says, "that your lover's family doesn't like you at all."

"That's true—especially his wife."

Q: How is a sea onion like a woman scientist?

A: As a sea onion has nothing in common either with the sea or with an onion, neither does a woman scientist—either with a woman or with a scientist.

"I decided to go back to my husband," a separated woman tells her friend.

"Why?"

"I can't stand seeing him get everything his way that easily!"

"How old are you, Sonya?"

"I'm thirty-three."

"I thought you were thirty-three last year."

"Well, I can't change my opinion every year!"

A paramedic is attending to the victim of a car accident. "He's dead," she says a moment later.

"No I'm not," the victim whispers to the surprise of everyone at the scene.

"Don't talk, dear," the victim's wife says. "She knows better!"

Q: Can a woman work as a diplomat?

A: No, because a woman and a diplomat use the words *yes* and *no* differently. If a diplomat says *yes*, it means *maybe*. If a diplomat says *maybe*, it means *no*. If a diplomat says *no*, what kind of diplomat is *he*?

On the other hand, when a woman says *no*, it means maybe. If a woman says *maybe*, it means *yes*. If a woman says *yes*, well, what kind of woman is *she*?

To understand a woman is hard; it's easier to find a new one.

—Mikhail Zhvanetsky

"**H**ey, Ivan, where are you running?"

"To the police station. I've lost my dog!"

"Why don't you tell my wife instead? In a few hours the whole town will know about it."

A woman tells her husband during an argument: "Okay,

I know I'm wrong, but you could at least ask me for forgiveness."

"Honey," he says, "am I your first man?"

"Of course, you are," she replies. "Why do you men always ask this damn question?"

A rich widow has married a young man:

"How did you manage that?" her friend asks.

"I told him I was seventy-five, but, as you know, I'm only fifty-seven!"

If a woman tells a man that he's the smartest man she ever met, that may mean that she thinks she's not going to find another fool like him.

Two young women stand in front of a cage at the zoo and look at a giant male gorilla. One woman asks the other, "Do you think you could live with him as a man?"

"Of course not. He doesn't make any money!"

Q: How is a woman like a parachute?

A: You're always better off if you have a spare.

Q: What can a woman make from nothing?

A: A hairstyle, a breakfast, and a tragedy.

"Where did you get this beautiful dress?" one woman asks another.

"That's my husband's present for my 30th anniversary."

"Amazing…are these still in style?"

One woman asks another about her fiancé:

In her twenties: "How does he look?"

In her thirties: "Who is he?"

In her forties: "Where is he?"

"Am I your first man?" he asks, embracing her gently.

She takes a long look at him and replies, "That's possible; you seem to look familiar!"

"Are you ready?" he asks. "We're going to be late."

"Why do you keep asking me that stupid question?" she wonders. "During last hour, I've told you a hundred times that I need two more minutes!"

"Oh, hi," one woman say to another. "I didn't recognize you at first."

"Why?"

"You look so good today."

It's the early eighties, and three women are having a conversation:

"My husband bought me the latest model of TV. Now I don't have to go anywhere—I can watch everything at home," says one.

"My husband bought me the latest model of VCR. Now I don't have to go anywhere—I can watch everything at home, and watch it as many times as I want," the second woman says.

"What about your husband?" they ask the third woman.

"He didn't buy me any of those things," she replies. "He said that I'm still in good enough shape to go out with him to the opera or theater."

Q: Why are women worse than the mafiya?

A: The Mafiya demands money or your life; women want both.

Woman wants many things, but from one man; man wants only one thing, but from many women.

MEN

Man's main erogenous zone is his wallet.

Two married men are talking:
"How do you tell when it's time to do the dishes or clean around the house?"
"Look inside your pants. If you can still see something, that means it isn't time!"

"There are so many beautiful women who just don't want to get married," one man tells another.
"How do you know?"
"I've checked it out for myself."

"You should see the girl I met yesterday," one man brags to another. "Oops! Look! there's another one!"

"Can you spare some change?" a beggar asks a passerby.
"No, I know you're going to spend it all on vodka."
"No, sir, I don't drink."
"Then you'll gamble it away."
"No, I don't gamble either, sir."
"Well then, you're going to spend it on women."

"No, sir, I don't spend money on women."

"Okay," the passerby finally agrees, "I'm going to give you 100 rubles, if you come with me. I want to show my wife an example of what can happen to a man who has no bad habits."

Adam and Eve are walking in the garden of Eden:

"Do you love me?" Eve asks him.

"Do I have a choice?" Adam says.

"Honey," she says, "tell me something warm!"

"A parka," he says.

"Do you guys know her?" one asks.

"I do," a second says.

"I know her too," the third says.

"Did either of you date her?" the first asks.

"I didn't," says the second.

"I didn't either," says the third.

"What a bitch!" says the first.

A local woman walks into a busy Paris hotel one night, while it is hosting a big Russian delegation. It's late, so she decides to take the best offer hotel management can come up with: to share a two-bed room with a Russian man.

At three in the morning the Russian enters the room, sees a woman in his bed, quietly crawls into the second bed, undresses himself under the blanket, and, without paying any further attention to the woman, falls asleep.

He is soon wakened by the woman's voice, who is trying to establish some sort of conversation. "Don't you think it's too hot in here, sir? Could you please open the window?"

"Yes," the man replies, in a sleepy voice. So he puts his pants back on under the blanket and gets up to open the window.

Fifteen minutes later, the woman tries again. "Sir, don't you think it's getting cold? Could you please close the window?"

The man frowns, mutters something in Russian, but he does it anyway. A little later, when the woman asks him to open the window once again, he tells her squarely, "Maybe you want it like husband and wife, madam?"

"Oh yes, I'd love to!" she answers excitedly.

"Alright then…get up and do it yourself, bitch!"

A man came home late one night, drunk and tired. "Where have you been?" his wife bawled.

"Honey, you're so smart. Can't you come up with a good answer yourself?"

"Here you can see a tiger," the man working as a zoo guide tells the visitors.

"Is it a man or a woman?" one woman asks.

"It is a male," the guide replies. "Now, over there, ladies and gentlemen, you can see a gorilla," he continues.

"Is it a man or a woman?" the same woman interjects again.

"Madam," the guide raises his voice, "It is a male. A man has money!"

A man is sharing a train compartment with a young woman in a mini-skirt.

"Excuse me, madam," he says, "why don't you cover your legs with this blanket? That way you'll be warm and I won't tremble."

Three men are walking down the street behind a gorgeous woman:

"I'd give a thousand rubles to spend a night with this woman," one man says.

"And I," the second man says, "I would give three thousand rubles to spend a night with her."

"Oh no, guys," the third man says. "I'd give *everything* to this woman! I'd buy her a good car, a lot of jewelry, and I'd take her out to the best places every night…".

"Excuse me, gentlemen," the woman says, turning around unexpectedly. "Which one of you said those last words?"

"Just keep walking and mind your own business!" the third man replies.

A middle-aged man tells his friend, "I'm getting married, but I'm afraid we won't be able to have children."

"Don't worry," his friend advises. "Get yourself a young secretary and you'll work it out."

"So, how are you? And how's the wife?" the friend asks the newlywed when they meet again, six months later.

"Everything's fine…my wife is pregnant."

"How's your secretary?"

"She's pregnant too."

Q: What's the safest contraceptive?

A: A telephone. And don't use anything else to get in touch with women.

A married couple are looking at a big male gorilla at the zoo.

"Why don't you give him a hot look, honey?" the man says to his wife jokingly. She thinks it's not such a bad idea. They might as well have some fun, and so she does it. The gorilla gets slightly excited.

"Now, shake your thighs for him," the man says mischievously. "Let's see his reaction to that!"

And so the woman does that too, and now the ape gets really excited. He starts moving back and forth, from one end of his cage to the other.

The man then grabs his wife and pushes her into the animal's cage. "Now, try to explain to him that you're too tired, that you have a headache, and you don't feel like it tonight!" he says.

"Come with me, please," a woman says to a man with a camera at a secluded beach. "My lady friend is drowning!"

"I'm sorry, but I can't," the man says. "I'm out of film!"

A single man has locked his keys and wallet in the car. He's late for work, and there's no payphone nearby, so he decides to ask his neighbor—an attractive single woman—to lend him some money for a cab.

The man climbs up the staircase, thinking to himself, "If she does me this favor, then I'll have to return it somehow. Then we'll start saying 'hello' to each other more often. Then she'll ask me out, and I'll have to do the same. That will lead to marriage. Then we'll have kids and they'll cry all the time. Then she'll have quarrels with me on a regular basis, and that will be the end of my freedom…".

On that thought, the neighbor's door opens and a smiling woman says, "Hi! I just saw you were trying to get into your car. Do you need any help?"

"No!" the man replies in a raised voice, as if someone has just disturbed his privacy. "I don't need your help!"

Q: What you call a man who's happily in love.
A: Single.

"All men are womanizers."
"All of them?"
"Oh, yes. You can't really call those who aren't 'men'."

"Such bluntness! I tell you in plain Russian that my wife is expecting a child and you're asking me who the father is?!"

"I'm sorry. I just thought you might know."

Two friends, both in their twenties, meet at a hotel:

"Do you always stay at this hotel when you come to Odessa?" one asks the other.

"Oh, yes! Where else can you find better girls!"

Twenty years later, they meet once again, this time in another Odessa hotel. One friend asks the other the same question.

"Sure," his friend answers. "I always stay here. Where else can you find better food?"

Another twenty years go by and they meet again in yet a different hotel in Odessa. To his friend's question, the man answers this time: "Yeah, where else can you find such peace and quiet?"

Before a shy young man heads off for his first date, he's being instructed by his friends:

"These are the three questions you must ask women if you want to make an impression: the first one should be about food; the second, about her family; and the third one, philosophical."

So, during their dinner, the young man asks his date, "Do you like blintzes?"

"No," his date answers.

"Does your brother like blintzes?"

"I don't have a brother."

"If you had a brother, would he like blintzes?"

A man walks into a drugstore and asks the pharmacist to give him one hundred condoms. He hears two young lady clerks giggling at him, so he adds, "Make it one hundred and two, please!"

"So, Ivan, how do you spend your nights nowadays?"
"At home, with my wife."
"Now, that's called big love!"
"No, that's called arthritis!"

"Sir, I'm afraid you must quit drinking, smoking, and having sex."
"But, doctor, I'm a man!"
"Well, you can still keep shaving yourself…".

A group of men manage to get themselves to a small island in the ocean after surviving a ship disaster. The next morning they see a group of women, apparently from the first lifeboat, on a small island a few hundred yards away. The men become excited and get right down to work, discussing their next actions.

"Let's swim there right now," say the men in their twenties.

"No, let's build a raft first. We can use that to get there," say the men in their thirties.

"Don't hurry, guys," say the men in their forties. "Let's wait for a few hours and the women will get here themselves."

"Why bother at all?" say the men in their fifties. "We can watch them from here!"

"Can you imagine?" a man asks his friend. "I've lost my sex drive recently. The world is so interesting! I've discovered so many great things: fishing, movies, sports…".

Q: What is a real man?
A: Someone who can stand up for himself and lay down for others.

MARRIAGE

Q: How is a marriage *not* like a lottery?
A: You have a better chance to win in a lottery.

"Honey," she says, "after our marriage I'll share with you all your troubles and problems."

"But, dear," he replies, "I don't have any."

"But we're not married yet," she says.

"So how does it feel to be married?" a man asks his friend, who has married just recently.

"I feel like a teenager again," the friend says. "I have to hide in the washroom to get a smoke."

"We've been married for just a week," he says, "and you're already starting quarrels with me?!"

"Don't forget," she says, "I've been waiting for this for three years."

A young man comes to visit his girlfriend's parents. "Sir," he says to her father, "I would like to ask you for your daughter's body."

"Well, young man," the father says, "when I was your age, a man used to ask for the daughter's *hand*."

"Hand!?... Why would I do that when I have my own!"

"What do you like most about your husband, Tanya?"
"His wife."

Many a single man is dreaming of a caring, beautiful, and intelligent woman. Many a married man is dreaming of the same thing.

A marriage is based on the balance of rights and responsibilities—the rights of the wife, and the responsibilities of the husband.

First year of marriage: He speaks, she listens.
Second year of marriage: She speaks, he listens.
Third year of marriage: They both speak, the neighbors listen.

"Let's get married," she says to her long-time lover.
"Oh, no!" he protests. "Who am I going to see every night then?"

If you want your wife to pay attention to every word you say, try talking in your sleep.

Another definition of an ideal couple: The wife is deaf, the husband snores.

The newlywed couple are having breakfast. The husband is nibbling on a plate of macaroni and cheese. The wife is sipping coffee.
"Do you love me, Ivan?" she asks him all of a sudden.
"Honey," he says, "how come you keep asking me this

question every day for a month, but you never ask me if I like having this for breakfast?"

"Mommy, daddy says we're descended from apes. Is it true?"

"I don't know, dear. He hasn't introduced me to his parents yet."

Q: How is housework like a crossword puzzle?
A: The wife is upright; the husband is across.

The phone rings at two in the morning:

"Honey, it's me, I'm coming home… You're not mad at me?" the slightly drunken man's voice says.

"No, dear," the woman's voice says on the other end.

"Can I bring my two buddies over with me?"

"Of course, dear."

After a short pause, the man's voice says, "I'm sorry, I must have the wrong number…".

A journalist is working on a report at the local marriage license office. She notices that every couple that leaves the office is strange in a way: every husband is much smaller than his wife. Puzzled, she decides to ask some of these women why they've chosen short men.

"We just love one another," one says.

"He's all I could find," says another.

"You know, honey," says the third, "all men are shit, so I just picked myself a smaller turd."

"To my regret, I have to postpone my wedding with Ivan."

"Why?"

"I'm marrying Sergei now."

"I can't believe that such a handsome young man as you is still single."

"Well, that's my luck. Every time I meet a girl that's as good as my mother around the house, she looks like my father."

"I've been telling you for two weeks not to buy me any presents for my birthday," she says to her husband. "Yet you still managed to forget about it!"

A couple are going on vacation. When they arrive at the airport and unload their numerous bags of luggage from the taxi, the wife says, "We should've taken our piano too."

"Very funny," the husband says, wiping his forehead.

"I left our tickets on it...".

"Honey, I want to have breast implants."

"It's too expensive. Why don't you take some toilet tissue and rub it between your breasts?"

"You think that will help to get them bigger?"

"Well, it seemed to work well on your behind!"

"Is it better when you're married?" an unmarried woman asks her lady friend.

"It's not better, it's just more often."

"Ivan, dear," she says, "Why don't we have dinner at a restaurant?"

"You must be kidding; it's too expensive," he says.

"Well, you forgot something, honey," she keeps trying. "It's the tenth anniversary of our wedding."

"Well, where are we going to get the money?"

"You know, I've been putting one ruble aside every week for ten years just for this. We have enough."

"But I have nothing to wear for the occasion."

"Here," she says, and she presents a garment bag. "I borrowed this for you."

"What about you?"

"I thought about that too," she says, and puts on a beautiful evening dress.

"Okay, let's go," he finally gives in.

When the doorman of the best restaurant in town sees them approaching the entrance, he quickly gets rid of his previous customer and runs toward them with greetings. "Hello Ivan! How are you doing…".

"Psst!" Ivan whispers into the doorman's ear. "I'm with my *wife* tonight."

"Your favorite table, sir?" the smiling manager asks as he meets them in foyer. "As usual…".

"Psst!" Ivan gives him a sign. "I'm with my *wife* tonight," he whispers as they're being escorted to their table.

A few seconds later a waiter rushes toward their table. "Hello, Ivan! I'm all yours," she declares, a big smile on her face.

Then a strip-dancer announces, "So, who's the hero tonight?" and she points to the last lace holding her bra.

"Ivan! Ivan!" the crowd shouts, turning to Ivan and his wife's table.

At this point, Ivan's wife gets up. She slams Ivan in the face, and then rushes outside. Ivan follows her. He jumps into the moving taxi as it's driving away with his crying wife.

After listening for some time to the woman's loud and somewhat hysterical comments, the cab driver turns toward the back seat and says, "What a bitch you got tonight, Ivan!"

They say the best way to remember your wife's birthday is to forget about it, just once.

A sixtieth wedding anniversary is being celebrated in a village. One of the members of a large family asks the hero, "Grandpa, you've lived with Grandma so long. Tell us the truth, have you ever had a desire to leave her?"

"To leave—never; to kill—yes!"

"As soon as you see a pretty woman you forget that you're a married man," she says.

"Quite the opposite, honey," he responds. "It *reminds* me that I'm married."

On their tenth wedding anniversary the husband confesses, "You know, dear, I've been thinking for ten years now about how to tell you this... Our marriage was the result of a mistake, which happened that night after the party ten years ago. Remember when I waved for a cab, and you thought it was meant for you?..."

A man returns home in the early morning hours. His wife reprimands him:

"Where the hell have you been? I couldn't sleep all night!"

"You think *I* was sleeping?"

"Do you promise me that, after our marriage, you'll quit playing *Preference* (a popular Russian card game)?" she asks.

"Yes, dear," he says.

"And that you'll quit smoking?"

"Yes, dear."

"And that you'll quit drinking?"

"Is that all?"

"Well, is there something else you're thinking of quitting, honey?"

"Yes! Our marriage!"

Heard at a payphone booth:

"Excuse me, sir, but for the last thirty minutes you've been standing there, and you haven't said a word! I need to use the phone!"

"Sure! Just as soon as I finish talking to my wife."

A man breaks up with his girlfriend and his friend asks him why:

"Well, would you like to marry 'a selfish, lazy, and useless loser'?"

"No, I wouldn't."

"She said the same!"

In a public *banya* (a Russian steam bath) a man sees a group of African men, one of whom has a white penis. He cannot hide his surprise. So in a moment when he sees that the strange man is alone, he walks over and asks him, "Excuse me, sir, but I've never seen an African with a white penis…"

"Oh, I'm not an African," the man says. "I'm a coal miner, and so are my friends. And this?" he points below his waist. "Well, my wife has come to town for a visit."

"Leave my father alone!" she says during a nasty argument with her husband. "What wrong did he do to you?"

"You!" he answers.

"Honey," a man asks a woman, "would you marry a rich fool?"

"It depends," she says. "How much money do you have?"

A man on a business trip is ordering his breakfast at a restaurant: "Yes, scrambled eggs are fine," he says to the waiter. "But please make one part uncooked; another, overcooked; and leave some eggshell fragments in it. I would also like you to toss it on my table in the frying pan with the words, 'Eat it, pig'."

"But I don't understand, sir…" the waiter stammers.

"After three weeks of traveling, I just want to feel at home."

"What did you stuff it with?" the husband asks his young wife, after he suspiciously smells dinner—a roasted duck.

"Actually," the woman says, "I was going to stuff it, but there was no space."

"**S**old!" the auctioneer shouts. "To the lady in the third row, holding her palm over her husband's mouth."

Two men are drinking at a bar:
"Ivan, you look sad. What happened?"
"I had a quarrel with my wife last night over some stupid clothes she wanted to buy."
"So, who had the final word?"
"Me, of course."
"What did you say?"
"I said, 'Hell with you, go buy them'!"

"**Y**our daughter is going to marry me!" an excited young man tells his future father-in-law.
"That's your fault; you've spent too many nights with her here."

A man comes home very late. He says to his wife excitedly, "You wouldn't believe where I was tonight…".
"No, I'm sure I won't," she interrupts. "But go ahead and tell me. I want to hear your version first."

"**I**'m running over to Tanya's, our neighbor, for ten minutes," the wife tells her husband. "Could you watch the chili on the stove? All you have to do is to stir it every half an hour."

"**S**ir, I would like to marry your daughter."
"Have you spoken to my wife?"
"Yes I have. But I prefer your daughter."

"**H**oney," a man says sleepily, "could you turn off the TV?"
"No, I can't!" she replies, "considering we're in a movie theater."

"I want ice cream, Dmitri," an elderly woman tells her husband at six in the morning. "Why don't you go to the store and buy some?"

The husband pretends he's still asleep. But, after repeated requests from his wife, he eventually gives in. "What kind do you want?" he asks.

"Raspberry with chocolate glaze."

"Okay, I'm going right now."

"Write it down; otherwise, you'll forget."

"No I won't, it's only one item: raspberry ice cream with chocolate glaze."

The man returns home a few hours later, as if he had done his shopping out of town. His wife unwraps a package and there she finds a hotdog.

"I *told* you to write it down!" she moans.

"What's wrong, dear?" he asks.

"You forgot to take extra ketchup," she says.

An old maid once surprised everybody when she got married.

"You were saying," her friend noted, "that men are foolish, and that you'd *never* get married."

"Yes, I was. Until I found one man who agreed to marry me."

"Why did you escape from the jail?"

"To get married."

"You have a strange perception of freedom, young man."

A man boards a plane and notices that the woman in the seat next to him is a well-known psychic.

They begin talking, and a little later he decides to test her: "I'll pay you 100 rubles if you tell me where I'm going and for what purpose."

"Your going to St. Petersburg to get a divorce," the psychic replies after taking a studious look at the man.

So he takes out his wallet and gives her 200 rubles.

"What's this other 100 for?" she asks.

"For a great idea."

"You know," an excited young man tells his girlfriend, "all this week I was going to ask you something…".

"Go ahead, dear," she interjects. "I had my answer ready last month."

"I'm wondering," the husband says, "why is it that the stupidest guys always marry the most beautiful girls?"

"Is that a compliment?" the wife asks.

"Dear," a mother says to her small daughter, "bring me some dishes from the kitchen, please."

"What for, mommy?"

"I'm going to have a conversation with your father."

"Why do you allow your wife to smoke that much?"

"That's the only way I can enjoy some quiet."

"I'm getting a divorce," one man tells another. "My wife hasn't talked to me for four months."

"Well, why would you want to do that? I just wish *I* had such a quiet woman."

"Mommy," a little boy whispers, "Dad is coming. So what are we going to show him first—your new dress or my report card?"

"What happened, honey?" the wife asks, waking up her husband. "Why are you crying so loud?"

"I had a dream that Tonya was drowning," he says, trying to catch his breath.

"Who's Tonya?"

"Well, you don't know her. I mean… she's from the dream."

"My wife left me for my best friend."

"I never thought Ivan was your best friend."

"He is now."

"What is your reason for seeking a divorce, madam?" the judge asks.

"My husband forces me to eat everything I cook."

Two women are speaking:

"He doesn't pay attention to me anymore," one complains. "I've tried everything; nothing seems to work."

"Try to wear a gas mask for an evening," her friend recommends. "That should work."

The two women run into each other again a few days later. "Did you try the gas mask?"

"I did, but it didn't help. He just asked me, before going to bed, if I had plucked my eyebrows."

"My ex-husband got custody of all four children," she brags. "The funny thing is, none of them is his."

"Sir," a secretary asks her boss, "why does your wife always give me that look?"

"Maybe because she used to be my secretary."

Ivan tells his friend Dmitri about his problems with wife:

"What size are your shoes?" Dmitri asks.

"Ten," Ivan says. "Why?"

"Buy yourself a pair of size eight's," Dmitri advises.

"But what for?" Ivan asks.

"This way, when you come home at night, you won't think so much about your family problems anymore," Dmitri says. "You'll think about taking your shoes off."

"**W**hy would you seek a divorce after thirty years with your wife?"

"Well, that's enough for me!"

During a quarrel, the husband, running from his wife, crawls under the bed. After few futile attempts to force him out with a broomstick, she yells, "Get out!"

"No I won't," he says.

"Get out of there!" she insists.

"No I won't."

"I'm telling you for the last time, get out!"

"Who's the boss here?" he says. "I told you I won't!"

"**H**oney, I had a beautiful dream about our youthful years and me asking you to marry me!"

"And what exactly are you so happy about, dear?"

"You refused me!"

"**H**ow much do you charge for a divorce?" a woman asks a lawyer.

"900 rubles."

"No thanks, I can get him killed for 500."

"**D**o you prefer mischievous, eccentric, and stupid women?"

"Of course not!"

"Then why are you seeing my wife?"

During a dinner, after noticing that the hostess isn't eating at all, a guest says to the host, "Your wife must be on a diet."

"No, she isn't," says the host. "My doctor recommended that I go to bed on an empty stomach."

A family of cannibals are having dinner by the fire. The father checks out the soup, frowns, and says to his wife, "How many times have I told you to take the socks off the meat before cooking?"

"Am I supposed to wear this old mink coat for the rest of my life?" she asks.

"Well," he answers, "if the minks can do it, you can do it too, honey."

"He looks exactly like his father," one woman tells another after seeing her baby boy.

"That's what I'm saying. But my husband insists that the boy looks like him."

"Dad," a teenaged girl says, running into her father's den, "I'd like to kiss you good-bye before I go to school!"

"You're too late, honey. Your mother just did that two minutes ago, and I don't have any cash left on me."

"Look at our neighbor, Mrs. Ivanova," the wife says. "Her husband gives her a kiss every time he leaves for work, and every time he comes back home. And you?"

"Well," the husband says, "I don't know her that well yet."

"If you can't prove that she's your wife, sir," a hotel manager says, "I won't be able to give you the same room."

"And if you prove that she's not my wife," the customer says, "I'll be grateful to you for the rest of my life."

"**W**hy don't you wear your wedding ring, honey?" the wife asks her husband, who is leaving for a long business trip.

"In this sultry weather?" he asks.

"**W**hy didn't you go shopping?" she asks.

"To go shopping is not a man's chore," he says.

"Well," she says and opens up her housecoat, "then go ahead and do your man's chores!"

"Okay, okay," he says, "give me the list! I was kidding!"

"**H**ow many times do I have to tell you," the wife asks her husband, "that when I say 'my dear' I mean the dog, not you, bastard!"

After surviving a ship disaster, a man finally manages to make it to a small island. Much to his surprise, his wife, alive and well, meets him and helps him out of the water. Says she: "The ship sank yesterday afternoon. Where have you been all night?"

"**C**ongratulations, Ivan!" a neighbor says. "I've heard you got married."

"Did you? I can't believe the lousy insulation they put in these buildings nowadays!"

"**W**hy is your daughter still single?"

"She's waiting for the man of her dreams."

"And what exactly is this man like?"

"Well, all he has to do is to be willing to marry her."

"**W**hy do you always go to the balcony when your wife starts singing?"

"I don't want anyone to think that I'm beating her up."

"Why do men gain weight after they get married?"

"That's easy. When a single man comes home, he checks his fridge, finds nothing, and goes to bed. Now, when a married man comes home, he checks the bed, and after he sees what's in there, he walks straight to the fridge to calm himself down."

"My wife is an angel!" one man says.

"You're lucky," another replies. "Mine is still alive."

"Okay, I'll take it. I really like the price," the buyer says after checking out a piano, for sale by a private party.

"Great! I have only one condition," the owner says. "You have to pick it up when neither my wife or my daughter are at home."

"You're such a fool," she says. "If they ever had a fools' competition, you'd be the second stupidest person on earth."

"Why second?" he asks.

"Because, you're such a fool."

During a divorce hearing the judge asks the husband about his motives for divorce.

"What do you think, your honor?" the petitioner says. "Can a family of two get by on one thousand rubles per month?"

"I guess so," the judge says.

"I think so too, your honor," the petitioner says, "but all she's been doing for years now is trying to set me up with a job."

An all too familiar scene:

The husband is reading something on the sofa, the wife is vacuuming. When she asks him to move his feet, he says, "You can't do anything without me!"

"Excuse me, sir," the neighbor asks, "who does your wife yell at all the time?"

"Oh, that… that's our dog."

"Poor animal. I heard her saying that she's going to kick him out of the house without the keys."

"You'll feel sorry when I leave you for another man," she warns.

"Yes, I will," he says, "…for the man you leave me for."

A man comes home from work and finds a note written by his wife:

"Honey, I went to see Tonya's new house. Fish is for dinner tonight. I left the tackle and the rods in the locker for you."

Two women are conversing:

"Last night he told me that I'm so beautiful, so intelligent, that I'm the best girl he ever met," one says. "And he said he's ready to marry me tomorrow!"

"I wouldn't marry him, if I were you," the other woman cautions.

"Why not?"

"How can you trust a man who's lying to you already?"

Early one morning, the husband is dressing to go to work. "Did you clean my jacket, honey?" he asks his wife.

"Yes, dear."

"What about my pants?"

"Yes, them too."

"What about my shoes?"

"No," she says, "I didn't know they have pockets."

"You don't even ask me why I'm crying," she wails. "Do you want to know?"

"No I don't," he replies. "I don't have that kind of money anyway."

"My wife just had triplets," a happy father tells a reporter for a local newspaper, over the phone.

But, due to a bad connection, the reporter asks, "Sir, could you please repeat that…".

"What?" the man protests. "No! That's enough for me!"

A man is at lost in a flower shop. When the shopkeeper, a man in his late sixties, sees this, he approaches the customer and asks, "Can I help you, sir?"

"Yes, please."

"Are you looking for something for your wife, or do you need something better?"

"What should I do?" one woman ask another. "My husband always talks about his ex-wife."

"You're lucky," says the other, "mine always talks about his future wife."

"I heard you broke up with Tonya."

"Yeah. She had that stupid laugh."

"I hadn't noticed anything like that."

"But you weren't around when I told her how much I was making."

"If you knew that he's a heavy drinker, why did you marry him?"

"I thought he must be making good money if he drinks that much."

"I'm so glad you finally decided to get married, Son. But why? She's not the one you've been going out with every night."

"Well, mother, I need a girl to go out with after I get married too."

"I'm not going to give you any more money, son. After you married that woman, you're dead to me."

"Well then, father, you wouldn't refuse to give some money for your son's funeral would you?"

"What happened, Ivan?" a friend asks Ivan, who looks very sad.

"My girlfriend is getting married," Ivan replies.

"Really," the friend says. "Who is she marrying?"

"Me," Ivan says.

"Is this fish fresh?"

"Can't you see it's alive?"

"So what? My wife is alive too."

A man is walking down the street. Suddenly, he hears a voice: "Jump off the sidewalk! Right now!"

As soon as he jumps, a brick falls very close to the spot he had been standing just a moment before.

"Who was it?" the man thinks to himself. "Whoever it was, he or she saved my life...".

"It was me," the voice says. "I'm your guardian angel. I'm in your pocket."

The man takes his guardian angel out of his pocket, squeezes his hand, and asks, "Where were you when I was getting married?"

"Doctor, I have a problem. After I got married, I can't see any money."

A man has recently buried his wife and he's still in shock

from the loss. Now he is having a drink with a friend:

"You cannot imagine," he says, "how hard it is to lose your wife."

"Tell me about it," the friend says. "It's almost impossible!"

"Honey, what would you like me to get for you for your birthday?"

"Well, I haven't decided yet, dear."

"Don't hurry then; you can have another year to think about it."

"What is your reason for seeking a divorce, madam," the judge asks.

"I ran out of causes for quarrels, your honor."

A wife is a housekeeping machine you wind up in bed.

Three men are talking:

"Do you help your wife around the house?"

"No, I don't."

"He's right. He does it all by himself."

The wife sends her husband to pick up their son from kindergarten. When he returns, the wife is in shock: "That is not our child!"

"Well," the husband replies, "I'm not going back. I can pick him up tomorrow; I have to take this one back anyway."

"How did you like my dinner tonight?" she asks.

"Are you looking for trouble again?" he replies.

"Honey, I can't find the money I've been putting aside for our vacation," he says.

"Well, I forgot to tell you, dear," she says, "I spent it to buy myself a new fur coat."

So the husband picks up the phone, dials a number, and says, "Hello, Sunny Travel? I'd like to cancel my reservation. Instead, I'd like to buy a trip to the Siberian tundra for one person."

He calls his wife a "treasure" because people often ask him where he dug her up.

The first night after their wedding, the wife looks at her husband, who's eating his breakfast, and sighs, "You *eat* like a rabbit too."

"Honey," a newlywed woman says to her husband, "I have to tell you that porridge and scrambled eggs is all I can cook."

"And which one is this?" he asks.

Two married men are having a leisurely conversation:

"Ah, yes, the honeymoon. What is a honeymoon, anyway?" one asks.

"Well," says the other, "I would compare my married life with a barrel full of tar, on top of which there's a thin layer of honey. That thin layer of honey is the honeymoon."

"I see," the first says. "Looks like I opened my barrel from the wrong end."

"As of yesterday," a newlywed man tells his friend, "my wife is on her honeymoon."

"Just her? What about you?"

"Not me, I have diabetes."

Two men, once close friends, meet after twenty years. One of them invites the other over to his house for a dinner. During dinner, the guest has to hide his surprise when he sees eighteen children in his friend's house:

"You must be happy in your marriage; the house full of kids. Isn't it nice!" the guest says to his friend when they step outside for a smoke.

"I wish. You don't know my wife. She eats at me day and night."

"Then, why did you father so many kids?"

"Well, I figured it's much easier to get lost in a crowd."

"Honey, when we get married, we'll have three children," she says.

"How do you know?" he wonders.

"Well, they live with my mother now," she says.

After he had saved a drowning woman, who later became his wife, the man completely avoided ever getting close to any large bodies of water again.

"Honey," he says, "after I compared my expenses for our wedding with your dowry, it looks as if I married you strictly for love!"

"My wife read somewhere that eating raw food is good for you."

"You know, mine doesn't like cooking either."

CHEATING

Q: What's the difference between a cosmonaut and a husband?

A: A cosmonaut always knows his backup.

"You know, I ran into your husband in the store yesterday," one woman tells another. "He told me such a funny joke, I almost fell off the bed…".

Q: Was Eve always faithful to Adam?

A: Nobody knows for sure, but, according to one theory, men were descended from apes.

A five-year-old tells his mother how much fun he and his father had when she was away:

"Every night our neighbor, Mrs. Petrova, visited us and brought candy for me. Daddy entertained her with cognac, and then they did the same thing you and Mr. Petrov do when father is out of town."

A woman who lives in a house close to the streetcar tracks calls for a carpenter to fix her closet doors, which keep opening whenever a streetcar passes by.

The carpenter tries one thing after another, but the doors still won't stay closed; they swing open every time another streetcar passes by. So he decides to check the doors from inside the closet.

Unluckily for the carpenter, just as soon as he steps inside the closet, the woman's husband comes home from work. He takes his jacket off, and opens the closet's door.

"Hey!" the husband shouts, turning red with anger. "What are you doing there?"

"You wouldn't believe me, man, but I'm waiting for a streetcar."

The husband comes home and finds his wife in bed with a lover. A big fight between the men ensues.

After the woman has pleaded many times for the men to stop fighting, she finally shouts to her husband, "Stop it! He is the father of your children!"

A crying woman comes to visit her mother:

"I just had a nasty argument with my husband; he wants me out," she says.

"But I thought he left the town on a business trip," her mother says.

"I thought so too."

A group of men are having lunch. One of them takes out his vacation pictures and shows them to his friends.

"See this one, the blond?" he says pointing to a woman. "She went out with every man on the resort. And this one was a bimbo too. And…".

"What about this one?" another man asks, pointing to a picture when he suddenly spots his wife.

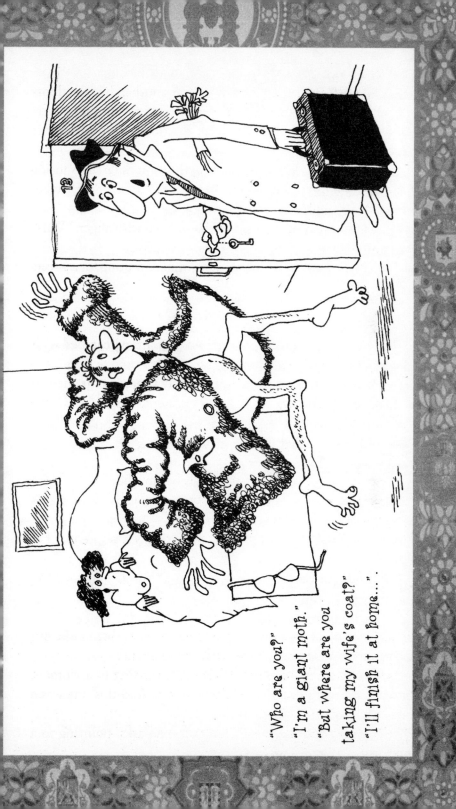

"Oh, this one. No… she came with her husband…the guy beside her."

A woman is in bed with her lover. She says, "Honey, you're so brave and strong. What would you do if my husband all of a sudden appeared in the doorway?"

"I'd beat the shit out of him. I'd break his neck, and then I'd throw him down the garbage chute…".

At these words, they hear a frightened voice from the doorway. "Well… actually… I'm still out of town for a couple of more days…".

A man comes to work and, soon enough, his co-workers notice that his socks are different. Later that day another co-worker makes a new discovery: The boss has also shown up wearing mismatched socks.

But the real fun starts once the two men compare their socks—only to find that they have two perfectly identical pairs of socks between them.

"**W**hat is this?" shouts the general, who wakes up in the middle of the night to find his wife in bed with a young lieutenant.

"Don't pay any attention, general," the lieutenant says. "This is just a dream."

So the general rolls over and mutters, "What can I do? The same dream over and over, and for the second week in a row…".

A telephone conversation:
"Honey, is it you?"
"No, it's me, your wife."

A man returns home from a trip to find another man's shoes near the door and his wife naked in bed. He starts searching around, enters the bathroom, and there he finds a man of Herculean proportions.

The wife asks from the bedroom, "So did you find anyone?"

The husband quickly shuts the door and says, "No, not really!"

Three months after marriage, the wife tells her husband that she's ready to give birth.

"So soon?" the man asks.

"Well, honey," the woman says, "we had sex for three months before we got married, and then for three months after. Three times three gives nine, right?"

The man nods and agrees. The next day, when he calls his wife at the hospital, she says that they have a little black boy. "How come he's black?" the man wonders.

"You remember," the woman explains, "when you drove me to the hospital, a black cat crossed the road in front of us? That's why our boy is black."

The man calls his parents and tells his father everything.

"Mother," the man's father yells, "do you remember seeing an ass on your way to the hospital twenty-four years ago?"

"She kicked me out of the house," one man tells another.
"Who?"
"The wife."
"I thought you were single."
"I didn't say my wife."

Fifty years ago, after their wedding, a young couple agreed that each spouse would keep a jar, and in each jar they would put one pea for each occurrence of his or her unfaithfulness.

Now, at their golden wedding anniversary, they decide it's time to reveal their jars to each other. So the man brings out his jar; it's full of peas.

"Now," he tells his wife, "show me yours."

"Well," says the woman, "it's empty."

"Oh, thank you," the man says. "I knew that, honey!"

"You're a fool," she says. "Why do you think my pea soup has always been your favorite?"

After finding his wife in bed with the postman, the husband just stands still and looks at them.

"Why are you standing there frozen, like an idiot?" his wife shouts at him. "Can't you ask him something... like... when he collects the mail?"

"Where did you get this nice designer suit?" one man asks another. "You must have spent a fortune on it!"

"No, actually, I got it for free; my wife bought it for me."

"What was the occasion?"

"Oh, there was none. She just bought it. I came home a couple of hours earlier than usual one night, and I spotted this beauty hanging on the back of a chair in my bedroom."

Two men are waiting for their turn at the pearly gates. One of them looks blue from frostbite and bruises; the other man looks happy.

"How did you die?"

"I froze to death. What about you?"

"Well, I came home and found my naked wife...who was supposed to be working...in bed."

"Was she with a lover?"

"No, I turned over the whole house and I didn't find any-body. And then I just died happily."

"You're a fool. If you had just looked into the fridge, we'd both be alive today."

A man comes home late and finds his wife in bed with a stranger:

"Where have you been so late, Ivan?" his wife asks him angrily.

"Who is this man?" the husband asks in turn, ignoring his wife's question.

"Oh, no you don't, Ivan," she insists. "I won't let you off this one so easily. Just tell me, where have you been, you bastard?"

A man threw a refrigerator out his apartment window and crippled a passerby. Now he's in court:

"Defendant," the judge says, "please tell us what happened that morning."

"I came home one day earlier than expected form my business trip," the defendant responds. "When I entered my apartment, I felt something was fishy. The bed was undone, there was an empty bottle of champagne, my wife was behaving kind of strangely. So I asked her, 'Where is he?' Then I looked out the window and I saw him running away, dressed only in boxer shorts. So I took the refrigerator and threw it down on him."

After a short pause, the judge says, "Plaintiff, please tell us your story."

"It was hot and humid that morning, so I decided to go for a run just wearing my boxers. As I was passing the defendant's building, I heard some noise and then I saw a refrigerator coming down on me. All I was able to do was to avoid it hitting my head."

"Bailiff," the judge continues, "please help the witness in."

The witness, a heavily damaged man in a full body cast, is

rolled into court in a wheelchair. Then he begins his testimony: "That night I happened to be inside my lady friend's refrigerator...".

"I just learned that my husband is seeing another woman," one woman tells another. "Do you think I should tell him about it?"

"What for? He probably knows it himself already."

A man applies for a divorce. In the courtroom, the judge asks, "Why do you want to divorce such a pretty and nice woman?"

"She doesn't satisfy me in bed, your honor."

At this the wife jumps from her seat and shouts, "Look at that bastard! The whole neighborhood is satisfied, but he's not!"

Wrapped in shopping bags and loaded down with electronics and various presents, a Russian tourist walks through a busy Tokyo airport. A Japanese man, who's late for his flight, bumps into the Russian and knocks the overloaded man down to the floor. The Japanese man begins to frantically apologize. Meanwhile, the Russian just quietly surveys the heap of broken souvenirs.

"I'm terribly sorry," the Japanese man says, and he pulls out some fancy glasses. "Here, these are for you. I don't want you to feel badly about your trip to my country."

Later, in the airplane, the Russian decides to check out the glasses. He puts them on, and—oh, a miracle!—everyone he looks at is completely naked! He doesn't care about the movies or sleep for the rest of his flight!

Back home, the Russian keeps his new glasses on, he's having so much fun. He enters his house to find his wife and a man both naked in bed. He takes the glasses off, but he still sees them naked. The man rubs his eyes, blinks frantically, and then, throwing the glasses to the floor, he shouts: "Hell, it looks like I've injured my eyes with these damn glasses!"

"I think my wife is being unfaithful to me."
"How do you know?"
"We moved to another town, but I've noticed the same plumber keeps coming to our house."

"Honey," the husband says to his wife over the phone, "I have to stay at work late tonight, at least until 10:30."
"Are you sure about that, dear," she asks. "Can I count on that?"

Ivan comes home late one night. While waiting for his wife to make his supper, he steps out on the balcony to have a cigarette. There he sees a man. "What are you doing here?" he asks the stranger.
"I'm waiting for the streetcar."
Ivan finishes his cigarette and goes back in to eat his supper. "Wait a minute..." he thinks to himself. "A streetcar, on the third floor, at two in the morning?" He returns to the balcony but finds nobody there.
"He must've gotten on the streetcar by now," Ivan concludes.

If a woman walks with her head turned slightly to the left, that means she has a lover. If a woman walks with her head turned slightly to the right, that means she has a lover too. In general, if a woman has a head on her shoulders, she has a lover.

Two men are fishing.

"Listen, Ivan," says one, "I know that you're seeing my wife. That's not good…".

"You Petrovs are a strange family!" interjects the other. "Your wife says it's good, you say it isn't…".

𝐀 blond, beautiful, and intelligent woman is looking for a husband for her daughter.

—From a dating column ad

𝐀 man comes home and finds his wife in bed with his best friend. The friend says to him, "We both love her. Since both of us are competitors, let's solve this problem by playing our favorite card game. Whoever wins the game wins her."

"Okay," the husband replies. "But you have to put some money up, too; I won't play just for fun."

𝐀 woman departs on a business trip. The next day she receives a telegram from her husband. It reads: "Where are our utensils?"

"Sleep at home," advises the return telegram.

The next day she receives another telegram from her husband, asking the same question. Again her reply is, "Sleep at home."

When she finally returns home, her husband asks, "Why didn't you tell me where our utensils were?"

"I told you to sleep at home." And with these words, she walks to the bedroom, lifts the bed cover, and shows her husband where she has put the utensils.

"Ever since I found about my husband's cheating," one woman tells another, "one thought is always on my mind."

"Who that woman is?"

"No, how he managed to do it."

A woman says to her husband, "Sergei, our daughter-in-law is being unfaithful."

"That's her problem," he answers.

"But she's cheating on our son!"

"That's his problem."

"But she's cheating on him with you!"

"That's my problem."

"What about me, Sergei?"

"That's your problem."

"Honey, you're the best woman in the world," he wrote to his wife. "Last night I had a chance to prove it once again."

A man comes home unexpectedly to find his wife in bed with another man. He challenges the stranger to a duel.

They walk into another room and close the door. The man then says to the stranger, "Why should any of us die? Let's both shoot into the air. Then we'll fall on the floor and wait. She'll rush in. Whoever she approaches first will have her."

The stranger agrees. And so they both shoot into the air and fall to the floor.

The wife walks in, looks at the two bodies and shouts, "Honey, you can come out! They are both dead."

A man knocks at the door of his apartment, but a stranger with a Herculean build opens the door and asks, "Who are you?"

"I'm her husband."

"What do you want?"

"I want to have my dinner."

"How about some of yesterday's soup?"

"Okay."

"Then come back tomorrow," 'Hercules' says as he shuts the door.

"It looks almost new," one woman says to another, pointing to a sofa. "Why would you want to get rid of it?"

"You see," says the other, "I was unfaithful to my husband on this sofa."

"If I had to get rid of everything I've used when I was unfaithful to my husband, all we'd be left with is our chandelier. On second thought, there was one odd fellow…".

"Tell me, honey," a dying man asks his wife, who's standing at his bedside, "have you ever cheated on me?"

"Yes, dear, but only twice. Once with an orchestra and the other time with a hockey team."

"Why did you divorce your husband?" one woman asks another.

"He was treating me like a dog."

"How's that?"

"He wanted me to be faithful to him."

LOOKS

Don't blame the mirror if you're ugly.
—An old Russian saying

"**W**ow! Where did you get that gorgeous body?" he jokes.
"I bought it at the store," she jokes back.
"What about your face?" he keeps on joking. "Did they give that to you for change?"

"**C**ould you help me?" a man asks a sales clerk as he looks for a birthday present for his wife. "What would be the right dress size for a woman who is a 5'9" tall and weighs 105 pounds?"
"Nina?" the clerk asks her more experienced coworker. "What does a 5'9", 105-pound woman need?"
"A statue," Nina replies.

On a visit to Tokyo a Russian lady steps onto a street scale. "One at a time, please," the computerized scale says in a metallic tone.

"**W**hen I see something funny, I can laugh till I cry…".
"Then shaving must be really hard for you!"

"**W**ho is this handsome man?" the little boy asks his

mother, pointing at the picture of an athletic young man with a full head of dark, wavy hair.

"That's your father," his mother says.

"Then who is that fat, bald man who lives with us?"

"They showed her on TV last night. She's 85 now," an elderly woman was telling another elderly woman, referring to her favorite movie star of days gone by.

"Yes," the second woman answers. "Finally, the dream of our youth—to look like her—has come true."

"I'll give you a thousand rubles," the bald man says to the hairstylist (who has a full head of hair), "if you can give me the same cut you have and if you can do it fast."

"Okay," says the stylist, and he gives himself a buzz cut.

An overweight woman enters the doctor's office sideways—the only way possible, given her dimensions.

"You have to cut your meals, madam," warns the doctor.

"Well, doctor," she replies. "I don't have any meals at all. All I do is finish the meals of the other members of my family."

"Well," the doctor says, "it seems to me you're overly concerned about leftovers. Why don't you get a pet pig?"

"You want me to be finishing up after it too?"

A hookworm crawls down a busy street, wearing this button: "Want to lose weight? Ask me how."

A man runs into a police station to report that his wife is missing. An officer asks him to describe what she looks like.

"Okay, but for heaven's sake, officer!" the man pleads. "If you find her, don't show her my description!"

"Your teeth are so beautiful!"

"Thank you. I inherited them from my mother."

"Isn't it something! You're lucky they fit you so well."

"Your hair is so beautiful! It looks just like a wig."
"It is."
"Really? I would have never thought so."

Two women are talking:
"I'm trembling when I think about my 50th anniversary!"
"Why, what happened to you then?"

"Your wife looks even prettier now!"
"How do you know?"
"I saw her with you in your car yesterday."
"No you didn't! That was our bulldog."

"What kind of chicken is this, waiter? It's nothing but skin and bones."
"That's the latest style, sir. It's on a diet."

"How would you like me to cut your hair, sir?" the hair-dresser asks his client.
"Quietly."

Once upon a time, a fisherman caught the Golden Fish.
"Let me go back in the water, good man, and I'll grant any wish of yours," said the Golden Fish.
"Okay," the man said, after taking some time to think. "I want you to stop the war in Chechnya."
"Well, good man," said the Golden Fish, "that may be too hard for me, because it involves a lot of people. Do you have another wish?"
"Okay," the fisherman said, "I want my old, ugly, stupid, and mad wife to become a young, beautiful, smart, and joyful woman."
"Let me see her picture," the Golden Fish said, and she

looked at the picture and pondered for a while. Finally she said: "Well…what did you say again about the war?"

"You are so white. Where are you from?" one woman asks another at a Black Sea beach.
"From Siberia."
"You don't have sun there at all?!"
"We do, but I was working that day."

Two middle-aged men are having a conversation:
"How are you, Ivan?"
"Like a watermelon—my stomach is getting bigger, but my tail is getting smaller."

"Did I shave you before, sir?" the barber asks his client.
"No, I got that scar during the war."

While riding a motor scooter, a boy hits an overweight man.
"Couldn't you go around?" the man protests.
"No," the boy says, "I was afraid I'd run out of gas!"

"Why don't all of those people who eat so much spaghetti gain weight?"
"Because some of them eat it crosswise, while others eat it lengthwise."

In a public sauna, two little boys approach a man with a big stomach:
"What's in your stomach?" one boy asks.
"A bomb," the man jokes.
"Let's explode it!" the second boy whispers into his friend's ear.
"No, that's too dangerous!" says the first boy. "The wick is too short!"

Everybody has a bald spot, it's just that most people keep it covered with hair.

"What is this? I'm not going to pay for it!" an angry customer complains to the tailor, talking about his new suit. "Look, the left sleeve barely covers my elbow!"

"Let me show you," the tailor says. "Here, lean your torso to the left and pull in your left arm… Yes, that's good."

"Now, what about my right sleeve?" the client says. "It's almost half a foot too long."

"Nothing wrong with that, sir. Just lean your torso forward and bend your right forearm like this… Yes!"

"Still, I can't wear these pants. The left leg is much longer than the right!"

"Well, why don't you squat just a bit… and now put your left leg slightly ahead of the right. Perfect!"

Sitting on a bench, two doctors see the man leaving the tailor's shop, wearing his new suit. "Poor fellow," says one. "That's quite a serious form of paralysis."

"Yes, I agree," says the other. "But look how perfectly his suit fits him!"

Baldness is the slow transformation of one's head into one's behind. It begins in *form* and finishes in *content*.

A farmer is invited to attend a wedding in the city. During the celebration he comments, "I've been to many a wedding, but I've never seen this before." He points to the bride. "Is that a he or a she?"

"Hey, be quiet!" someone says. "That's my daughter!"

"I'm sorry, sir!" the farmer says. "I didn't know you were the bride's father."

"Actually, I'm her mother!"

"Where do you want me to part your hair, sir?" the hairstylist asks his almost bald client.

"In the middle, please," the client says.

"That's not possible, sir," the stylist says. "You have an uneven number of hairs."

"Why does our father have no hair?" the little boy asks his mother.

"Because he thinks a lot."

"Now I know why you, mommy, have so much of it."

Two men are sharing a compartment on the train. To strike up a conversation, one man says, "Take the mustaches out and you'd look exactly like my wife!"

"I'm sorry," says the other, "can't you see that I have no mustaches?"

"Yes, I can see that. But my wife does…".

A hunchback and a blind man walk along the street. The hunchback decides to make fun of the blind man. "Look at that blonde's legs!" he jokes.

A moment later the blind man asks, in his turn: "Do you have any smoke?"

"No, I don't," the hunchback replies.

"Could you please check in your knapsack?"

A hunchback tells his friend, who stutters, that a TV station is looking for announcers with speech defects. The friend goes to the station, only to find out that he has been duped. He calls the hunchback and says, "Come over and take your picture back!"

"Why?" asks the hunchback.

"Because I can't close my picture album."

"Ivan, my boss tells me that I'm very beautiful," she says.

"I told you!" he says. "This guy is a pervert."

"I've been swimming for more than six months now, but I still can't lose any weight," one overweight woman complains to another.

"Why would you think that swimming helps?" the second woman asks. "Have you never seen a whale?"

"Your hands are so dirty," the client tells his small-town hairdresser.

"Yeah, I still haven't washed a single head today."

Q: How is a fat girlfriend like a motor scooter?
A: You love to have them, but you don't want your friends to know about it.

Mother fly is walking with daughter fly on a bald man's head:

"When I was your age," she says, "there was only a narrow trail here."

Two women run into each other on the street:

"You've changed so much after these twenty years!" says one, "If it wasn't for your dress, I wouldn't have recognized you!"

"Honey, I don't want you to cut your hair that short!"

"Well, Ivan, you didn't ask me for an opinion when you lost yours completely!"

Two women are talking:

"Can you imagine!" says one, "Today, on the subway, two young men offered me their seats, both at the same time."

"So was there enough space for you after that?"

"Do you have breasts?"

"Yes?! Why?"
"Then why don't you wear them?"

Two old friends meet at a reunion:
"I heard you got married. How's your wife? Is she pretty?"
"She's very beautiful. Her right eye is hazel and looks to the left. Her left eye is blue and looks down, toward her nose. Her left arm is short and crooked, and her right arm is long and thick. She also has a twisted neck. And her legs! You should see her legs... Well, why am I telling you all that—you never understood Picasso anyway!"

"You don't look well at all, madam."
"How can you say such things to a woman?!"
"I'm sorry, madam. I thought women your age stopped paying attention to such things."

"You need to put something on, honey," he says. "I know it's hot, but our neighbors may think I married you for your money."

"You're lucky," she says. "I still look great for my years, and I don't even have to wear a bra."
"Yes," he agrees, "you look better when you don't wear one: It makes all the wrinkles on your face disappear."

Q: What's better—to be bald or to be a fool?
A: To be fool—it's less noticeable.

"Daddy, is it true that you got that big stomach from drinking a lot of beer?"
"No, that's not true, son. Remember, a stomach doesn't get big *from* drinking beer, but *for* drinking it."

Q: What's better—to be bald or to be a fool?
A: To be a bald fool—you have nothing to lose.

"This drink makes you irresistible," he says.
"But I didn't drink any," she says.
"I did," he explains.

"How did it go last night?" one woman asks another.
"That guy was so rude and arrogant! When I told him that I didn't want to see him anymore, he just turned off the light…".

"Who is that frump you were talking to?"
"That's my wife."
"Oh, I'm sorry, I made a mistake!"
"That's okay. It was me who made the mistake…".

A woman goes to confession:
"I'm so sinful, father!" she says.
"Tell me about your sins, daughter."
"Every time I look in the mirror I think, 'I'm so beautiful, I'm so beautiful..'.".
"Go in peace," the priest says. "It is no sin, my daughter, it is a delusion."

"I love nature!" one woman says to another.
"Even after what it's done to you?"

BUSINESS AND COMMERCE THE RUSSIAN WAY

Don't let yourself be fooled by others—buy here!
—From a sign in a store

Two former classmates, a dropout and the best student, meet ten years later. The dropout is driving a Mercedes, wearing expensive clothes and jewelry. The best student, meanwhile, is barely surviving in the new economic reality.

"How did you manage to do so well in life, Ivan?" the best student asks. "I recall that you didn't even know the multiplication tables."

"Well, that's simple, Sergei," the dropout explains. "I buy goods for 200 hundred at one place and resell them for 400 at another. This two percent—the difference—is what I keep for myself!"

Q: What is business the Russian way?
A: You steal a case of vodka, pour the contents of every bottle down the drain, return the empty bottles for a refund, and then get drunk on the change.

A man asks his six-year-old son, "What is two times two?"
"Seven."

"No, you're wrong! It's four."
"I know that, dad, but don't I have to haggle?"

People in other countries have therapy; we have shock.

If you must steal, at least do so from profits, not from expenses.

—Mikhail Zhvanetsky

A businessman sends a telegram to his partner. "Accept your offer. With respect, Rabinovich."

The post office clerk checks the text, and then lends some cost-saving advice: "You don't really have to say 'with respect', Mr. Rabinovich."

The man thinks for a moment, then replies, "I guess you're right. But how do you know my partner?"

Two future *New Russians* (please see chapter ten) meet to talk business during the days of Perestroika. "I have a railroad car full of vodka. Are you interested?"

"How much?"
"One million."
"Deal."

They both leave—one to search for the vodka, the other for a million.

"Ivan, have you finally settled down?"
"No, I'm still working."

At a job interview:
"I have a wife and three children."
"What else can you do?"

𝐀 bum walks into a posh store that sells expensive home hardware. He heads toward the bathroom fixtures department. There he finds a gold-plated toilet bowl that he likes, takes his pants off, and commences to 'test drive' the bowl.

Alarmed, a salesman runs from the other end of the store, shock written all over his face. "What are you doing!? You can't do this here!" he shouts at the homeless man.

"Why?" asks the bum. "It doesn't work?"

"Of course not!"

"Then why are you selling it?"

𝐐: What starts with an *R* and never ends?

A: Reorganization.

𝐓he boss calls in his secretary, undresses her, and starts making love to her.

The secretary protests. "Sir, let's close the door first!"

"No, we can't, Tanya," the boss says. "They will think we're drinking vodka in here!"

"𝐄xcuse me!" the customer complains to the store manager. "I asked for Swiss cheese, but instead they gave me the Russian!"

"But how could you know the difference, sir?" the manager wonders. "Did you talk to it?"

𝐀 guest, who stopped by for a cup of tea, informs the hostess, "I would like to wash my hands."

"Are you going to use soap?" she asks.

"Yes, I need some."

"Then you won't get any sugar with your tea."

𝐀n elderly woman inquires of a farmer selling produce on the market: "How come your cucumbers are so crooked, withered, and yellow?"

The farmer, a middle-aged macho man, gives the woman a look of despise and says, "Look at yourself, old lady!"

Q: Will people steal under Communism?
A: No, there won't be anything left.

"Hello, do you sell dollars?"
"Yes, we do."
"What is your exchange rate?"
"Two rubles for one dollar."
"What? That's impossible! Is this a bank?"
"No, sir, this is a print shop."

Ivan comes to Abram and asks if he can borrow one hundred rubles until next month. He promises to pay back two hundred and offers his ax as collateral.

As Ivan is leaving with the money, Abram asks, "Listen, Ivan, why don't you make it easier for yourself and pay me one half of your debt now?"

Ivan agrees to give the money back. On his way home, he thinks to himself, "Isn't it something? I have no money, no ax, and I have to pay one hundred again next month. But yet it all seems to work out right!"

"Hey girl, do you wanna be in business?"
"Yes I do, as long as my mother doesn't find anything out."

"I had to work two shifts in a row yesterday," one worker says to another.
"Why is that?"
"Well, I dozed off at my workplace and nobody woke me up."

There were two friends: Ivan and Dmitri. Ivan was doing okay; he had a small business. Soon he expanded and started to do even better.

Dmitri wasn't that fortunate, although he wasn't trying all that hard either. And soon he got into some heavy drinking.

To help his friend out, Ivan offered Dmitri a job. "All you have to do, Dmitri," he explained to his friend, "is to take cash to the bank before five o'clock every day. You will deposit one half of it, and keep the other half for yourself."

Six months down the road, Dmitri was doing just great: a new car, a new house, etc. But he still wasn't happy.

"Something wrong, Dmitri?" Ivan asked him one day. "You look disappointed lately."

"Yes I am, Ivan," Dmitri complained. "Look, I'm the one who goes to the bank all the time. Why do I have to share with you?"

A drunk man stumbles into his apartment, where he barely manages to give his explanation to his demanding wife. "I spend all my pay on alcohol in protest to the International Monetary Fund's policy toward our country!"

A woman enters a bakery to buy some *baranki* (a type of Russian pretzel). "How much is your baranki?" she asks the owner.

"Five rubles per dozen," the owner replies.

"The bakery across the street sells them for only three rubles per dozen."

"Then why you didn't buy them there?"

"Because they don't have any left."

"Well, when I don't have any left, I sell them for only one ruble per dozen."

"I've heard you hired a new secretary. Is she cute?"

"Yes, she is."

"How does she dress?"

"Quickly."

"**W**hy are you late for work?"
"I left my house late."
"Why didn't you leave earlier?"
"It was too late to leave earlier."

A New Russian is being questioned by the Tax Inspectorate officer:
"Do you really think we believe that you've bought all those mansions, jewelry, and fancy cars with legally earned money?"
"What other money could it be?" the New Russian asks.
"I can tell you, this is the Russian workers' money!"
"Are you sure the workers have this kind of money, officer?"

"**D**on't you know everything in America is owned by the Jews?"
"Well, after all, that's not a bad investment of the proceeds derived from selling out Russia."

The secretary walks into the office and finds some workers there, who carry out her boss's sofa. She turns to her boss and asks him, her voice trembling, "Does this mean I'm fired?"

Q: How are a naked businessman, a naked politician, and a naked street peddler alike?
A: They all have one thing that hangs down below their knees: a businessman, his belly; a politician, his tongue; and a street peddler, his arms.

"**H**oney, I've invited my colleagues to have dinner with us," a man says to his wife. "Could you make something up for seven o'clock?"

"Sure, dear," she answers. "Should I make it so that they'll want to come more often, or never again?"

A successful multinational corporation is looking for a psychic. For a confidential interview please call the number... You know the number, don't you?

"**W**here's my old jacket, the one with a big patch and a stain?"

"I threw it out, honey."

"Why did you do that? What am I going to wear when I go to the tax office now?"

A dialogue at the market:

"How much?"

"Nine ninety nine."

"What nine ninety nine?"

"What how much?"

*A*fter learning that she's fired, the secretary walks into her boss's office. "With my two universities" (she points to her breasts), "broad erudition" (she pats her lower back), "and narrow specialization" (she puts her hands around her waist), "I'm a welcome asset in any organization. But you, sir, with your weak character" (she shows her small finger), "will only disappoint your future secretaries!"

A businessman is being questioned at a Tax Inspectorate office. "We've checked your income tax return," an officer tells him. "Could you please explain how were you able to buy the latest model of Mercedes?"

"Well, I used to have a *Lada* (a Russian car)," the businessman explains. "I sold it for a good price, borrowed the rest, and bought this Mercedes."

"Then where did you get the money to buy a Lada?"

"Before the Lada, I used to have a motorcycle. I sold it for a good price, borrowed the rest, and bought the Lada."

"Well, sir, we still need to know where the money came from that you used to buy the motorcycle."

"I don't have to tell you that, officer."

"And why is that?"

"Because for that, I already did the time."

A businessman comes to the mayor's office. He is greeted by a bureaucrat, who leads him to his office. In the office the businessman sees two signs prominently displayed at the city official's desk. One says "No smoking"; the other says "I don't take bribes."

"I would like to talk to you about some property that I would like to privatize," the businessman begins.

"Well," the city official ponders, as he takes the "No smoking" sign from his desk. "Why don't we have a smoke first?"

Q: What is the richest country in the world?

A: Russia. They have been selling it off for a long time, but it still has a lot that's up for grabs.

A boy buys a hot dog from a street vendor. He hands over his money and takes the hot dog without saying anything.

"Do you know the magic word, son?" the vendor, a full-bodied lady, asks him.

"Yes I do," the boy replies. "Where's my change?"

A man returns from his business trip to Russia. "I'm declaring bankruptcy," he informs his wife. "Before I went to Russia, I was thinking that, if the Russians live well, they would need bread, and if they don't live well, they would need caskets. So I went over there with a shipload of bread and caskets. And now

I'm broke, because those bastards are neither living nor dying."

"How is that possible?"

"Apparently, it's possible in Russia. They're just barely surviving."

Heard at the market:

"How much do you want for your chicken?"

"One thousand."

"Wow! Does it lay golden eggs?"

"No, I just need the money."

Ivan goes into business. He buys a hotdog cart and sets it up on a busy downtown corner, near a large bank.

One day, his friend Sergei approaches him and asks Ivan if he can lend him some money. Ivan refuses.

"Why?" Sergei asks. "Everyone knows you're doing well, and I'm not asking for much."

"Well, Sergei, you see, in order to get this spot, I had to sign a Non-Competing Agreement with this bank. And according to the terms of the Agreement, they're not allowed to sell hot dogs, and I'm not allowed to lend money."

Heard at a farmers' market:

"So, where's your horse?"

"What horse? I'm selling a rabbit. What are you looking at?"

"I'm looking at the price tag."

MONEY

The government doesn't know where all the money goes. The *New Russians* (please see the next chapter) don't know where to put it. And the rest of the Russians don't know where to get it.

"I wish I had enough money to buy an aircraft!"
"What do you need an aircraft for?"
"I don't need an aircraft, but I need a lot of money."

"Can I borrow some money from you?"
"I don't have any on me."
"What about at home?"
"At home, everything is okay, thank you."

The head of the national bank visits his doctor. "I don't know who can help me, doctor," he says. "The ruble is falling steadily. I'm going nuts!"

"Well, sir," the doctor says, "if it's falling you need to see a sex therapist. And if you're going nuts I'll send you to a psychiatrist."

Q: What is the difference between one ruble and one dollar?

A: One dollar.

A man discovers that some of the money in his wallet is missing. He asks his son, "Kolya, why did you take my money without asking me first?"

"Why do you think it's me?" the son asks. "Why don't you ask mother?"

"It wasn't mother: there's still some money left," the man replies.

"**W**hat is your problem, sir?"
"Money and women. I don't have either!"

"**T**he doctor told me that I'm going to lose my memory. What should I do?"
"Why don't you lend me some money?"

"**W**hen are you going to pay me back, Ivan?"
"As soon as my rich uncle from the States comes to Russia to visit me."
"Well, that's an old story, one I've been listening to for years."
"I can show you his letter."
"So what does he write?"
"He's asking me to buy him a ticket."

Q: What is a paycheck?
A: Well, nobody really remembers—so long ago it was.

"**W**hat could you buy for the old ruble?"
"Nothing!"
"What about the new one?"
"A hundred times more!"

An elderly man sees a well-endowed young woman tanning on a beach. He approaches her and says, "Excuse me madam, your breasts are so beautiful. May I touch them only once? I'll pay you one hundred rubles."

"Are you crazy," she explodes. "Leave me alone before I call the police."

"Please calm down, madam," the old man says. "I'll pay you one thousand rubles if you let me touch…".

"Get lost, old fart!"

"How about two thousand!?" The man is persistent.

"Okay, grandpa," the woman finally agrees. "But do it quickly, I don't want anybody to see!"

The man touches her breasts, murmuring, "Oh my god, oh my god!..".

"What's wrong?" the woman asks.

"Oh my god," the man says. "Where am I going to get two thousand rubles?"

"**R**abinovich, can I borrow ten rubles?"

"From whom?"

"**T**here must have been *something* attractive in your husband," the divorce judge says to a woman. "Otherwise, you wouldn't have married him."

"There was," the woman replies. "But, to the last ruble, it has all gone somewhere else by now."

"**M**y husband is so disorganized: Every day he puts his wallet in a different place!"

"**M**y wife is bugging me every day: 'Give me some money, give me some money'!"

"What does she do with it?"

"I don't know, I haven't given her any yet!"

A young man inquires in a bookstore: "Do you have the new book *How To Make A Million In Five Days?*"

"Yes we do, sir," the clerk says. "And if you care to hear my advice, I would strongly recommend buying the *Criminal Code* too."

"Ivan, Dmitri is asking me to lend him some money. Do you think I should do it?"

"Of course you should!"

"Why?"

"Because if you don't, he'll come to me."

A stranger approaches the farmer, whose bicycle has just been stolen. The stranger says, "If you buy me a drink at the local bar, I'll tell you who stole your bicycle."

The farmer is glad to hear this, and so he says to the stranger, "I'll buy you two drinks if you tell me who did it."

The stranger slowly consumes the alcohol. Finally, the farmer asks impatiently, "So, who did it?"

"Thieves!"

"I'm asking you one last time: When are you going to pay me back?"

"Oh, I'm so glad I won't hear this stupid question anymore!"

Q: Why don't people like paying back their debts?

A: The money that people borrow is somebody else's money, borrowed for a short time. The money that people return is their own money, given away forever.

"Why did Robin Hood rob only the rich?"

"Well, what could he take from the poor?"

"Ivan, how did you manage to spend one thousand rubles that fast?"

"Well, you know, honey…one hundred here, one hundred there… Then I was going to buy you some flowers with the rest—and there goes one thousand!"

Walking down the street, a young man sees an elderly lady sitting on a bench and crying.

"What happened, babushka?" he asks her.

"Someone just stole my wallet and it had all my money in it!" she wails.

"Well, how much money did you have in there?"

"One hundred rubles!"

"Here's the money. You don't have to cry!"

"Thank you, son… Maybe you could give me my wallet back too?"

News from abroad:
The first issue of dollars printed in the Russian language was announced today in Washington.

"Doctor, my husband has a strange disease," the woman says. "I think it's from stress and overwork. Every time I start asking him for money, he can't hear me at all."

"Well, dear, it's not a disease—it's a talent."

Q: What is the exchange rate between a ruble, a dollar, and a pound?

A: One pound of rubles equals one dollar.

"Is your salary small too?" she asked him in bed.

NEW RUSSIANS

The youngest category of jokes in Russia, these New Russian stories came into existence in the early nineties, which are known as the period of Wild Capitalism. These jokes target a new stratum of Russian society—the newly rich. While most New Russians are hardworking entrepreneurs and professionals, there are stories in abundance about overnight rags-to-riches success, or sudden wealth acquired by bribing authorities, through protectionism, extortion, and/or illegal deals with newly privatized state-owned property.

The image of the New Russian depicted in these stories can be somewhat confusing for someone who is unfamiliar with Russian life. These jokes reflect the Russian public's ambivalence toward the rich and the accumulation of wealth in general. One joke may portray a New Russian as a smart businessman. Another may picture him as dumb and showy, spoiled by riches, like a grown-up kid.

Yet a third type of joke tends to synonymize the New Russian with the mafioso. It targets the shoddy side of this stratum, the criminal jargon, the massive, flashy jewelry (such as golden 'dog chains' and 'fastening nut' rings), along with a scary manner of speech, which involves some pointing of bent fingers in front of the listener's face.

Q.: What do you call a man surrounded by three New Russians?

A: A prey.

Q: What do you call a man surrounded by a dozen New Russians?

A: A banker.

Q: What do you call a man surrounded by three dozen New Russians?

A: A godfather.

Q: What do you call a man surrounded by ten dozen New Russians?

A: A prison guard.

Q: Why are there so many New Russians acting as sponsors and benefactors?

A: For them, it's easier to give money away than to explain how it was earned.

Q: Why do most New Russians look foolish?

A: A fool takes first; then he thinks.

A New Russian is in a church, where he is distracted by a beggar standing next to him. The beggar is continuously crossing himself while murmuring a prayer.

Finally, the New Russian loses his patience. He asks the beggar, "Hey man, what are you praying for?"

"For some food tonight," the beggar explains.

The New Russian pulls out a 100-dollar bill. He gives it to the poor man and says, pointing to the exit, "Here, this should last you for a week or two. And don't bother god with this small stuff anymore!"

Of all cultural events, cuisine is my favorite. Of all theaters, I prefer a restaurant.

A New Russian comes to an old Jew and says, "Father,

can you lend me some money?"

"In your income statement, sir," the Tax Inspectorate officer says to a businessman, "you declared your income to be five million. But we have some documents showing your expenditures for the same period to be at least ten million. How would you explain that?"

"Well, officer, that means only one thing: I am working very hard to make ends meet."

Four New Russians are sitting in a sauna. After one of them finishes a conversation on his cell phone, another says to him, "That's an old model cell phone you have there. Do you see this scar on my hand? I have a cell phone implanted right into my hand."

"So what?" the third man says. "I have a virtual cell phone! There's no hardware at all. I dial the number in my mind and speak mentally without ever opening my mouth!"

At this moment, the fourth man's eyes start to pop, and his tongue is coming out of his mouth. "I'm receiving a fax," he explains to his amazed colleagues.

A New Russian visits the dentist. The dentist looks into the man's mouth and nearly falls off his chair. The New Russian's top jaw is made of 24-K solid gold. His bottom jaw is made of pure platinum.

"How can I help you, sir?" the dentist asks, finally gathering himself for a question.

"Can you install an alarm system, doc?"

Two children of New Russians are playing in the sand box. One of them breaks his scoop. He pulls out a cell phone, flips up the mouthpiece, and starts using it as a scoop.

The other kid looks at him disapprovingly and says, "What are you doing? You'll break it!"

"Well, so what?" the kid with the cell phone says. "My dad will buy me another one tomorrow."

"Yeah. And today you're gonna walk around with just a pager, like a loser!"

Climbing out of his Mercedes 600, a New Russian runs into his old school classmate.

"Hi, Ivan," the classmate says. "How are you? We haven't seen each other for at least ten years."

After they hug each other, the New Russian says, playing with his Rolex, "Well, you know, Sergei, it's really tough to be in big business nowadays. Meetings, presentations, business lunches, etc. What about you and your wife?"

"Well, we're both unemployed and, to tell you the truth, Ivan, we haven't eaten for two days."

"That's not good, buddy!" the New Russian says, as he makes a move indicating that he's leaving. "You have to eat, guys, you have to force yourselves!"

A restaurant manager walks over to a man who is known to be one of the city's most powerful crime barons. The manager whispers into his ear, "Sir, your people just killed one of our waiters."

"Don't worry," the baron says. "Just put him on my bill."

Two New Russians meet at a Mercedes dealership. "Hi, Ivan. Say, what are you doing here, any way? You just bought a '600' last week. Did you wreck it?"

"No," says the other, putting out his cigarette, as he slowly replies, "but the ashtray is full already."

Ivan returns from his first trip to the States. His friends ask him, "So, Ivan, tell us. How did you find America?"

"You wouldn't believe me, guys," Ivan says. "They have everything we have here in Moscow. They even use the same money."

A New Russian walks into a Swiss bank and asks to see a manager. "I'd like to get a loan," he says.

"Yes sir," the manager says, "and what would be the amount?"

"One hundred dollars."

"I am sorry, sir, but the sum you're asking for is one hundred times below our minimum loan amount."

"I'll pay good interest. Just name it!"

"That's not enough, sir. We will need collateral as well," the manager continues, thinking that, by asking for collateral, he will probably be rid of this customer.

"No problem," the New Russian says. "Will my Mercedes do?"

"Okay, then, please sign the contract. Here's $100. We'll see you next year, at which time you will need to bring $200. And I will require the keys for your Mercedes."

The next year, as the New Russian is picking up his car, the manager could not resist asking him, "Don't you find this whole deal a bit strange, sir?"

"Not at all," the New Russian explains. "Where else would I find parking for $100 a year in downtown Zurich?"

"**I**s this a quiet place?" the man who was shopping around for a house asked the neighbors.

"Yes indeed, sir," one woman replied. "When they killed the previous owner, nobody heard a thing!"

A Zaporozhec (Zapor)—the cheapest and ugliest car in Russia—rams into a Mercedes that is stopped at a red light.

A New Russian jumps out of the Mercedes. He walks over to the Zapor's driver and shouts, "Are you blind? You know how much this is going to cost you?"

"Frankly, sir," the Zapor's owner says timidly, "I thought you probably didn't have to stop on red."

Two New Russians are sitting in a sauna. "How many bodyguards do you have?" one asks the other.

"Eleven. What about you?" says the other.

"I have eleven too. So, why don't we play some soccer?"

Q: What are the three most popular cars among New Russians?

A: Mercedes, BMW, and a hearse.

"**I** just came from Barbados," one New Russian says to another. "I had so much fun. What about you? I've heard you've been somewhere too."

"Yeah, I have. But I can't remember the place's name. I guess I'll have to wait until they develop the film."

Two New Russians are having a conversation. "So, how did you sleep last night? I wouldn't want to have your problems."

"I slept like a baby—I was waking up every other hour and crying."

A New Russian is visiting a Mercedes dealership in Moscow. "Hey, brother, I need some help over here. Tell me more about this car," he says to a salesman, pointing to a newer model.

The salesman names the gamut of all possible options and features.

"What about the speed?" the New Russian asks.

"It's a very fast car, sir," the salesman continues. "For instance, if you leave in this car right now, you'll be in St. Petersburg at exactly 11:00 tonight…".

"No, thanks, brother," the New Russian interjects, and he heads for the exit. "Think about it. Why the hell would I need to be in St. Petersburg tonight?"

A New Russian has been badly injured in a car accident. He's talking to his friend in a hospital.

"How did it happened?" the friend asks him.

"I was doing over a hundred in my Mercedes when, all of a sudden, I saw this man riding on a horse in front of me. I hit the brakes as hard as I could, but I couldn't avoid the collision. Too bad, the car is a total wreck now…".

"What happened to the man on the horse?"

"What could possibly happen to him? He and his horse were made out of bronze!"

A man is signaling for a cab at a busy road. Suddenly, a Mercedes 600 pulls over and an apparently charged-up New Russian gets out. He walks around his Mercedes, closely inspecting it for something. Then he beckons the man.

When the man comes closer, the New Russian grabs him, slams his face against the Mercedes, and yells, "Now tell me, what made you think this is a taxi?"

A boy and his family are invited to attend a party at a New Russian's mansion. The boy is amazed to see a huge TV, which looks as if it's been cast from solid gold. He takes a deep breath and asks the host, "Excuse me, sir…is this TV made of gold?"

"Yes it is," the New Russian replies casually. "Twenty-four-carat solid gold, to be exact."

"But how do you watch it?" the boy asks, obviously confused.

"It's not for watching, son. It's for showing."

One New Russian says to another: "I went to the *Bolshoy Theater* yesterday; I had so much fun!"

"Watching an opera!? How is that?"

"Our hockey players beat the Canadians in the final game!"

"In a theater?"

"No, I was watching TV in the theater's snack bar."

POLITICS

In addition to fools and poor roads, Russia has another ailment—fools giving directions at crossroads.

Last night, without gaining his sobriety, the President dismissed the entire government.
>   —From an alternative Russian news flash

In the middle of a *Duma* session (the Russian parliament), a man is plowing his way closer to the presidium from a distant row.

"Could you please move aside," he asks a woman in front of him. "I can't see from here."

"I can give you my binoculars."

"No thanks. My rifle has a scope."

The Communists once sent their agitator to a hospital for the mentally ill. After finishing his harangue, the agitator asked the only person who had not applauded him, "Why didn't you cheer like everybody else, madam?"

"Because I'm not sick, thank you," the woman explained.

"I'm a nurse here."

Q: Why have the Baltic states—Latvia, Lithuania, and Estonia—been knocking on NATO's door since the breakdown of the USSR, and yet they're still not members?

A: They're too small to reach the doorbell.

Q: How will we know when Cuba has finally constructed Communism?

A: They'll begin to import sugar and cigars from the States.

A policeman approaches a motorist, who has parked his car in Red Square.

"Don't you know you can't park here?" the policeman demands. "The government is just a few yards away."

"That's okay, officer," the motorist says. "My car is equipped with the latest theft-deterrent system."

"Russians, how do you live?" jokes the President.

"Very well!" the Russians joke back.

The Czar once sent his tax collectors out to visit his subjects. When they had returned with all the gold they could manage to collect, the Czar asked them, "How are my people?"

"Your majesty, the people are crying, and they're drinking in despair. They say we took their last."

"This is far from the last!" the Czar declared. "Go again and bring me more!"

This time, the tax collectors took all the silver they could take. "How are my people?" the Czar asked when they brought

him this tribute.

"Your majesty, the people are in despair, they're selling their last shirts, they're drinking even more heavily. They say we've taken all they had."

"I know my people, and I know this is not all!" the Czar declared. "Go again and bring me more!"

When the collectors returned once more, they brought with them mostly copper. They told the Czar, "Your majesty, the people do nothing but drink and have parties like there's no to-morrow…".

The Czar finally smiled. And he said, "Now I know you've brought me everything!"

"How's life?"
"Just like Lenin's!"
"And how's that?"
"They don't feed me, but they don't bury me either!"

To justify their defeat in the Chechen war, the Russians used the Olympic creed: "The most important thing is not to win, but to take part."

"Excuse me, young man, how could you sell this garbage?" a customer asks a newsstand owner after buying an ultra-national-ist newspaper.

"Well, unlike you, sir, I don't read it, I just sell it."

A corrupt politician, sensing an end to his days in power, cut the school budget. In its place, he issued a decree to spend more funds on improving the living conditions of prison inmates.

A train stops in the middle of Russia, because no more tracks have been laid ahead. On board are Czar Nicholas II, Lenin, Stalin, Khrushchev, Brezhnev, Chernenko, Andropov, Gorbachev, and Yeltsin.

Czar Nicholas stands up and says, "I will make this train move." He gets off the train, mounts his horse and rides off to Paris.

Lenin then stands up and says, "I will make this train move." He leaves the car and says to the passengers, "Come on people, don't just sit there! Let's work hard, let's do something! Eventually we will manage to get the train moving again." The agitated passengers kick the wheels, jump around the train, even chant some things, but the train still doesn't move.

Stalin stands up and says, "I will make this train move." He leaves the car and returns a few minutes later. "I shot two passengers, and I let them know that I will shoot the rest of them if the train isn't moving by tomorrow morning," and he sits back down again. The train still doesn't move.

Khrushchev then stands up and says, "I will make this train move." He leaves the car and returns a few minutes later. "I've told them to move the tracks from behind the train to the front of it," he says as he sits back down. The train doesn't move.

Brezhnev then stands up and says, "I will make this train move." He instructs everyone to act as if the train is moving, and he sits back down. The train is shaking, but it doesn't move.

Gorbachev now stands up and says, "I will make this train move." He paints big signs that say "We don't have tracks!", "We need help!", gives the signs to the people, and orders them to go outside and protest. The train doesn't move.

Yeltsin, quite put out, finally orders a military attack on the Russian parliament, hoping that this entire railroad incident will be soon forgotten.

A politician tells his wife, "You know, dear, I received two votes in yesterday's election."

"I knew you had a lover!"

Q: What's the difference between the heads of state in Great Britain and in the United States?

A: When meeting with the former you're supposed to kneel on only one knee.

SON: Daddy, what is a president?

FATHER: A president is a person who is in charge. For example, I am the president of our family.

SON: Then who is our mom?

FATHER: She is the Finance Minister.

The Russian prime minister is visiting Saddam Hussein in his personal bomb shelter. All of a sudden the Americans start bombing Bagdad.

"Who built this bunker?" the prime minister asks Hussein, trying hard to hide his fear.

"Relax, it wasn't Russians!"

After a heavy round of drinking, the president is lying down with a terrible headache, bubbling stomach, and throbbing heart.

"Mr. President," his secretary says, knocking at the door, "here's the Prime Minister to see you."

"To hell with him!" the president moans. "I'm sick."

And next morning the papers bring news about another government dismissal by the president.

"What is a mini-skirt?"
"It's a small or short skirt."
"And what is a mini-computer?'
"It's a pocket PC."
"Then why is such a big mess called a Mini-stry?"

Q: Why did they appoint Yeltsin's daughter Tatyana Dyachenko as the president's aide?

A: Because she knows what the president means better than he does himself.

Q: What is the Kremlin's most popular play today?
A: *Live Corpse*, directed by Tatyana Dyachenko.

A poor Russian wakes up in the middle of the night to answer the call of nature. Walking down a hallway that's crowded with huge sacks and cartons, he hits one of them. "Must be potatoes!" he thinks to himself. A few steps later he hits another sack. "Damn rice! Couldn't they move it closer to the wall?" After he hits something once again, this time a box of canned food, he exclaims, "I wonder when the food shortages will be over in this country!?"

A foreign leader makes an official visit to the Kremlin. Yeltsin is helped to the room prepared for their one-on-one meeting, but when he arrives he immediately begins to undress.

"What are you doing, Mr. President?" the foreign leader asks Yeltsin.

"I'm getting ready for your examination, Doctor Debakey."

Q: What is the largest mishap of the century?

A: The disaster of the *Titanic*, not the cruiser *Aurora* (the battleship from which the first shot of the Bolshevik Revolution was fired, in October of 1917).

"How do you know that Russia is the richest country in the world?"

"Look, even the people's servants here are driving Mercedes."

Two drunks are having a conversation in Red Square. "Tell me, Ivan," says one. "Why is the Kremlin wall so tall and wide?"

"That's to make it harder for the enemies to climb over it."

"Which enemies? Those from outside, or those from inside the wall?"

An Estonian approaches an ethnic Russian and says, "How much time do you need to pack up and leave my country?"

"I'm not sure about my belongings," the Russian replies, "but to get my *Kalashnikov* ready (the famous AK-47 Russian assault rifle), I need only 45 seconds."

The President tells his Defense Minister, "The Americans offer their assistance in our disarmament. They want us to send our armored vehicles and tanks over to the States."

"It would be better to send our missiles, Mr. President; at least we can save on shipping costs."

"How?"

"Well, we can simply aim and fire them."

Q: What's the difference between Communists and democrats (Russian democrats, that is)?

A: Communists kill the intelligent, democrats beget fools.

Nixon once asked God, "When will the unemployment situation improve in the US?"

"In 20 years."

"Too bad it won't happen during my lifetime," Nixon regretted.

Brezhnev, in his turn, was asking, "When will the Russian people finally have a happy life?

"I regret to report it won't happen during my lifetime," was God's reply.

Episodes from Russian political life:

1907. A policeman takes a revolutionary to jail. They don't talk.

1917. The revolutionary takes the policeman to jail. They don't talk.

1937. The former revolutionary and the former czarist policeman serve time in the same jail. They don't talk.

1999. The former revolutionary sells hot dogs on a busy street. The former policeman walks over and says, "What did you need that revolution for? Couldn't you just sell your hot dogs under a monarchy?"

Two government officials are having a chat:

"Life is hard for honest people nowadays," one sighs.

"How does it affect you?" says the other.

President Yeltsin comes to his Finance Minister:

"I need your help immediately. I'm loosing my sleep, and I can't look the Russian people strait in the eyes, simply because I cannot understand our economic reforms."

"Nothing to worry about, Boris Nickolaevich," the Minister comforts him. "I will explain everything to you as we have some tea, if you don't mind…".

"Don't bother to explain, I can do that myself," Yeltsin cuts in. "My point is I don't understand them!"

"They say the president has a great many supporters."
"That isn't true. He can still walk by himself."

Y2K for Russians: Will we be alive by then?

Columbus, son of a bitch, why do the Serbs have to suffer because of your curiosity?
—From a demonstrator's sign outside the US embassy in Moscow

LAW AND DISORDER

He is right who has the most rights.

Visiting his father at work in a police station, a boy asks him, while looking at the "most wanted" pictures, "Why didn't you arrest them when you were taking their pictures?"

"Excuse me sir, have you seen a policeman around?"
"No I haven't."
"Then give me your money!"

A corrupt cop stops a car and says to the driver, "You have to pay a fine!"
"But why, officer?" protests the driver. "What did I do wrong?"
"And why do you think my children should wait until you do something wrong?"

A cop stops a car and asks the driver to show his documents.
"Why are they so dirty?" the cop asks disgustedly, holding a heavily soiled license and registration.
"Well, officer," the driver says, "guess who touches them all the time!"

*A*n ugly woman rushes into a police station. Looking scared to death, she manages to gasp, "I'm being followed by a drunk man... I think he wants to sexually molest me."

A duty officer takes one look at her and offers his conclusion, "I wouldn't argue with you that the man is drunk, very drunk indeed, madam."

A cop visits a doctor: "Doc, every time I have sex with my wife, her hair turns that wild red color. I want to know what's wrong?"

"Do you take off your hat during sex, officer?"

"No, why?... Now you gonna tell me to take the whistle out of my mouth too!"

A corrupt cop stops a motorist. He checks the vehicle, then he checks the driver's papers. Unable to find anything wrong either with the papers or with the vehicle, the cop decides to go for his favorite trick in just such cases. And so he pulls a bottle of liquor out of the trunk of his own car and offers it to the driver. "Would you like a drink?"

"No thanks, I'm driving, officer," the motorist responds, puzzled.

"Are you sure?"

"I can't—I'm driving!"

"Well, sir, it's your choice. The fine is 800 rubles for impaired driving, or 1,000 rubles for not following the orders of an officer of the law."

"**H**ow do you call your Tax Inspectorate officer?"
"We don't call him; he shows up himself."

*A*n excited man, carrying a gun with a scope, rushes into a police station shouting, "I need to talk to the chief! I just killed

a New Russian!"

"Yes, I know about the murder already," the chief says to the killer. "But why did you come here? Go to whoever it was that ordered the murder; let *them* pay you for it."

Late one night a man is cautiously walking down a deserted dark alley. He looks around and listens to every sound. Then he spots a policeman.

"Excuse me, officer," the man pipes up, a major look of relief on his face. "Is this neighborhood very dangerous at this hour?"

"If it was dangerous," the policeman answers, "do you really think you would see me here?"

A man is on a trial for moonshining. The judge says, "Defendant, do you admit that you were producing alcoholic beverages illegally?"

"No, your honor," the man replies, "I don't."

"But police officers found distillery equipment in your house."

"In that case, you can also charge me with rape."

"You've also raped someone?"

"Not really, but I have the equipment!"

Walking his dog one evening, a police chief runs into a live penguin. Willing to help a poor animal, he takes the leash from his dog and leashes the penguin so it won't run away. Then he calls a police officer who's patrolling a nearby street. "Officer," the chief says, "please take this animal to the zoo."

The next day, much to his surprise, the chief sees the same cop walking down the street with the penguin. "Didn't I tell you to take him to the zoo yesterday?" he asks the cop.

"I did, sir."

"Then why is this penguin still here?"

"Well, sir, we had such a good time, today I've decided to take him to the movies."

A cop stops a car. While checking the driver's papers, he catches a whiff of alcohol on the driver's breath. So he asks the driver to step out of his car for a breath test. Sure enough, the test indicates the presence of alcohol.

"That must be a mistake, officer!" the driver protests. "You can test my wife…she never drinks."

The cop tests the driver's wife as well. Again, the test is positive.

"Your wife has been drinking as well, sir," the cop says. "Looks to me like you've had a nice family dinner with a bottle of vodka…".

"Officer, I'm sure something must be wrong here," the man pleads. "Why don't you check your equipment? Here," the man says, and he carefully produces his four-year-old boy out of the child's seat behind him. "You can check my son."

"Okay," the officer agrees once again.

When even the child's test shows alcohol, the officer simply scratches his head and lets the driver go…

"I told you!" the man says to his wife, smiling, as they drive off. "And you were scolding that I shouldn't give beer to the baby!"

*A*n elderly lady runs into a police station to report a sexual assault.

"When did it happen?" an officer asks her.

"Forty years ago," she says.

"Well, madam, this will be hard. You should have reported this much earlier."

"Why would I do that? I enjoyed it so much…".

"Then why are you here?"

"Because I have nobody to share my memories with."

*T*wo men were once telling each other cop jokes at a local bar:

"Do you know what separates a cop from a donkey?" one

asked.

And just as he spoke these words, an officer who had been patrolling the area overheard the men. He approached them and said, "So tell me, what?"

"Well, nothing, officer, nothing!"

"That's better; and watch your mouth next time!"

During one of his visits to Russia, David Copperfield was performing for customs officials. The great magician was surprised to see so many unimpressed faces in the audience, so he decided that he should try to work with something more familiar to the customs officers.

A large truck happened to arrive right on the scene. Copperfield waved his magic wand and—presto!—both the truck and it's trailer disappeared. The audience remained quiet once again.

Intent on saving the show somehow, Copperfield then asked the officers if they would like to share a trick or two of their own. A customs officer named Ivan stepped up and asked, pointing to the trailer, "What's in it?"

"Oranges," the magician's assistant replied after checking inside.

"Bring me the papers for the load," Ivan ordered. He crossed out the word "oranges" in the declaration, pulled out his stamp, and, in one graceful motion, he turned a truckload of oranges into a truckload of apples.

Q: How fast can you go before the police will stop you for speeding?

A: Over 120 miles an hour; otherwise, they'll be able to catch you…

Q: Why do Moscow cops always patrol the streets walking in pairs?

A: You need one cop who knows the city, and another who can speak Russian.

(Other versions of this story: Because the first cop can only read, and the second one can only write. Or: So one cop can protect the other whenever they're attacked.)

During a customs inspection, the customs officer says to the traveler, "Please open your suitcase for inspection."

"But, officer, I don't have a suitcase with me," the traveler explains.

"It doesn't matter! This is the rule here."

A woman calls the police to report that her husband has been missing for three days. The operator asks her for a description. "Does he have any special marks, madam?"

"No, but I can bet you that as soon as that bastard gets back home, he will!"

It's three o'clock in the morning and a drunk man, barely standing on his feet, is staring at the streetcar tracks.

A police cruiser pulls over nearby. An officer approaches the drunk, and asks him, "Can I ask you what you're doing here, sir?"

"I'm waiting for the streetcar," the drunk answers.

"It's three in the morning, sir. There's no more service until six o'clock."

"Then why did they leave these tracks here?"

"Can I see your ID, please!"

The man hands his documents over to the cop. As the cop checks the papers his manner changes in a flash. He snaps to attention and reports sharply, "I'll make some arrangements right away, sir!"

"How could you mount a motorcycle, being so drunk?"
"I was helped by my friends."

When he spots a car driving through an intersection on red, a young policeman pulls the car over. "Why were you driving through a red light, sir?" he asks.

"Well, officer, to tell you the truth, when I'm drunk I can't tell them apart. Red, green, yellow…they all look the same to me!"

"Step out of the car!" the cop barks, and he takes the impaired driver down to the station for a blood test.

"Are you sure he was drinking?" his supervisor asks the young cop.

"One hundred percent!"

"But the test shows zero alcohol," another officer says, bringing in the results.

The driver then turns to the supervisor. Pointing to the arresting officer, he says, "Listen to him, officer. Now he'll tell you that I went on red too!"

A police officer stops up to another car that has driven through an intersection on red. Much to his surprise, he recognizes the driver—an elderly woman, his former Russian teacher.

The officer immediately tears up the ticket. He then hands the woman a blank sheet of paper and his pen. "Hello, Mrs. Ivanova!" he says. "Please take this pen and paper and write for me the following sentence on every line of both sides of the sheet: 'I will always obey the road signs!'"

A cop stops a truck and says to the driver, "Your right rear turning light doesn't work, sir."

The driver gets out of his truck, walks to the rear, and freezes, standing entirely still.

"You can see for yourself, sir; that light doesn't work," the officer says, breaking the silence.

The driver, slowly regaining his senses, finally responds: "To hell with the light! Where is my trailer???"

"Did you hear? Ivan took his brother's car for a drive yesterday."

"But Ivan doesn't have a license."

"Oh well he was driving the entire day yesterday—until he was pulled over by a cop. But the cop saw another cop in Ivan's car, so he let him go!"

"Ivan had a cop with him?"

"No! The car's windows had mirrored film on them!"

Q: Why do Russian police officers carry AK-47 assault rifles?

A: To protect their handguns, in case someone tries to take them.

A motorist is stopped by a cop. The cop looks inside the vehicle and says, "Sir, you have to pay a 100-ruble fine for not wearing a seatbelt."

The man pays his fine, pulls the seatbelt over his shoulder, and drives on. Twenty minutes later, he sees flashing lights and pulls over again.

Another cop walks over, takes a look inside the car and says, "You can't have your seatbelt loose like this, sir. You need to fasten it. You'll have to pay the fine—100 rubles."

The man pays his fine, fastens his seatbelt, and drives on. Half an hour later, he is stopped once again.

The third cop takes a look inside, checks the seatbelt, and says, "Look, sir, your seatbelt is not adjusted properly. It's too loose. See, you can put another person your size between you and the belt. That means, during a collision, it wouldn't help you at all. I'm afraid you'll have to pay the fine."

The man pays another 100 rubles, fastens his belt so tight he can hardly breathe, and drives on. Not for long. Less than half an hour after his last encounter with the police, he's stopped yet again.

This time, the fourth cop checks the seatbelt but lets the driver go. "What a people!?" he mutters disgustedly. "To save a hundred rubles, they're willing to strangle themselves to death!"

Ａ policeman stops a speeding car. "Why were you going 55 miles an hour on a city street?" he asks the driver.

"Fifty-five miles *an hour*!?" the driver protests. "That's impossible, officer! I just got into the car fifteen minutes ago!"

Ｒesponding to the alarm at a jewelry store, the police arrive at the scene of the crime. Most of the jewelry is already long gone. So, rather than leave empty-handed, the cops pick up a drunk walking nearby, and call him their only suspect.

When they bring the drunken and confused passerby to the station for questioning, they stick his head into a toilet bowl, and they hold it there for as long as the poor man can hold out without drowning. Then they commence to ask him the same question, over and over again: "Where are the pearls? Tell us! Where are the pearls?"

After an hour or so of this questioning, the drunk finally sobers up, and manages to say, "Hey guys, why don't you find yourselves another diver... I can't see anything in here!"

"Ｏpen the door! Police!"

"Look what they've done to this country: They can't even break in anymore!"

Ａ donkey was once put in charge, as the chief of police out in the woods. He got down to work right away, arresting the fox.

"Where did you get this luxurious fur coat?" the donkey questioned the fox.

"That's mine, I've always had it!" the fox replied.

"No, Fox, you've stolen it!" the donkey insisted, and then he ordered the fox to be arrested.

Sharing her cell with a goose, the fox asked, "What did they charge you with?"

"The damn donkey keeps asking me," the goose explained, "how it is, with my income, that I can afford to go for such a long vacation down south every year!"

One morning citizen Ivanov went to buy himself a pack of cigarettes. No one has seen him since. This is the kind of tobacco products they're selling in our country these days.

"Where are you running to so fast?" a bear asks a rabbit, who is rushing through the woods.

"Didn't you hear the news, Bear? To implement the new Higher Efficiency Law, they're going to cut off one paw from every animal who has five paws."

"What do you have to worry about then, Rabbit? Do you have five paws?"

"No, I have four. But they put the donkey in charge, and you know him; he cuts first, then counts."

Q: What's the tallest building in the world?

A: *Lubyanka* (KGB and its successor *FSB* headquarters in Moscow)—you can see Siberia from there.

A police officer comes home from work hungry, tired, and very angry. "Let me see your report card!" he shouts, when he sees his daughter.

The girl leaves the room, and goes immediately to her mother. "Mom, I don't know what to do. Dad is so angry and he wants to see my report card. But when he sees my grades, I'm afraid he's going to kill me."

"I'll tell you what to do," the mother comforts her. "Here. Take this hundred-ruble bill, put it between the pages of your report, and then give the report to your father."

The cop takes his daughter's report. When he sees the money he says, with a smile on his face, "Well, at least everything is okay at home…".

The CIA had spent a lot of money and time training their next agent. Finally, it was time to get down to work. They dropped the new agent somewhere over the vast Russian territory, armed with a parachute and all the necessary papers.

The agent landed in the woods, destroyed his chute, and dressed himself in a worn-out quilted cotton jacket, a cheap synthetic fur hat, military khaki pants, and military-style boots. Looking just like an ordinary villager, he headed for a nearby village.

He approached an old log house, one that seemed to be standing somewhat apart from the others. He knocked on the door.

An elderly woman opened the door. "Can I have some water please, mother," he began in perfect Russian. "I've been travelling for three days…".

"Are you a spy?" the woman cut in suspiciously.

"What makes you think so?"

"Well, son, the last time I saw a black man around here was twenty years ago, and that was on my TV."

While the people at NASA were searching for some answers about why the space shuttle Challenger's right solid rocket booster had exploded, the people at KGB were searching for some answers about why the Challenger's left solid rocket booster didn't.

Q: What's the name of the new material that was used to build the American embassy in Moscow?

A: Microconcrete. It was fifty percent concrete and fifty percent microphones.

After the tragic death of a Russian official, Russian authorities concluded that he was murdered by three CIA agents. According to a reliable source, their names were Jack Daniels, Jim Beam, and Johnny Walker.

MAFIYA AND CRIMINALS

He laughs best who shoots last.

 Passing through a dark alley at night, a man is stopped by two young men, who display rather unfriendly attitudes.

"Hey, man!" one says. "Do you wanna buy a crowbar?"

"No! What would I need a crowbar for?" the man replies.

"Are you sure you don't wanna buy a crowbar?"

"I've already told you no!"

"Well then, give us your wallet!"

"Okay, okay, you guys…how much did you say you wanted for your crowbar?"

"Oh no, smart ass; it's not for sale anymore!"

 A woman is visiting her husband in jail. Her husband, a professional criminal doing his third term, asks her to tell him about things back at home.

"Our youngest boy didn't pass exams, and he's going to have to go through fourth grade for another year," the wife says.

"Impossible!" replies the man, placing his head in his palms in despair. "What a shame for the family!"

"Someone walked out of the movie theater wearing my

coat last night."

"Unbelievable. Who would want your old, worn-out coat?"

"I don't know, I left first!"

Two moonshiners run out of sugar in the middle of a batch. One leaves to fetch more of this necessary ingredient, the other stays with the still to keep an eye on the process.

Half an hour later, the man who stays with the still gets really bored and decides to bring some more of the spring water that their favorite recipe calls for.

When he returns to the still he is arrested by two cops who had raided the place in his absence.

A month later, in court, the man gives the following testimony:

"My friend and I got together at my place to have some tea. He went to get some sugar, and I went to get some spring water. When I returned, I saw two strangers, who are present here and dressed in police uniforms. They were brewing moonshine right there in my house…".

"**W**here do you keep your money?" a robber yells at the owner of the house, holding her at gunpoint.

"I'll tell you if you promise that you won't harm me," the scared woman replies.

"I swear I won't touch you," promises the robber, letting the woman go. "I need the money!"

"Okay," she says, running out of her house. "It's in the bank safety deposit box…".

Two gangsters are having an argument. One says, "Do you like flowers, Ivan?"

"Yes I do, why?"

"Soon you'll have a lot of them," answers the first gangster, as he pulls the trigger on his AK-47.

Armed with sniper rifles, two killers are hiding on top of a building, watching the entrance of the building across the street. One man looks nervously at his watch and says, "The target is late. I'm starting to worry about him; what if he was in an accident?"

Q: Why does the latest model of BMW have such a small steering wheel?

A: To make it easier to steer in handcuffs.

There's a knock at the door:

"Anybody home?" a low and unfriendly man's voice says.

"My parents are busy right now," a child's voice replies. "They're loading their guns."

A customs officer is clearing a cargo ship. After he finishes with the ship's papers, but before he's ready to inspect the holds, he customarily asks the ship's master, "Are there any illegal drugs onboard your ship?"

"Yes there are," the master says this time, and he pulls out a briefcase. "Here they are!"

"What about firearms?" the officer continues after checking out the drugs.

"Ivan, bring in that suitcase," the master orders, and Ivan carries in a huge suitcase full of various weapons and ammo.

"What about foreign currency? Do you have any of that onboard?"

The master pulls out another briefcase. "Here it is—one million US."

The officer checks the money. Finally he says, pointing to the drugs, the arms, and the money, "This all belongs to you?"

"No, officer," the master explains. "This is all *yours*. Mine is down in the cargo holds."

Two hoodlums are having a chat in their favorite restaurant:

"Did you hear? Ivan the Terrible took five pistol shots in his head yesterday while having an argument with the cops!" one says.

"Is he okay?"

"Yeah, his doctor says he'll live: Not one of the bullets reached his brain."

A group of criminals, all belonging to an organized crime clan, are having a good time on the beach. One of their friends catches a fish and, to everybody's surprise, it turns out to be the magical wish-granting Golden Fish.

"I will grant three wishes to everyone of you if you let me go back into the sea," announces the Golden Fish.

"Okay, it's a deal," the criminals' leader says. "As my first wish, I want you to get one Mercedes 600 for each of my men."

"Done," the Golden Fish says and thirty shiny new Mercedes appear out of nowhere.

"As my second wish," the leader continues, "I want you to fill the trunk of every one of these Mercedes with 100-dollar bills."

"Done," the Golden Fish says and all the cars' rear-ends begin to sink from the weight of the cash.

"Now, as my third wish," the criminal says, "I want you to make the most powerful clan from *Solntsevo* disappear; this will make our lives much easier."

"I'm sorry, chief," the Golden Fish sighs, "but that's impossible! This clan is the most powerful in all of Russia—they control everything!"

"You're *the Golden Fish*, aren't you?? You can make wonders!"

"Well, I am, but the people from Solntsevo control *me* too.

A little girl asks a thug, "Mister, why do you have such big hands?"

"For beating up anyone who refuses to pay me protection money!"

"And why do you have such long legs?"

"Long legs are needed to be able to catch anyone who doesn't want to pay protection money and tries to run away from me!"

"And why do you have a head that's so small? Because it makes it harder for them to hit it?"

"Yeah, and I also eat in it."

A criminal is spanking his little son. "I'm punishing you not because you ate all the chocolates, but because you managed to leave your fingerprints all over the place!"

*T*here's a knock on the door:

"Did you call for a gang of racketeers?"

"Oh god forbid, we didn't!"

"Then you have to pay for a false alarm!"

"*H*ow is your husband? I haven't seen him for a while."

"He became a victim of science."

"Oh, no! Radiation? X-rays?"

"No, DNA. He's in jail now."

*A*n average-looking girl on a bus whispers to a man, who is slowly moving his hands around her thighs: "Excuse me, sir, but you can't do that right here."

"Stop drooling, baby. All I need from you is your wallet."

*I*n a dark alley at night, a man sneaks up on a shapely woman dressed in a mini-skirt and fur coat. He pulls out a knife and barks out his orders: "Just be nice and quiet! Take off your coat!"

The woman takes her coat off and asks the man, "What about you? Aren't you going to do the same?"

"No, I'm working," the man says as he carefully folds the

expensive coat.

"What do you think *I'm* doing here, idiot?"

A customs officer is having a chat with his friend:

"For my wife's birthday, I gave her a pearl necklace."

"Why didn't you buy her something more practical, like a car?"

"Well where would I get a fake car?"

In a poor neighborhood apartment, a woman wakes up her husband in the middle of a night:

"Ivan, listen! Do you hear someone inside?" she whispers. "We have to do something."

"Okay," the husband whispers back. "Let them find something first. We'll catch them on their way out!"

"**D**efendant, why did you kill your husband instead of his lover?"

"I figured it was far more practical to kill one man once, instead of a new woman every week."

A mugger forces a pretty woman at knifepoint into a dark alley. "Take if off!" he orders.

Fearing for her life, the shocked woman quickly undresses herself from the waist down.

"What do you think I brought you here for? To take a pee!?" the man shouts impatiently, "Take off your jewelry and get lost!"

"**D**o you have any money?" a mean-looking man asks another man one night as he pulls out a knife.

But the attacked man suddenly pulls out a gun. "What do you need it for?" he asks.

The attacker puts his knife away. He takes out a one-hundred ruble bill and says (now in a much friendlier voice), "Sir, I was wondering if you could make some change for this…".

"**W**hy do you always ask me to hold your ears when we're kissing, dear?"

"Because I don't want to lose my wallet again!"

Driving through an infamous part of the city because it's controlled by street gangs, a man gets a flat tire. Putting on a spare tire, he is approached by two unfriendly youngsters.

"Hey you," one says, trifling with a knife. "Got a smoke?"

The man grabs his tire jack and hits the mugger over the head. The attacker falls to the ground, motionless.

The man then turns to the second mugger, and says, "What about you? Do you want some smoke too?"

"Oh no, thanks, I'm going to share it with my buddy!"

On a dark street one night a man is approached by a group of muggers:

"Got a smoke?" one of them asks.

"When are you going to quit smoking, jackals?" the man complains, as he takes off his fur hat, his fur coat, and a gold watch.

Walking down the rows of merchants' kiosks at a flea market, a man is shouting, "A drill for sale! A drill for sale…".

"Can I see the tool?" a customer asks him.

The seller undoes his long coat and pulls out an automatic rifle. "Here it is," he says.

"Wow, man! You call this a drill?" the potential client exclaims. "This is an AK-47!"

"Whatever its name is," the seller says, scratching his head, "it sure makes some nice holes!"

"Okay, I can understand why Ivan's partner took all the company's money, but why did he run away with Ivan's wife, too? That old, grungy woman?"

"That's simple; he didn't want Ivan to go after him."

"I was just robbed on this street, officer!" an angry man exclaims. "They took my gold watch!"

"Why didn't you cry out when they were taking your watch? It's only nine o'clock; the people could have heard you and called the police."

"I couldn't cry out officer," the victim explains. "I have golden crowns…".

A man is being questioned in court:

"Do you know Sergey Ivanov?"

"No, I don't."

"What about Boris Petrov? Do you know him?"

"What?… No, I don't. But, your honor, I think I know Sergey Ivanov!"

A man is visiting a fortune teller. She studies his palm for a moment and says, "I can see the death of your wife in the near future."

"I know that," the man says impatiently. "What I need to know from you is whether they'll catch me or not."

A cop stops a heavily mud-covered Jeep Cherokee along a secluded village road. "You need to clean the lights and the license plates," he says to the driver. "You can't drive like that."

"Okay, officer," says the driver, a tall and strong young man in dark glasses and leather.

The cop, either not willing to let the driver go without getting some money from him, or smelling something fishy, then asks the driver to open up the Jeep's trunk.

The driver opens the trunk, exposing a man's corpse inside. "Here's the document saying that this is a funeral car, officer," the man says simply, before the stunned policeman can could do anything.

"Well, okay…" the officer says, after checking the papers. "But why does this poor man have a soldering gun sticking out of his ass?"

"I guess, officer, that was his last will."

Two classmates meet ten years later.

"Hi Ivan, where do you work now?" one asks.

"I'm a contract killer, Sergei," answers the other. "And what do you do these days?"

"I'm a banker."

"That means we may meet at work one day!"

A knock at the door at two o'clock in the morning:

"Open the door! We need to talk!"

"How many of you are there?"

"Just two of us!"

"Then why don't you talk to each other!"

"Defendant, why didn't you hire an attorney to represent you?"

"Well, your honor, I approached quite a few lawyers, but once they take a look at my case and saw that I didn't steal those millions, they all refused to defend me."

"Defendant Ivanov," the judge proclaims, "the court grants you the last word."

"Two million dollars, your honor!"

A group of men approach a car that's waiting for a green light at an intersection. "Get out of that stolen car!" they order the driver.

"What? This is my car!" the driver protests.

"It was until now," one of the criminals says as he pulls out a knife. "Do I need to repeat myself?"

"**W**itness, you saw the defendant hitting her husband with a marble rolling pin," the judge says. "What did you do at that point?"

"I called my fiancée and told her that I had changed my mind about marrying her."

"**W**hy didn't you help your wife when she was drowning?"

"I thought she was just yelling at me, as usual."

A man is tried for the sexual assault of two people. During the entire trial he sits quietly, his eyes fixed on the floor.

"Defendant, why did you assault this woman?" the judge asks him.

"I lost my head over her, your honor," the defendant replies without looking at the judge.

"And why did you assault this man?" the judge continues.

"I lost my head over him, your honor," the defendant replies, his eyes still fixed on the floor.

"Defendant, why don't you look at me?"

"I'm afraid of losing my head over you too, your honor."

"**D**efendant, you insist that your husband battered you. But he's hardly able to move in his cast and bandages."

"Well, he was able to move very well before he attacked me!"

"**D**efendant, do you insist that the objects you used to throw at the plaintiff were tomatoes?"

"Yes, that is correct."

"Then how do you explain these scars and bruises all over his body?"

"Well, they were pickled tomatoes—they come in jars."

"Plaintiff, the defendant called you an idiot. Is that true?"

"Yes, it is."

"Then why are we all here today?"

"Defendant, is this the man you attacked and beat up last week?"

"No, that man was without cast and bandages."

"Defendant, do you plead guilty to the crime of robbery that you are charged with?"

"No, I don't!"

"Do you have an alibi?"

"What's that?"

"Do you know of anyone who might have seen you at the time of the robbery?"

"Thank god, no!"

A thief, caught selling 'hot stuff', explains himself:

"I don't need anything that doesn't belong to me. That's why I'm selling it."

"Defendant, where did you get this money?"

"I found it."

"Where?"

"In the plaintiff's pocket, your honor."

"Where does your family plan to spend the summer?"

"My wife is going to Paris, my daughter to America, my son to India, and me... Well, most likely, I'll be going to jail."

"Defendant, do you have an alibi?"
"I need some time to think about it, your honor."
"Will five years of hard labor be enough?"

I've been working hard to have a nice house along a warm seashore. My dream finally came true, although with a bit of a twist: I'm in a Siberian jail with a nice view of the Arctic Ocean.

Late one night a cop stops a car. He looks into the window to find thirteen drunken men stacked like sardines inside. The policeman, a middle-aged veteran, has never seen anything like this, but he lets the men go on one condition: All thirteen men must report to the local police station the next morning and demonstrate their 'art of car packing' to his fellow officers.

At the station the next morning the men are busily packing themselves into the car. All but one mange to wedge themselves in. They try many different layouts, but they still cannot find enough room for the thirteenth man.

Finally one man says, "Ivan, are you sure you were with us last night?"

"Sure I was!" Ivan says. "Who do you think was playing the accordion when the officer pulled us over?"

In today's *cultural* news, we have a report about the assassination of the director of the city's symphony orchestra.

—From an alternative Russian news flash

MOTHERS-IN-LAW

Mothers-in-law may be even a more common topic of jest in Russia than they are in the West. Mothers-in-law serve as the heroines of many extremely popular jokes in Russia, especially among Russian men.

This phenomenon owes partly to comparatively closer family ties in Russia, which create both a cult of children and a more respectful approach to elders (placing an elderly parent in a retirement home is still frowned upon). It is also partly due to the eternal lack of decent housing in Russia. Many Russians have had to share their roofs with their in-laws—sometimes well into retirement.

Q: Why does the rooster always sing?
A: Because he has ten wives and no mother-in-law.

"Why did you marry your ex-wife's sister?"
"I just couldn't stand getting used to another mother-in-law."

A woman is bitten by a dog on the street:
"I'm very sorry," the blameworthy owner explains. "My dog would have never done that, if you weren't wearing the same perfume my mother-in-law wears!"

"**I**n order to get my daughter to study music, I bought her a violin," one man tells another. "Unfortunately, it didn't work out."

"I did almost the same when I bought my mother-in-law a suitcase," the other man says. "It didn't work out either."

"**R**emember," a man tells his newlywed friend, "never argue with your mother-in-law. Just let her talk as much as she wants. Soon enough she'll be contradicting herself."

A doorbell rings. A man opens the door and there he sees his mother-in-law. Trying gamely to hide his disappointment, he asks her, "Hello, mother. So, for how long do you plan to stay with us?"

"Well, until you get fed up with me," the woman jokes.

"So," the son-in-law replies excitedly, "you're not even going to have a cup of tea with us?"

"**Y**ou're so boring," a woman says to her husband. "Every time we have my mother here visiting us, you don't even take her out to show her the town."

"I've tried, but it's useless," he answers. "She always finds her way back."

After yet another quarrel with his mother-in-law, the quick-tempered Georgian grasps a large kitchen knife and tells the woman to step out onto the balcony with him.

"Givi," he asks his neighbor on the left, "what did you do to your mother-in-law?"

"I killed her," Givi replies.

"Vano," he asks his neighbor to his right, "what did you do to your mother-in-law?"

"I drowned her," Vano answers.

"You see?" the son-in-law says, turning to the woman, "And I'm letting you go!"

"That sign must be hurting your sales. Why don't you get rid of it?"

"Oh, no. On the contrary—it's the best ad I've ever had. You'll see how many men buy them for their mothers-in-law."

"I will pay you one hundred rubles if you pick my mother-in-law up at the railroad station."

"What if she doesn't show up?"

"Then I'll pay you two hundred rubles."

"... Which means that you saw how the defendant killed your mother-in-law?" the judge asks.

"Yes I did, your honor," the witness replies.

"Why didn't you help, then?"

"At first I was going to, but then I decided that he could manage to do it himself."

A man brings his dog to the vet and asks him to cut off the dog's tail.

"Why now, sir?" the vet asks.

"Well," the man says, "my mother-in-law comes to visit us tomorrow, and I don't want any friendly exhibits extended to her."

A man tries to push an elderly woman over a fifth-floor balcony railing. A crowd of onlookers down on the street is growing angry.

"Stop him! Help the poor woman!" they protest.

"She's my mother-in-law," the man on the balcony explains.

"Oh... Look at her!" the crowd shouts. "She even resists!"

If a man wants to learn the rich vocabulary of Russian curses, he must share his house with his mother-in-law.

"Honey," she says, "what can we get for my mother for her birthday this year?"

"What did we get for her last year?" he asks.

"A chair," she answers.

"Why don't we add electricity for her this year?" he suggests.

"I will poke myself in my eye," he said. "Let her have a crippled son-in-law."

A woman once ate some wild mushrooms and then came down with a serious food poisoning. Upon the arrival of the ambulance, the paramedic asked her son-in-law why the woman had so many bruises.
"Well," he said, "she didn't want to eat them at first."

A mother-in-law is sitting on a sofa beneath a large clock on the wall. The moment after she gets up, the clock falls down on the sofa.
"That clock is always late," is the first thought of her son-in-law.

Deciding to please his mother-in-law, a man wears one of the two ties that he has received from her as presents. "You didn't like the second tie I bought you, did you?" the mother-in-law comments when they meet.

Two men are drinking:
"When our house caught on fire," one man sighs, "I entered the flaming kitchen and saved my mother-in-law."
"Don't worry, Andrei," the other man comforts him. "Everyone makes mistakes."

A policeman pulls a car over and asks the driver, "Why did you speed up when you were passing this town?"
"Well, you see, officer, my mother-in-law lives here."

The hardest moment for a man to control his emotions comes when he is seeing his mother-in-law off on her way.

Two women are having a conversation:

"How's your daughter?" one asks.

"I'm so happy for her. They are an exceptional couple. My son-in-law always does the dishes and the laundry, and he cleans up after the kids. He's such a sweetie."

"What about your son?"

"Oh, my poor boy! That witch forces him to do the dishes and the laundry, and to clean up after the kids!"

"**I**'m sorry, sir," the pharmacist says, "but that picture of your mother-in-law is not enough reason to allow you to buy this powerful medication."

Off on a business trip, a man receives a message from his attorney:

"Your mother-in-law passed away last night. What should I arrange for: a burial, a cremation, or an embalming?"

The man replies immediately: "Arrange for everything. I don't want to take any chances."

A man was once standing on a street corner, watching a strange funeral procession. Behind the hearse followed a man leading a goat on a rope. The man and goat were closely followed by a line of men.

Approaching the man with the goat, the bystander inquired, "Excuse me, sir. Can you tell me who has died? And why this strange following?"

"Well," the man answered, "the person in the hearse is my mother-in-law. Yesterday, while working in our garden, she was struck from behind by this goat and killed instantly."

"Really!" the bystander said eagerly. "Do you think I might borrow your goat for a day or so?"

"Sure," the man replied, "but you'll have to go to the back of the line like everyone else."

"**H**oney," she says, "I can't find our book, *How To Live To*

Be One Hundred."

"Well," he replies, "when your mother asked me if she could borrow it, I donated it to the library."

An elderly woman is filling out a telegram form. Having some problems without her glasses, she asks a clerk for some help.

"I think, madam," the clerk suggests, "that it'll be much easier and cheaper if you just put 'all of you' in your congratulations, instead of mentioning each of the seven members of your family."

"What do you mean 'all of you'?" the woman protests. "What if I don't want to congratulate my son-in-law!"

How can you constantly have quarrels with your wife, but at the same time respect your mother-in-law?"

"Well, she was the only one who was against our marriage!"

Have you met the man who saved my life when I was drowning?" the mother-in-law asks.

"Yes I have," her son-in-law replies. "He came to apologize to me this morning."

Doctor, how is my mother-in-law?"

"I'm afraid she's much better now, sir."

For the price of one ticket, our entire family had a wonderful vacation this year."

"Where did you find such a deal?"

"Well, I bought the ticket for my mother-in-law, and the rest of the family had a great time at home."

A man receives the ashes of his mother-in-law after her cremation:

"Let's put the urn on the piano. Grandma always used to

like my playing," his little daughter suggests.

"No," the man objects, "we're going to put her ashes in the hourglass. Let her work for a bit yet."

Q: What is the definition of a mixed feeling?

A: Watching your mother-in-law plunge down a cliff in your car.

A woman asks her son-in-law: "What would you like as a present for your birthday?"

"Your absence would do just fine, mother."

"**Y**ou say that I'm always in your way," the woman says to her son-in-law. "But you were the one who made me your mother-in-law."

A man is shopping for a gravestone for his mother-in-law. "I need something decent but cheap," he tells the salesperson.

"Well, we have a nice monument that has gone unclaimed, although it does have some lettering already."

"Oh, that's fine," the man says and pulls out his wallet. "My mother-in-law was illiterate anyway."

On his way home from his mother-in-law's funeral, a man is struck by a falling icicle. "I can't believe she's in hell already!" he thinks to himself.

"**I** have an exemplary mother-in-law."

"What do you mean?"

"There's no mother-in-law joke that wouldn't fit her."

MOTHER-IN-LAW: When does my train leave?

SON-IN-LAW: In two hours, twenty-five minutes, and ten seconds.

CHILDREN-OUR FUTURE

"So, Kolya, how do you like your new mother?" a newly remarried father asks his little son.

"You know, Daddy," the boy replies sadly, "I think they fooled us; she doesn't look new at all!"

"You're a big boy now," says father. "You should know that Santa doesn't exist. It was me."

"Yes, I know that already, Daddy," his son replies. "I also know that you're the stork who brought me."

"Mommy, is it true that God gives us our food?"

"Yes, you could say so."

"And is it true that the stork brings children?"

Yes."

"And that Santa brings presents?"

"Yes, dear."

"Then, tell me, what do we need our father for?"

"Are your parents afraid of cartoons too?" one preschool kid asks another.

"No."

"Mine are. As soon as they let me watch some, they hide

under the blanket in their bedroom and start shaking."

"**Y**ou need to eat well, dear!" the mother says to her seven-year-old daughter. "You know what happens to girls that don't…".
"Yes, I know," says the girl. "They become models."

"**W**hat major event took place in 1870?" a history teacher asks.
"Lenin was born."
"Correct. What about 1873?"
"In 1873 he was three."

A father is having a problem getting his five-year-old daughter to fall asleep. Finally, she suggests, "Daddy, why don't you just whisper something into my ear the way you do with Mommy?"
The father does just that, and the daughter falls asleep murmuring, "No, not tonight, honey; I'm so tired."

"**S**o, what did you like most at the zoo?" the mother asks her five-year-old son.
"I liked the tiger, and Daddy liked a pussy cat."
"A pussy cat?! They don't have those at the zoo."
"I didn't see them either, but I heard daddy saying, 'What a pretty pussy cat they have working in the ticket booth.'"

An orphan boy is writing a letter to Grandpa Cold (*Dedushka Moroz*, the Russian Santa Claus):
"Hello Grandpa Cold! Please help me. I have no daddy and I have no mommy either. I live with my grandpa, who often drinks and spanks me. Please send me a warm coat, pants, and mittens."

Postal workers soon read the letter and, feeling sorry for the boy, they pool some money and buy him a winter coat and a pair of pants. Either short of money, or simply because they forgot, they send the little boy everything he has asked for, except the mittens.

Much to the workers' surprise, few days later they receive a thank you note from their beneficiary. It says:

"Hello Grandpa Cold! Thank you very much for your presents. I received the coat and the pants. I didn't get the mittens; probably, they were stolen at the post office...".

"**H**ow can you read like this, son?" asks his mother. "You're skipping so many pages."

"This book is about spies. I can't wait to see them get caught!"

"**M**ommy, who do I resemble?" a girl asks her mother.

"You resemble me, dear." the mother replies.

"And who do you resemble?"

"I resemble your grandma."

"What about my grandma?"

"She used to resemble her mother."

"That's too bad," the girl says sadly. "That means we all look alike, just like Russian dolls."

For the first time in his life, a city boy visits his relatives on a farm. Finding three empty milk cartons in the grass, he runs home and says, "Grandma! I just found a cow's nest!"

"**W**hat happened, dear?" mother asks her crying daughter.

"Daddy hit himself with a hammer while he was trying to hit a nail."

"He'll be okay. But why are *you* crying?"

"I laughed when he did it."

"Would you like a candy?" a little boy asks a women sitting on a park bench.

"Thank you, boy," says the woman, accepting the treat.

"Do you like it, madam?" the boy asks her.

"Oh yes, it's very tasty."

"I wonder, then," says the boy. "Why did both the cat and the dog spit it out?"

"Kolya," says his mother, "I'd like to see your report card, please."

"I don't have it today; Sasha borrowed it to scare his parents."

A young couple were going out, but they couldn't find a babysitter to stay late. So they decided to follow their friends' advice. They turned on an old record of their daughter's favorite fairytales, and they had her wear headphones.

When they returned home they found their girl hitting her little head against the crib and crying. "Yes, I want, yes I want…".

The parents turned the speakers on: "Would you like to hear a fairytale, zzz…kh…Would you like to hear a fairytale, zzz…kh…Would you like to hear a fairy-tale, zzz…kh…"

"Shame on you!" mother says to her son, Kolya. "They called me again and they want to see me in the school. Your father will be really upset that you're not following his advice and behaving so poorly."

"But my father is in jail," protests the boy.

"Well, in his last letter, he wrote that because of his good behavior, they'll be letting him out earlier."

"Okay, children," the physics teacher says, "today you learned that all bodies expand at high temperatures and constrict at low temperatures. Who can illustrate this phenomenon with an example? Yes please, Sasha."

"Take, for example, summer and winter breaks…".

"Daddy, can you tell me, how did people finally learn that the earth is round?"

"Well, son, haven't you ever seen a globe?"

A woman and her eight-year-old daughter climb into a cab, not far from the city's most infamous joint. When the girl sees some prostitutes, she asks her mother, "Who are these brightly dressed women?"

"Just ordinary women, dear," answers her mother.

"Don't listen to your mother," intrudes the cab driver. "These are not ordinary women, they're prostitutes."

A few minutes later, the girl asks her mother, "Do they have children?"

"Yes they do, dear," her mother replies. "Their children are mostly taxi drivers."

It's cold. Soon it'll be dark and we'll become extinct, just like dinosaurs.

—From a school essay

"Mommy, come here, quickly please! I knocked down the big step ladder!"

"We have to put everything in order before your father finds out," mother says, hurrying on her way to help.

"He knows already," the son answers. "He's up there, hanging onto the light fixture…".

A seven-year-old girl asks her mother, "Mom, what does it mean, 'abort'?"

Her parents talk it over with each other and, thinking that, sooner or later, the girl will find out everything on the street anyway, they decide to tell her the truth.

An hour later, when the parents have finished their speech, the father asks his daughter, "Where did you hear about this, honey?"

"At school, Daddy. We read a poem that had these words: 'The huge waves were jumping aboard the ship.'"

Sasha," says mother, "if you play piano for us, I'll buy you a big chocolate bar."

"Well, I can't. Daddy promised me *two* big chocolate bars if I don't play the piano."

After seeing a movie with Indians who had painted their faces, a little boy asks his father what the paint was for.

"They were preparing for war," his father explains.

One night soon after, the son runs into his father's room, very excited. "Daddy! Let's flee the house!! Mommy is preparing for war!"

Can't you people control your dog? It growled terribly last night; my daughter couldn't finish her singing lessons."

"I'm sorry, but your daughter started first."

Who was that young fellow who kissed you last night, daughter?"

"At what time last night, Dad?"

"Don't you think your friend Ivan is staying here too long lately?" a father asks his teenaged girl.

"Oh no, father," she says. "I just offer him a cup of tea and he leaves."

"Well, in that case, please at least ask him not to take my morning paper."

"About three months ago you introduced me to a fellow you'd been dating for quite some time now, daughter. So, when are you guys going to get married?"

"I hope soon, Father, but definitely not at the same time."

"Do you know what happened to Sasha when you asked him to rake the leaves in the garden?"

"I hope he didn't step on the rake!"

"No, he didn't. He fell out of a tree."

"Daddy, is it true that military men are very able?" a little boy asks his father, a military officer.

"Yes, Son. That's true."

"Then let's go to the washroom. I'd like to see how you put your shaving cream back into the tube."

"Dad, what is freedom?" a little boy asks his father.

"You'll know it when you get married. But, unfortunately, then it will be too late," the father explains.

"Mom, what is happiness?" a little girl asks her mother.

"You'll know it when you get married. But, unfortunately,

then it will be too late," the mother explains.

"Dad, why do they say that children under 14 can't watch this movie?"

"Just take a seat and be quiet, son, and you'll see why."

"Daddy, where do little elephants come from?"

"Well…".

"Just don't tell me the stork brings them. That bird wouldn't be able to lift a little elephant!"

"Mommy, I found our father," a little boy yells from outside.

"How many times have I told you not to play in the trash."

"I had a dream that I got an A," the boy tells his father, "and you bought me a small candy bar."

"Behave yourself," his daddy says, "and you'll dream of big candy bars."

A teacher asks her student's mother, "Why do you send your son to this musical school to learn to play piano? He doesn't have an ear for it."

"That's not important!" the student's mother replies. "We send him here not to listen, but to play."

"How many times do I have to explain to you," the teacher says, "that one half, compared to another half, cannot be smaller or bigger?! And yet the bigger half of this class doesn't understand it!"

"Are you sure, boy," a grocery sales clerk asks a little customer, "that your mother sent you to buy six pounds of candy and one pound of potatoes?"

"When is your birthday, Katya?" the teacher asks her little student.

"July 21, Ms Ivanova," the student answers.

"And what year?"

"Every year," the student reports.

One New Year's Eve, a daughter says to her mother: "Instead of midnight, let's shout 'Happy New Year!' at 11:30 tonight."

"What's that for?"

"Just to let our neighbors think that the new year came to us earlier."

"Tell me, Dad," a pre-school boy asks his father. "The man who is getting married is called a fiancé. But what do they call a man who is married already?"

"It's too early for you to know those words, son," replies his father.

A family is expecting a new baby. The happy father asks his older son: "What would you like to have? A little brother or a little sister?"

"Well," the boy answers, "even if I didn't want *anybody*, it's too late now."

Mother asks her little daughter, "How much is three plus four?"

"Seven," the girl replies.

"How much is seven plus four?"

"I don't know, Mommy. We didn't learned to count past ten yet."

"Tell me, Daddy, how does the brain work?"

"Not now, son. I have other things in my head."

"I can't believe your boy goes to school."

"He does."

"Wow! He's only three and he's already reading papers."

"No, he doesn't read them, he just solves the crossword puzzles."

"Why are you so wet?" a mother asks her little son.

"We played dog."

"You were the dog?"

"No, I was the tree."

"Do you have any complaints about your ears or nose?" a doctor asks his little patient.

"Yes I do, doctor. They're in the way every time I put my T-shirt on."

"Which chocolate figure do you prefer?" the mother asks her daughter at the store. "A boy or a girl?"

"The boy, of course! It has more chocolate in it."

"Why weren't you present yesterday, Petrov?" the teacher asks her student.

"My family got a new member," he explains.

"Marvelous! Do you have a baby brother or a baby sister?"

"Oh no, Ms Ivanova. My mother finally got married."

"Daddy, do you know how much toothpaste is in one tube?"

"No, I don't."

"Well, I do: from the washroom sink to the tub."

Mother and her little son are watching father while he fixes the roof.

"When you grow up," says mother, "you'll help your daddy."

"Isn't Daddy going to finish that work by then?" he wonders.

"Your father is going to turn gray when he sees your report card," a teacher says, handing the papers to her student.

"No, he won't," the student says.

"He doesn't care how you do at school?" the teacher asks.

"It's not that he doesn't care," the student explains. "He's just bald."

"Honey, I forgot to tell you," a woman says to her husband, "that you have a meeting with Vasily's teacher this afternoon at the school. He broke the window again."

"Damn! How many windows do they have down there?"

A daycare center worker has spent half an hour putting underpants on a little girl and dressing her up for outside activities. Finally, after the girl is dressed, she says, "These are not my underpants!"

The poor woman undresses the girl again, only to find that there's no other underwear in the girl's bag. So she asks the girl if she's sure about her underwear.

"These are my brother's underpants," the girl explains. "I don't know why Mommy put them on me this morning!"

"Mom, can I go to the washroom?"
"Did you finish your homework?"

"How did mother find out that you didn't wash your hands this time?" the father asks his son.
"I forgot to wet the soap."

"So, how did your exams go?" the parents ask their son.
"Not bad, I guess," he answers. "Except that the teacher was a bit too religious; every time I spoke up he was saying, 'Oh, my God! Oh, my God!'"

"Mommy," a little boy wonders, "is it true that you bought me on support money that my father sends you every month?"

"We just got a parcel from Grandpa!" the little boy says to his twin brother. "He sent us ten chocolate candies—seven for me and seven for you. Here…".
"But how can each of us have seven candies, if you say Grandpa sent only ten?"
"I don't know. I had my seven candies already."

A grade five class is visiting a construction site. Before the children begin their tour, one of the workers explains the necessity of wearing hard hats:
"Last year, on one of our sites, a girl was hit by a brick. But

because she was wearing a hard hat she wasn't injured. So she left the site smiling."

"I know the girl you're talking about, sir," one boy pipes up. "By the way, she's still wearing a hard hat and she's always smiling."

As a punishment for poor behavior, a man decides to make his son repaint all the windows around the house.

After a couple of hours, the boy walks in, covered in paint from tip to toe. He notifies his father: "I've finished painting the glass. Should I do the frames too?"

"Daddy, why is it that when I blow on the candle it stops burning?"

"Well, just don't blow and it won't."

"Yesterday I found a wallet with some money in it," the father says to his son. "So I took it to the police. What would you do, son, if you were me?"

"I would've lied too, father."

"How's everything at school, son?"

"I don't talk to the father of a drop-out."

"Why does a giraffe have a long neck?"

"So that it will be easier for it to eat leaves off the tall trees."

"And why are the trees so tall?"

"Well, that's because the giraffes can eat their leaves without bending over."

"Daddy, did your mommy spank you too?"

"No, she didn't. But yours did."

"Did you wash your hands after you came in, Katya?"

"I didn't need to. It's raining outside."

"Honey, if you eat one more piece of that cake, you're going to explode," the woman warns her little son.

"Okay, Mom, just give me one more piece and you go hide in another room."

"Why are you crying?" the policeman asks a little girl in a big shopping center.

"I lost my parents."

"Do you know their names?"

"Yes. Honey and Dear."

A teenaged girl comes home from a party. Her grandma takes one look at her attire and says, "That's how you dress nowadays?! Okay, put something on and let's have dinner."

"Do you have an English-speaking parrot?" a boy inquires at the pet shop.

"No, but we have a woodpecker."

"What language does it know?"

"None, actually. Although it does know Morse code."

A woman asks her grandson, "Why is it that we first see the lightning and then we hear the thunder?"

"That's because we have eyes in the front and our ears are toward the back," the boy explains.

"Who do you want to be when you grow up, Petya?" a daycare worker asks a boy.

"I want to be a policeman," the boy replies.

"What about you, Kolya?" the worker asks another boy.

"I want to be a criminal," Kolya says.

"That's bad!" the worker responds. "Why would you want to be a criminal?"

"So Petya and I can play together, even after we grow up."

"Is it true that I was born at night?" a little boy asks his mother.

"Yes it is, honey."

"I hope I didn't wake you up, Mommy."

"Mommy, can you tell me where children come from?"

"It's a long story, dear."

"Please, tell me at least the beginning."

"What is that?" a little boy asks his naked mother in the sauna, pointing below her waist.

"Well," says the mother, "that's sort of a sponge."

"Father has a better one," the son concludes. "It has a handle."

Two boys are talking:

"Do you know when your sister is ready to get married?" one asks.

"Always," replies the other.

"I need shoelaces," a boy says to the store clerk.

"What kind do you need?"

"One left and one right."

A postman rings the bell and the door is opened by a boy who has a huge cigar in one hand and a drink in the other.

"Ah… are your parents home?" the postman asks, dazzled by the sight. "I need their signature."

The boy gives the postman a studying look and says, "What do you think, moron?"

"Why do you use those bad words?" the first-grade teacher asks a boy when she overhears him swearing. "You don't even know their meaning."

"Yes I do, Ms Ivanova," the student explains. "They mean my father can't start his car."

"What good did you do today, my dear children?" mother comes home and asks her kids.

"I washed the dishes," says the first child.

"Very good, Kolya!" she says.

"I dried the dishes," says the second.

"Great, Sveta!" she says.

"And I," says the third child, "swept the broken glass from the floor and took out the garbage."

"Who did you get this beautiful hair from, Tanya, your mother or your father?"

"I think from my father: he doesn't have any left."

"What is it?" a little girl asks the pregnant woman, after taking a long look at the woman's stomach.

"This is my little baby boy," the woman explains.

"Do you love him?" the girl says.

"Oh yes, I do love him; very much."
"Then why did you eat him?"

"Who would you like to stay with, Katya?" the parents who were going through a divorce asked their little daughter.
"With whoever keeps the TV."

"Why is your baby sister is crying so loud?" a woman asks a boy.
"Madam," the boy says seriously, "I'd like to see you when you're missing your teeth and your hair, and when you can't control your hands and legs."

"Kolya, why are you lying on the sofa all day long?"
"I'm getting ready to be a father."

"Who can tell me?" the teacher asks. "Is the word 'pants' singular or plural?"
"It's singular at the top and plural on the bottom," one sharp student replies.

"Mommy can I go out to play with Ivan?"
"No, Ivan is a bad boy."
"Then, can I go out and beat him up?"

When a young mother was asked why she allowed her five-year-old son to play in the mud, she explained: "First of all, I have no problem finding him. Second, he doesn't get any bruises or scratches. And third, I don't have to buy batteries."

"Mommy, they taught us how to write today!"

"And what did you write, honey?"

"I don't know; they didn't teach us how to read yet."

One morning, at the request of his wife, a man took his little son to kindergarten. But everywhere he took the boy, they refused to take him in. After about the eighth kindergarten, the son turned to his father and said, "Daddy, if you take me to one more kindergarten, I'll be late for school."

Two writers meet:

"What happened? You look so sad," one asks.

"Yes, an awful thing happened," says the other. "My son burned the only manuscript of my latest novel."

"Your son? How old is he?"

"Three."

"What a wunderkind! That young and he can already read!"

Two four-year-olds from different families, a boy and a girl, are playing naked on a beautiful Black Sea beach. After staring at the boy for some time, the little girl says, "I never knew that there's such a big difference between Russians and Ukrainians…".

A group of children is playing outdoors:

"I have a sister and each of us has her own room," one girl says.

"I have two sisters and one brother, and each of us has a bike," a boy brags.

"Well, there are eight children in my family," another girl says, "and each one of us has his or her own father!"

"When I was your age," an elderly man tells his teenaged granddaughter, "girls used to know some shame."

"I can only imagine, Grandpa," says the girl, "what you used to tell them."

MEET VOVOCHKA—RUSSIA'S "LITTLE JOHNNY"

"Father, I need to talk to you."

"Okay, go ahead, Vovochka. But be brief and to the point."

"One hundred rubles."

"Dad, we're invited to a private meeting at my school," Vovochka says.

"What do you mean, a 'private' meeting?" his father asks.

"I mean only you, me and the principal are invited."

"Do you use spanking or any other form of corporal punishment, sir?" a teacher asks the father of one of her students.

"Well, if you're talking about my Vovochka," the man replies, "I use it strictly in self-defense."

"What is it?" an art teacher wonders, looking at Vovochka's papers. "You didn't draw anything. All I see is a small checkmark."

"But I did. That is a picture of 'no panic', Ms Ivanova," Vovochka explains. "You see, my older sister puts a checkmark on the calendar every month. So last month, my parents were in a big panic when she didn't do it."

Tired of hearing the children calling one another names, the teacher decides to try a new trick:

"Attention, class," he announces. "Anyone who thinks he or she deserves to be called any of those bad names I'm hearing in class, please stand up!"

After a long pause, only Vovochka stands up. "Do you really think you're a fool?" the teacher asks him.

"No, I just wanted to share the company with you, Mr. Ivanov."

"Tomorrow, at 4:15 PM, you'll be able to watch a total eclipse of the sun," the astronomy teacher tells her class. "Don't miss it; this phenomenon doesn't occur very often."

"On which channel can we watch it, Ms Ivanova?" Vovochka asks.

Vovochka sees his neighbor getting into the car. So he comes over and says, "Mr. Sidorov, could you give me a lift to school?"

"Unfortunately, Vovochka, I'm going the opposite way," the neighbor says.

"Well, that's even better!" replies Vovochka.

"Do your parents know that you smoke?"

"Does your husband know that you ask too many questions from men you don't know?"

"Please name the person whose personality struck you most," a history teacher asks her class.

"Napoleon!"

"Peter the Great!"

"Lenin!"

"My father," Vovochka says in his turn, "when he saw my report card."

"Father," Vovochka says, "they want to see you at the school. I blew up a desk during chemistry class."

The next week Vovochka tells his father, "Father, they want to see you at school. I blew up the whole lab."

One week later, he says once again, "They want to see you at school, Father."

"I'm not going to your school anymore," his father protests.

"Well," Vovochka says, "there's not much left anyway."

"Vovochka, dear, don't hit your friends with that heavy stick; you can work up a sweat and catch a cold."

"Wake up, Vovochka!" his mother calls, knocking on her son's bedroom door.

"I want to sleep longer today, Mom."

"The early bird catches the worm," his mother insists.

"Do you really believe in that, mother?" Vovochka asks skeptically.

"Of course I do," she answers. "Take, for example, our

neighbor boy. He found 100 rubles while walking the dog at six in the morning last week."

"Well," Vovochka says, rolling over in his bed, "that means the guy who lost the money must have waken up even earlier."

"Don't talk to me that way!" Vovochka's father reprimands him. "Am I your father or not?"

"How would I know that, man?!" answers Vovochka.

"Why didn't you go to school yesterday, son?"

"My teacher's birthday was yesterday, so I decided to make her a present."

"What present?"

"I thought I'd let her enjoy her job for one day."

"Who do you want to be, Sveta, when you grow up?" a fifth-grade teacher asks her student.

"I want to be a ballerina."

"Very good, Sveta."

"What about you, Victor."

"I want to be a cosmonaut."

"Good."

"And you, Vovochka? Who do you want to be when you grow up?"

"I want to be a sex therapist, Ms Ivanova."

"Oh?! Could you explain to us why?"

"That's simple," says Vovochka, and he asks his teacher to come closer to the window. "Can you see those two women walking down the street and eating ice cream? Now, can you tell me which one is married: the one that's licking her ice cream bar, or the one that's sucking on it?"

"Well, I think the one that's sucking on it," the woman says and blushes.

"No, you're wrong, Ms Ivanova," Vovochka explains. "The married woman has a wedding ring on her finger. But here's my point, Ms Ivanova: You're not the only person who would answer like that—and that's why I want to be a sex therapist!"

"**W**hat do you need to read *War and Peace*?" his mother asks Vovochka, implying the time it would take.

"A hundred bucks will do," he replies.

"**W**hat happened?" a woman asks her son.

"I got into a fight with our neighbors' boy."

"Your new suit is all torn up. Now we have to buy you another one," the mother complains.

"Well, after what I did to him," the boy brags, "his parents need to buy a new son."

"**M**ister, would you like to pat a dog?" little Vovochka asks a man in the park.

"Sure. Nice dog," the man says, patting the animal. "Why is he so skinny? Do you feed him?"

"That's not my dog," Vovochka replies, murmuring disapprovingly, "and they say he could bite off a hand so quick…".

THE HUNGRY STUDENT

A student is floundering during an exam. "Your mind is like a desert, sir," the professor tells him in frustration.

"Every desert has an oasis, professor," the student replies. "But not every camel is able to find it."

During an exam on agriculture, and tired after so many attempts to save his student from an F, the professor decides to give him one last chance.

"Okay, Mr. Ivanov," he says, "my last question to you: Can an abortion be performed on a cow? I understand that this is not a typical question; therefore, I'm giving you an hour to prepare your answer."

The student leaves the auditorium, puzzled. But, instead of going to the library, he goes to a bar to buy a sandwich. There he meets his old friend, who has just finished his semester and is celebrating this accomplishment.

Our hero walks over to his friend's table, refuses his offer of a drink, and says, "Do you know if a cow can have an abortion?"

Nearly choking on his wine on hearing these words, the friend sobers up for a second and says, "I know a doctor. But you're in a very *big* shit, man!"

A math student goes to bed with a sex problem on his mind. When he wakes up the next morning he holds the solution in his hand.

"What would you choose—money or knowledge?" the professor asks one of his students during class.

"Money, of course," the student replies.

"I would choose knowledge," the professor says. "And do you know why?"

"Yes I do, professor," the student replies. "Everyone chooses what he lacks most."

A student walks into the examination room, pulls out an expensive bottle of French cognac and places it on the desk in front of his professor.

"D," the professor says.

The student then puts a box of Cuban cigars on the desk. The professor takes one look at it and says, "C."

Now the student reaches into his pocket, pulls out a thick wad of money and places that on top of the cigar box.

"A," says the professor, and he begins to write in the student's report card.

As soon as the student gets his card back, he grabs everything from the professor's desk, shoves it inside his book bag, and rushes out of the room with these words: "Sorry professor, but I have two more exams to pass, you know!"

"Why do you worry so much," the professor asks his student before the exam. "Are you afraid of my questions?"

"No, professor," the student explains, "I'm afraid of my answers."

"You must be the best student in your class," an older lady on the subway asks a student, who's carrying a long overcoat in his hand. "You're so skinny. Would you like to take my seat?"

"No, I'm only the second best," the student answers. "And thanks for offering me your seat, but I'd prefer to stand up."

"Well," the woman says cordially, "I can hold your overcoat if you want."

"It's not my coat, ma'am, it's my classmate," the student

"Doctor, I haven't been to the washroom for four days. Can you give me something?"

"Here, take this and get something to eat."

explains. "He's the best student in my class."

A young drama student is heading out of town to perform. His friend offers some help:

"I know you don't have a suitcase; you can take mine."

"What for?"

"So you can take your clothes with you."

"Then what am I going to wear? I can't go naked."

A woman arrives at a mental institution to visit her grandson. Right after she walks in, a girl, dressed like a nurse and imitating a witch with a broomstick between her legs, approaches the woman and cackles an offer: "Would you like a ride?"

The woman agrees, feeling pity for the girl.

"You owe me five rubles for the fare," the 'witch' announces after their 'ride'.

Next, a guy, dressed up like a doctor and holding a spray bottle in his hand, walks by and makes this offer: "This is magic water," he says, pointing to the bottle. "It cures all diseases. Would you like me to spray you, ma'am?"

Again out of pity, the woman agrees. When he is finished, the 'doctor' collects ten rubles for his service.

"Why do you keep your patients this way?" the woman finally asks a nurse.

"We keep all our patients well supervised, madam," the nurse replies. "Those are medical students, laboring for their pocket money."

"... *A*nd to illustrate my thesis," a Psychology professor concludes his lecture, "I would like to perform a little demonstration." He walks over to a telephone, turns on the speaker phone, and dials a random number.

"May I speak to Ivan, please?" the professor says.

"You've got the wrong number," a man's voice answers.

"This is the first and the mildest stage of anger," the professor says, and then he dials the same number again. "Could you please call Ivan to the phone for me?"

"I told you, there's no Ivan!" the same voice replies.

"This is the second stage of anger," explains the professor, and he dials the same number once again. "May I speak to Ivan, please?"

"Get the…!" the man on another end of the line shouts.

"And this is the third and final stage of anger," the professor says. "Any questions?"

"I know the fourth one, professor!" one student pipes up. "Could you please demonstrate it for us?"

The student walks over to the telephone, pushes the re-dial button and says, "Hi, this is Ivan. Are there any messages for me?"

"**W**hich one of hell's departments do you prefer?" a devil asks the freshly arrived student. "The regular department or the one for students?"

"The regular one," the student answers. "I've been to stu-dent hell already; nothing could be worse than my days at the university."

Once he arrives there, the student is amazed. He finds everything he could have only dreamed of during his student life: lots of women and free booze, and no studying.

The student barely begins to enjoy this new life when the devil walks in and drives a big nail into the student's back. The same thing takes place the next day, and then the day after, and the day after that. Realizing he has made a mistake, the student asks the devil about a transfer to hell for students.

"Okay," the devil says, and he grants the student's request. When he arrives in the hell for students, our hero finds better women and more free drinks and—most important of all—no nails in the back.

This routine continues for three months. Suddenly, in the fourth month, however, the student hears a noise behind his back. He turns around and there he sees the devil with a bucket of nails. "What's that for?" he shrieks, pointing at the bucket.

"Get ready, student. This is your mid-term exam."

"**E**xcuse me, sir, you can't sleep during my lecture."

"I'm not sleeping, professor, I'm blinking. Very slowly."

"My piano exam is next week," a conservatory student tells his friend. "But I just can't produce a line."

"Why don't you take one of your professor's compositions?" his friend advises. "Just rewrite it backwards. He won't notice anything."

"I've tried that; all I got was Tchaikovsky."

A professor in a busy student cafeteria finally finds an empty seat. He reserves it by placing his briefcase on the chair, and then he goes to the buffet. When he returns with his food, he is surprised to see a student occupying his seat and eating.

The professor glares at the student, picks his briefcase up from the floor and, just before leaving, he says, "Do you know the difference between a man and an animal, young man?"

"Sure I do," the young man grins. "A man sits when he eats; an animal stands."

"Do you know what exam we have tomorrow?" the linguistics student asked his classmate, who isn't studying.

"I'm not sure. Tell me."

"Chinese!"

"Well, I have the whole night ahead."

"What are you having for dinner tonight?" one cannibal asks another.

"A student."

"Bad choice," the first cannibal says. "Last time I barbecued one, all I got was skin and bones, and while he was cooking, he ate all the vegetables from the grill next to him."

Some graffiti from the wall of a public washroom on campus:

"Look on your right," the writing on the door says.

"Look on the left," the writing on the right wall says.

"Look behind you," the writing on the left wall says.

"Hey, buddy," the writing on the back wall says, "I don't

get it. Did you come in here to just look around or what?"

Having finished a successful sex counseling session, the sex therapist who has just saved a young couple from divorce shares in detail his recent professional experience with his colleague:

"What was the couple's name?" the colleague interjects.

"The Ivanovs."

"I know them. They're both students, they have no place to do it, and you must be the last doctor in town whose room they haven't used yet."

"I'll do anything, professor," a pretty female student says with a bright smile, "to get a good grade."

"Very well, madam," replies the professor, "then study the material."

"You can keep a good beer for about six weeks at room temperature," a student says, reading an article aloud.

"Well," his roommate responds, "I don't know about that. I've never been able to keep it for longer than a day."

"What do we get if we multiply 458,723 by 14,533, then take the square root of the product and divide the result by 125.56?"

"A headache."

"What would you prefer," the professor asks his student during the exam, "one hard question, or two easy ones?"

"One hard one, professor."

"Okay, where on earth were the first apes discovered?"

"In Red Square."

"Why would you say that?"

"Now you're asking me the second question, professor."

"Do you think I'm an idiot?" the angry professor says to his badly floundering student.

"I don't know, professor," the student says, "I've only been in your class for one term."

Two roommates, a man and a woman, have to share one washroom. One day while taking a bath, the woman catches her roommate peering into the gap.

"Why are you looking at me? You've never seen a naked woman?" she asks.

"I'm not looking at you," he replies. "I'm just checking to see which razor you're using to shave your legs."

"I don't think my son is going to pass his university exam tomorrow," a father tells his friend sadly.

"I can bet you 10,000 rubles that he will," replies his friend, who is a professor at the same university.

"What's the difference between a French student and a Russian student?"

"The former is clean-shaven and slightly drunk. The latter is poorly-shaven and very drunk."

God sends an angel to check out the students:

"It is only the beginning of the term," says the angel. "All the students are studying, except the engineering group—they're partying."

Two months later, God sends the angel again. "It's the mid-term," says the angel. "All the students are studying, except the engineering group—they're partying."

After two more months have passed, God sends the angel once again. "It's the night before exams," reports the angel. "All the students are studying hard, except the engineering group—they're praying."

"Very well," God says. "Then they're the ones I'm going to help."

"Please give us an example of deceit," a law professor

asks his students.

"Professor," one student volunteers, "we'll have an example of deceit if I fail this exam."

"Please elaborate."

"According to one definition, if one person uses another person's lack of knowledge and causes him or her damage by doing so, that's deceit."

"**W**hat's the difference between a professor and a student?"

"The professor is a student who passed all the exams."

A hard-nosed fellow is taking an entry exam, trying to enter one of Moscow's prestigious universities. Using his familiar tactics of 'greasing the palm,' he places $5,000 inside his papers, along with a note: "$1,000 for each grade."

The next day, when he returns for his exam results, he opens his envelope and there he finds his papers, marked: "Failed", along with $4,000 and this note: "Here's Your Change."

A leisurely strolling student couple passes by an expensive restaurant:

"Wow!" she says. "It smells so nice."

"You like it?" he says. "Then let's turn around and pass by again."

"**P**rofessor, what do you think of the use of make-up by your female students?"

"I have no problem with that. The students who use it are less prone to cry during exams."

A veterinarian is the only doctor who can do a diagnosis without asking any questions. You'd go to see her if you were tired like a dog, hungry like a wolf, and working like a horse; in other words, if you were a student.

A student is failing his oral exam miserably. Finally, the tired professor takes his report card and writes in it: "An arrogant fool."

The student takes the report, looks at it and, unable to find his grade, says to the professor, "I don't see my grade, professor—just your signature."

The CIA once sent a mole, posing as a Russian student, to one of Moscow's technical universities. Two months later he was uncovered.

"Well," the spy explained to his superiors at the American embassy, "I couldn't drink that much. Firstly, it was almost physically impossible, and secondly, even if I could, it would have been against your instructions."

The CIA changed the instructions and sent in another mole with the same orders. But three months later, they were facing a similar disaster.

"Have you been drinking like everybody else?" they asked the mole.

"Yes I have," the mole replied.

"How did they get onto you then?"

"They got suspicious when they found out my attendance rate was the highest in the entire university," the mole explained, "but I was only following your instructions."

The CIA changed the instructions one more time, and they sent in their third mole. Unfortunately, during the mid-term exams, they received the devastating news of his failure. When the expelled "student" arrived at Langley, he explained, "I had been drinking and partying just like everybody else, and just occasionally showing up at lectures."

"How did they get you then?" his superiors asked.

"I was the only one who failed the exams."

Two hungry students are drinking beer: "Somebody is having a BBQ," says one, sniffing around.

"Stop drooling," says the other, "and get that fly off your cigarette tip."

CHUKCHIS

Two Chukchis were playing hide-and-seek—and got lost.

It is still largely unknown why the people of this small nation in northeast Siberia managed to become a butt of so many jokes in Russia. Skilled reindeer herders and sea hunters, people who live in the harsh weather of the Siberian tundra, the Chukchis are known as kind and generous people.

Their rough, tradition-breaking encounter with 'white people' in the beginning of the seventeenth century, holds some parallels to the experience of the natives of North America. The Chukchis are the target of some quite bad ethnic jokes. People who are repelled by ethnic humor in general may want to know the following popular Russian saying: Chukchi is not a nationality. Chukchi is a diagnosis.

Q: Why does a Chukchi always smile when he sees lightning?

A: He thinks someone is taking his picture.

A Chukchi shows up at work wearing different shoes: one is black, the other is brown.

His boss stops him in the hall and says, "Go home and

change your shoes."

An hour later, when the Chukchi returns, his boss notices that the man's shoes are mismatched again. "I thought you were going to go home to change your shoes," says the boss.

"I did," our Chukchi explains. "This is the other pair I had at home…".

A Chukchi comes into a store and asks, "Do you have color TVs?"

"Yes, we do."

"All right. Give me a green one."

A Chukchi wants to buy a refrigerator. "What do you need that for?" the salesperson asks him. "You live in Siberia."

"Well, to warm up during the winter. Imagine the comfort: it's minus forty outside and plus thirty-six (°F) in the fridge."

During the Second World War a Chukchi was a suspect in the robbery of a large shipment of gold, so he was questioned by the police. Another Chukchi was helping the police, acting as a translator. "Ask him where he hid the gold," the police officer began.

"He says he didn't take it, officer," the Chukchi translated.

"Tell him if he doesn't tell us where he keeps the gold, he'll be executed. The country is at war, so nobody will bother trying to prove his innocence."

When the translator told the accused about the prospect of execution, the Chukchi decided to admit his crime, and he explained where he had hid the gold.

Here is how the man's statement was translated: "Officer, he says you can shoot him; he will never tell you where he has hid that gold."

After Brezhnev's death, a Chukchi called the Kremlin to

ask, "Hello, do you need a new General Secretary?"

"Are you sick?!" the voice on the other end shouted.

"Yes, yes, I am," the Chukchi replied. "I am sick and very old."

A Chukchi brings a TV into his *yaranga* (a Chukchi teepee). "Why did you bring it here?" his wife asks him. "We don't have a power outlet here."

His reply: "Chukchi is smart. Chukchi bring an outlet too."

A Chukchi, visiting the big city, loses his wife. He goes to the police for help. "We need her description," an officer explains.

"What description?" the Chukchi wonders.

"Here, for example." Trying to explain, the officer pulls out a picture of a young woman. "This is a picture of a woman. You can see she is young, slim, tall, she has blond hair...".

"Oh," Chukchi says. "Mine is old and ugly. You better find me this one!"

A Chukchi returns to his village. His clothes are torn, his face, hands, and body covered with blood and bruises.

"What happened to you?" the villagers ask him. Pointing to a boomerang, the village elder says, "What is that thing in your hand? Throw it out!"

"You take it, please," our Chukchi says. "And try to throw it out yourself!"

One Chukchi says to another, "I have bought an inflatable latex woman. It improves my sex life."

"How is that?"

"Well, I leave it with my reindeer to scare off the wolves, and then I go home to my wife."

A gold miner approaches a Chukchi and asks, "Can you lend me a pound of gold? I am short of my norm this year and, you know, I can't go back without completing my norm." Chukchi has helped the white man many times, and he does so again.

The miner returns again next year. Instead of paying his debt, however, he asks Chukchi, "You have to help me out. This year was even worse. Can you lend me one more pound of gold?" And once again, Chukchi helps him out.

One year later the miner knocks on Chukchi's teepee.

"If it's the gold miner, tell him I went to a distant pasture and will be back next month," the Chukchi says to his wife, and he hides under the bed.

"Where's your husband?"

"He went to a distant pasture."

"Looks like he's out of luck then. I brought him two pounds of gold, my debt for the last two years. Okay, get me some vodka, and let's have a quickie, I'm leaving tonight."

Lying under the bed, the Chukchi is eating himself alive. "I have to get my gold! I have to beat up the miner for sleeping with my wife! What am I doing at a distant pasture?"

Chukchi and his wife are swimming against the current in a kayak. Chukchi is sitting at the stern, smoking a pipe; his wife is rowing. He lets out a puff of white smoke and thinks to himself, "She's lucky. All she has to do is row; I have to think about the future."

Once upon a time a smart boy was born in a Chukchi village. The envious villagers expelled him, however, just for being too smart. That gave birth to a new nation—the Japanese.

A Chukchi, visiting Red Square for the first time in his life, is standing and looking at St. Basil's Cathedral. "Do you like it?" a passerby asks him.

"Very much," Chukchi answers.

"Well, I can sell it to you for only one hundred rubles. Here, I'll give you a rope, which you can use to pull it back home to Siberia with you."

"Okay, I'll take it."

A policeman sees the Chukchi pulling on the rope frantically. So he asks him, "What are you doing, sir?"

"I just bought this cathedral and I'm taking it home."

"Have you made any progress?"

"Yes I have, officer. In fact, I can't see my suitcases already."

"**H**ey, Grigori, I slept with your wife last night!"

"So what? I do it every night."

"**W**hat do Chukchis do when they're cold?"

"They get together in a teepee and sit close to one another around a candle."

"And what do Chukchi do when they're very cold?"

"They light the candle."

A Chukchi returns to his village from a trip to Paris. "What a nice bunch of people the French are: cheerful, kind, and very intelligent," he tells his friends. "I was in a bar the other day. There was a beautiful woman sitting at a table next to mine. I knew no French, she knew no Chukchi, not even Russian. So I took a napkin, drew a wine glass on it and showed it to her. She smiled and joined me at my table. Next I drew a fork and a chicken. So she agreed to have dinner with me. After dinner, she took a napkin and drew a bed on it. Now, tell me, how, just how did she know that I was a carpenter?"

A Chukchi goes to an information booth and asks, "Tell me please."

"Please."

"Thank you."

A Chukchi walks into a small electronics store and tells the shopkeeper that he wants a stereo. The store owner decides to pull a quick one—he sells him a huge old floor model of a loud-speaker.

When the Chukchi gets back to his remote village in Siberia, the entire village gathers in a local club to listen to the stereo. Chukchi plugs the loudspeaker into an outlet and all they can hear is the hissing sound of burning insulation, accompanied by a cloud of smoke.

Watching this for some time, an elder voices his verdict: "Patience people, they'll start playing after the conductor finishes his pipe."

Q: Why do Chukchis never water-ski?
A: They can't find a lake with a slope.

"**D**o you like your new car better than a dogsled?"

"Yes, except that it takes me one hour to get to town and four hours to get back."

"Why is that?"

"You see, I have a car with four speeds forward and only one in reverse."

Q: What do they call smart people on Chukotka peninsula?

A: Tourists.

"**S**top! Who goes there?" a Chukchi sentry yells out. "Say the password!"

"Black sky."

"Not right. The password is 'white earth.' Go ahead.

And try to remember that next time."

Q: Why don't Chukchi drink boiled milk?
A: They can't plug the cow's horns into the power outlet.

A Chukchi takes a cab. "Twenty rubles, please," the driver says at the end of their ride. But Chukchi gives him only ten.

"It's twenty rubles, sir," the driver repeats.

"But you got a ride too, didn't you, driver?" protests Chukchi.

Q: How do the Chukchi drink coffee?
A: They put on their darkest sunglasses and drink hot water.

"Chukchi, what do you think is the stupidest nation in the world?"

"The Russians, of course!"

"Oh, why?"

"Well, every time I come home and see my neighbor Ivan in bed with my wife, I explain to him again and again that she's *my* wife. And yet that stupid Russian just keeps coming back!"

A Chukchi and an explorer were looking for some minerals along the ocean shore when they spotted a disturbed, and hungry, polar bear approaching them. The Chukchi quickly took their only pair of skis and began to put them on.

"It won't help," the explorer said. "You can't run faster than the bear anyway!"

"I don't have to run faster than the bear," our Chukchi explained. "All I need to do is run faster than you!"

ODESSA AND JEWS

A beautiful city on the northwest coast of the Black Sea, now part of Ukraine, Odessa was considered a cultural capital of Russian Jews. No wonder why this is where a very unique, refined, and undisputedly one of the best brands of Russian humor—Odessan humor—was born.

"Abram, you have a brother in Israel? Why haven't you told me before that you have a relative abroad?"

"Abroad? He's not abroad. I am the one who is abroad."

Two beggars are sharing a busy street corner. One has a sign that says: "Please help a crippled WWII veteran!". The other carries this sign: "Please help a poor Jew!"

The first beggar sees a steady flow of change coming into his old, shabby military hat. The second gets only scornful looks.

A warm-hearted woman then approaches the beggars. She gives some change to the Jewish beggar, and then gives him a little advice. Says she: "Good man, get rid of that sign."

"Did you hear that, Moishe?" the Jewish beggar says to the other, and he straightens his sign as soon as she leaves. "She thinks she can give us a business lesson!"

Two women inspect some dresses brought from Paris. "Isn't it something? Two thousand miles from Odessa and such quality!"

"There are about ten million Jews around the world," a Jewish man tells a Chinese man. "What is the world's Chinese population?"

"Over a billion," the Chinese man says proudly.

"Then tell me," the Jewish man says, "how come you Chinese aren't as visible?"

Q: How many times does a Jewish man laugh after a joke is told?

A: Four times. The first time because everybody else is laughing. The second time because now he gets it. The third time because he didn't get it right away. And the fourth time is because someone still doesn't get it.

An elderly man walks down the street in Odessa. Passerby point their fingers at him while chattering to one another. A girl then runs over to the man and asks, "Sir, is it true that you're the last Jew in Odessa?"

"No, I'm the last fool in Odessa."

There's a knock on a door in Odessa after the Revolution.

"Rabinovich," the Bolsheviks say, entering his house. "Do you have any gold?"

"Sara, my gold," Rabinovich says to his wife. "They have come for you."

Immigrating to Israel, a man is carrying a large framed picture. "What is it?" the Soviet customs officer asks him.

"It is not 'what', officer, but 'who'," the man replies, unveiling a picture of Lenin. The officer, afraid to disagree with that statement, lets him pass by.

Once in Tel Aviv, the newcomer is asked about this pic-

ture by an Israeli customs officer. "Who is that?"

"Not 'who', but 'what', officer," the man replies. "A gold-plated picture frame, to be exact."

Q: What was the Sputnik's nationality?
A: Jewish. Who else would leave the USSR that fast?

A man is running behind a bus. When the bus stops, someone asks him, "Why are you running behind the bus?"

"I'm saving a ruble—the bus fare," he explains.

"Then why don't you run behind a taxi—you'll save much more."

Pointing to a picture of one of the famous Russian military leaders while on a tour in a museum, a Jewish man asks another visitor, who happens to be a general, "Excuse me, sir, is this Marshal Suvorov?"

"Yes, Suvogov, Suvogov," the general replies rudely, mimicking the man's accent.

"If you could only copy him instead of me, General."

"**W**hat are all these people lining up for?" a foreign tourist asks Rabinovich when she sees a long line near the *GUM* (the State Department Store, the Soviet Union's largest department store) at Red Square.

"They're lining up to buy government bonds, madam," Rabinovich answers.

A KGB informant then tells his superiors about that encounter, and Rabinovich is invited to visit the Kremlin.

"Comrade Rabinovich," begins the official. "On behalf of the Soviet government and on behalf of all Soviet people, I would like to thank you for that heroic speech. That was a remarkable explanation?"

"I'm a patriot, Comrade Commissar!" Rabinovich replies solemnly.

"How can we thank you for that, Comrade Rabinovich?"

"May I have an exit visa to the States?"

"Moshe, what's wrong? Why are you so quiet?"

"In this cold!? Thanks, I'd better keep my hands in my pockets."

"Sara, were you ill?" one woman asks another, her neighbor.

"No, why?"

"I saw a doctor leaving your house yesterday morning."

"So what! I'm not asking you if a war broke out just because I saw a lieutenant leaving yours!"

At a concert: "Ladies and gentlemen, please welcome the quartet *Friendship of Nations*. Let me introduce the performers: Pilipenko - Ukraine; Arapetian - Armenia; Musrepov - Uzbekistan; Rabinovich - violin."

In the early days of the telephone, an elderly man is being taught how to use the new invention. "You take the earpiece in one hand, and you take the mouthpiece in the other…".

"Wait a moment," the old man interjects. "How am I supposed to talk with my both hands tied up by these things?"

"Hi, Moishe! First of all, I slept over with your Sara. And second of all, let me ask you how you like the 'first of all'?"

"First of all," Moishe replies, "I haven't seen Sara for a year. Second of all, she has syphilis. And third of all, tell me, how do you like the 'second of all' now?"

Q: Is there a symphony orchestra in Papua New Guinea?

A: No. No Jew would ever agree to put a ring into his nose.

Moishe comes home unexpectedly and finds his wife Sara in bed with a stranger. The stranger quickly gets up, puts his clothes on, and quietly slips out of the room.

"Sara, who was that man?" Moishe asks.

"I don't know. But he sure was some kind of rude," Sara replies. "He could have at least said hello to you or good-bye to me."

Rabinovich applies for a job, but he is denied the position. "This is anti-Semitism," he complains to the personnel manager.

"I don't think so, sir," explains the executive. "Why would we hire someone who will soon leave for Israel?"

"But I have no intention to emigrate."

"In that case, I'm afraid, we can't hire you at all!"

"Why?"

"We don't need fools."

"Are you going to attend Rabinovich's funeral?"

"Why should I? Do you think he will go to mine?"

A Jewish man comes to a store and sees this sign: 'We don't sell meat to the Jews.' He begins to complain to the manager.

The manager then looks around and whispers into his ear, "If you try this meat you'll know why, dear sir."

It's early Sunday morning, in an apartment building in Odessa, where everybody knows everything about everybody. A woman walks out onto the balcony and begins talking to her neighbors.

"Hey, Rose, did you see my Abram?"

"Why?"

"Rahil, is Abram at your place?"

"No. Why?"

"Sara, can you hear me? Did you see my Abram?"

"No. What happened?"

"Well, he said he was going to see a hooker yesterday; he's still not home…".

"How can you say that? Are we hookers?" the neighbors protest.

"Okay, okay," says the woman. "I can't even ask you anything?!"

Moishe meets his friend Abram, who is pacing back and forth repeating, "But why? What for?"

"What happened, Abram?"

"One thing bothers me, Moishe. Why is there a 't' in the word 'bread'?"

"Abram, but there's no 't' in the word 'bread'."

"Okay, but let's just say we have a 't' in the word 'bread'."

"But, what for?"

"That's what I'm thinking about."

A man named Rabinovich is looking for a job. He tells the prospective employer that, despite his name, he is Russian. The interviewer thinks about this for a moment and then says, "Well, in that case, I'd better hire a Jew."

Q: What does Rabinovich do while spending time in a minimum-security Siberian prison?

A: He marries a Chukchi woman and brings up some winter-proof Jews.

An OVIR (External Passport and Visa Office) officer asks a man, "Why do you want to go to Israel?"

"My wife bugs me all the time, 'Let's go, let's go!'"

"Well, let her go."

"You know, officer, my daughters insist also."

"So what?"

"And my mother-in-law and father-in-law want to leave as well…".

"Are you a man or not? Let all of them go and you stay here."

"I wish I could. But I'm the only Jew in our family."

From a newspaper ad: A respected, intellectual Russian family is seeking a Jewish son-in-law for immigration purposes.

Brezhnev asks one of his top aides, "What is the USSR's Jewish population?"

"Around four million, Comrade Brezhnev," is the reply.

"And how many, do you think, will leave if we open the borders?"

"At least ten million."

"Moishe, I heard you married a Russian girl?"

"Yes, I did."

"But why?"

"You know, Abram, our women get sick so often."

"So what? You think the Russian women don't get sick?"

"Well, they do, but I don't feel sorry for them as much."

When Khrushchev was presented with a list of candidates to be the new rabbi of the Moscow synagogue, he studied it for a moment, and then exclaimed disapprovingly, "Are you out of your mind? These are all Jews."

A Jewish man fills out an official Soviet form:

...

84. Have you ever been a member of any other political party?

No.

85. Have you ever been in any enemy-occupied territory?

No.

86. Have you ever been charged with an indictable offence?

No.

87. What is you nationality?
Yes.

An OVIR officer asks Rabinovich why he wants to leave the USSR for Israel.

"The first reason, sir, is my neighbor. Whenever he sees me he keeps saying, 'Damn Jew, I'll get you the first thing once the Soviets are washed up'."

"Comrade Rabinovich, there's nothing to worry about. The Soviets will never be washed up."

"Well, officer, that is my second reason for leaving."

"**I**s Israel a big country or a small country?"

"Of course it's big. If it were small, it would be called *Izya*.

The tourist is visiting a village. She sees a monument and asks an elderly man about whose tribute the monument commemorates:

"Haim Rabinovich," he answers.

"Then why does it say on the stone 'To the Unknown Warrior'?"

"Well, you see," the man explains, "everyone knew him as a storekeeper, but nobody could vouch for him as a warrior."

On their golden anniversary the Ivanov's invited their friends. According to tradition, the guests were to bring presents that, if not made of gold, would at least have something golden in them.

Rabinovich arrived with a stranger. "Ladies and gentlemen," he declared, unveiling his 'present', "Allow me introduce to you my distant relative, Moishe Goldman."

During his tour of Eastern Europe in the late seventies, Rabinovich sent a few telegrams:

"Hello from free Bulgaria. Rabinovich."

"Hello from free Romania. Rabinovich."

"Hello from free Hungary. Rabinovich."

"Hello from Austria. Free Rabinovich."

Q: Will there be any Jews under communism?

A: No, they'll manage to slip away.

When Rabinovich heard about Yuri Gagarin's space flight he had this to say, "Isn't it stupid? He's given a chance to leave the Soviet Union, to fly around the world. And after all that, he comes back?!"

Rabinovich's son asks, "Dad, what is Proletarian Internationalism?"

"I'm not quite sure what it means, dear boy, but my guts tell me we should start packing up."

The Soviet Jews were generally divided into two categories: the brave ones, and the desperate ones. The former were leaving, the latter stayed.

The Soviet Jews were sometimes also divided into three categories: the leaving, the willing to leave, and the 'thinking that they don't want to leave'.

It's a cold winter day. The manager of a store makes an announcement to a huge line outside: "Citizens, we won't have enough meat today. Therefore, all Jews can leave."

Two hours later, the manager shows again: "Comrades, unfortunately, it looks like we'll receive very little meat today. Therefore, all non-party members can go home."

Three hours later, another announcement: "Comrades communists, we won't have any meat today."

"Those Jews again," someone says. "While we're standing in this damned line, they're able to stay warm at home."

A woman tells her lover, "Listen, Abram, my husband is going out of town tonight, so we can have some fun at my place."

"Sounds great. But how would I know he's really gone?"

"I will throw a coin out the window. As soon as you hear it hitting the ground, come on up."

"Okay, Sara."

Sara does as she says, but Abram isn't coming up. An hour later, she's starting to worry, so she takes a look out the window. There she sees Abram, on his knees, searching for something in the dark.

"What are you doing down there, Abram?" she asks. "I've been waiting for you for the whole hour!"

"I'm looking for the coin, Sara."

"What a pinchpenny you are. I pulled it back on a string an hour ago!"

*A*bram has an argument with his boss. During the heat of the discussion he tells the boss everything he thinks about him. His wife, Sara, isn't happy with that. So she insists that Abram go back and apologize.

"Abram," she says, "you have to go back to the office and tell your boss that you feel sorry for what you said and that he is a good man."

Abram dutifully goes back to the office. "Excuse me, Mr. Goldman," he says. "You are a *good* man? I am sorry!"

"*E*xcuse me, sir. Are you from Odessa?"

"Why? Is something missing?"

"*R*ebbe, is it possible to talk to the dead?"

"It is, but they won't talk back."

"*I* visited Goldberg's last night," one woman says to another.

"What was it like?"

"Well, I played piano for the entire night."

"I don't like that family either."

A conversation takes place in a synagogue in a pre-revolution Russian city.

"I don't know what to do, Rebbe. If I register my newborn son a year younger, he will be drafted sooner. But if I register him a year older, he'll have to go later to school. What should I do?"

"Why don't you register him as is?"

"Yes! I hadn't thought about that!"

An elderly Jewish man is in his car in the middle of a busy intersection. After he allows the lights to change three times without making any progress, a police officer walks over to him and asks why he isn't driving through.

"You know, officer," the man says, sounding rather suspicious. "Somehow, I just don't trust them today."

Two friends, Abram and Moishe, walk down the street. "I am so thirsty, I am so thirsty," Moishe keeps saying. "If you only knew, Abram, how thirsty I am."

Tired of his friend's whining, Abram buys him a soda pop. "How thirsty I was," Moishe says when he's finished his drink. "Oh, how thirsty I was. You can't imagine how thirsty I was, Abram...".

"**A**bram, what would you do if you won a million dollars?"

"Nothing."

"What do you mean 'nothing'?"

"But why?"

Falling off the roof of his house, Rabinovich shouts to his wife as he's passing the window on his way down: "Sara, don't cook for me, I'm not having dinner tonight!"

A man answers his door. The woman outside asks, "Excuse me, sir, did you save a Jewish boy by helping him out of the ice on the river yesterday? I am his mother."

"Yes, that was me."

"Then you must have seen his hat?"

A chief rabbi comes to a small-town synagogue for an inspection.

"It is impossible, what you have done to this holy place!" he complains to the congregation. "It looks like a whorehouse."

"Oh!" someone says from the back.

"What, Abram?"

"Nothing, rebbe. I just remembered where I left my umbrella."

---

*A*n old Jewish man makes a phone call to an ultra-nationalist political organization. "Excuse me," he says into the receiver. "Is it true that the Jews have sold out Russia?"

"Yes they have. Now what do you want?"

"Well, I just wanted to know where I can get my share."

---

*A*n elderly man is sharing a train compartment with a young man. The young man asks the elderly what time it is. The older passenger says nothing, however, as he is making himself comfortable for the night.

The next morning the older man says, just before he's ready to leave, "It's eight thirty in the morning, young man."

"Why wouldn't you tell me the time last night, sir?" the surprised fellow asks.

"Well, if I'd answered you last night, we could have had a conversation, from which you could have learned that we were going to the same town. Then you would have asked me to let you stay overnight with my family. And since I have a young daughter, you would have seduced her, and later, as a well-bred man, you would have married her. Now, tell me, why would I need a son-in-law who doesn't even have a watch?"

"Rebbe, can I smoke on Saturdays?"
"Of course not, Abram."
"What about you, rebbe? I've seen you doing it."
"Well, I don't ask anyone."

A Jewish man shares a train compartment with an African man. "Excuse me," the Jewish man says, "are you Jewish, by any chance?"
"No, I am of African descent," the African man replies.
"Oh, I'm sorry."
Thirty minutes later, the Jewish man says, "Are you sure you're not Jewish?"
"No, I'm not. I told you that half an hour ago."
Another thirty minutes passes by. The Jewish man then says, "You know, I am Jewish myself. Come on, you can tell me."
"Sir, I've told you many times I'm not Jewish."
One hour later the Jewish man says once again, "You know, I still think you're Jewish."
"Yes, okay, okay, I'm Jewish. Now just leave me alone!"
"Excuse me, sir, but if you are Jewish, why is it that you look like an African?"

"Do you love your Fatherland, Private Ivanov?"
"I do."
"Will you give your life for her, if needed?"
"I will."
"What about you, Private Goldman? Do you love your Fatherland?"
"Yes, I do!"
"Will you give your life for her, if needed?"
"No."
"Why not?"
"Well, I can't give my life for her and love her at the same

time."

A knock on the door. "Excuse me, does Abram Rabinovich live here?"

"No."

"Okay, who am I talking to, please?"

"Abram Rabinovich."

"Well, why did you say you don't live here?"

"You call this living!?"

An elderly Jewish man is dying. He is surrounded by his grieving family. "Would you like something, dear?" his wife asks, wiping away her tears.

The man gathers himself and says, "I would like to have a cup of tea with two cubes of sugar."

"Why would you want something like that, grandpa?" his youngest grandson asks.

"Well, all my life I've had my tea with one cube of sugar at home, and with three cubes when offered free. But I really like my tea with two cubes of sugar."

Rabinovich's wife comes home from the market.

"Abram," she says, with great excitement on her face. "You should hear how they were offending me at the market. They called me the dirtiest names!"

"I told you not to go where everybody knows you."

God was giving away noses. The Roman requested, "I need something distinctive." God gave him a Roman nose.

"Give me something simple," said the Russian when his turn came up. And so he got a plain snout.

The Jew was slightly late. "How much is it?" he was asking people as he made his way through the thick crowd of nations.

"It's free."

"Then give me the biggest!"

A tourist from Odessa is bargaining over a stereo with a merchant in Rome. Before he had left Odessa, the tourist had been instructed by his friend to cut every asking price in half.

"I will give you five thousand," he tells the merchant.

"No, I told you it's ten thousand!" the merchant says.

"Five thousand is all I have!"

"Ok, nine thousand."

"Forty-five hundred!"

"I can't… Okay, eight thousand."

"Four thousand."

"Listen, where are you from?"

"From Odessa."

"Oh, Odessa… Ok, take it for free and leave my store."

"In that case, give me one more."

The last wish of Abram, a successful businessman, was that all the money owed to him be brought to his funeral by the borrowers themselves and put into his casket.

This turned out to be a problem. With all of Abram's money finally pouring in, it was quite a task to fit Abram's body and his money into one casket. Finally, the rabbi came up with a solution.

"Count the money and put it in my trunk," he said. "I know Abram would be glad to take my check instead."

A woman is crying over her baby son's casket at a cemetery. "And ask God to heal uncle Haim," she is pleading. "Also, ask God to send a good man as a husband for our Sara, and ask him to save Moishe from the military…".

"Excuse me, madam," the grave keeper interrupts her. "But if you have so many requests to God, why, instead of sending a baby, don't you go there yourself?"

A sign in a Soviet store: "Temporarily, we sell TV sets only to the veterans of the Napoleonic War of 1812."

"I didn't know there were any still alive!" one curious customer remarks.

"Yeah," the sales clerk says, "We had two Jews yesterday with papers signed by Kutuzov himself." (the Marshal who commanded the Russian opposition to Napoleon)

The more the Soviet Jews used to gather in one place, the more they wanted to leave for another.

As Moishe and Abram are talking, a boy walks over to them and asks, "Dad, who is Karl Marx?"

"Well," Moishe replies to his son. "He is the man who liberated us from our chains." Moishe then turns to the other man and says, "Abram, do you remember my golden chain?"

Three soldiers—a Russian, an Uzbek, and a Jew—were on guard duty at an important military location during the civil war that ensued shortly after the Bolshevik Revolution of 1917.

To kill some time, and despite the regulations, they decided to play a quick game of cards. As soon as they'd started their game, an inspecting officer noticed them grouped together, and quickly approached the soldiers.

"What's going on here?" he demanded. "Don't you know you're not supposed to cluster like this? Are you playing cards?"

"No, Comrade Commissar!" the Russian answered.

"Are you an Orthodox Christian, soldier?"

"Yes, I am, sir."

"Then swear on the Bible that you didn't play."

"I do."

The officer then turned to the Uzbek and asked him if he had been playing cards.

"No, I didn't, Comrade Commissar," the Uzbek responded.

"Are you a Muslim?"

"Yes, I am, sir."

"Then swear on the Koran, that you didn't play."

"I do."

"Rabinovich," the commissar continued, turning to the

Jew. "I know you're going to say you didn't play either. Will you swear on the Torah?"

"Comrade Commissar," Rabinovich said, "Why should I swear? If neither of them were playing, that means I'd have been playing by myself!"

Two Jewish men are sitting on a park bench. A bird, flying over, discharges its drop, which hits one of them on the shoulder.

"Did you see that, Abram?" the man who was hit asks, rubbing his arm. "And for the Russians, they sing."

An elderly man pays a visit to his friend. They talk late into the evening.

"Wait a moment, Abram. Let me put out the candle," one says. "We can hear each other without the light; I'd better save it."

When the time comes for the friend to leave, the host gets up to light up the candle again, but his guest stops him. "Wait, Moishe, don't light it yet. Let me put my pants back on: I didn't want to put them through any extra wear while we were talking."

"Moishe, where did you get that nice watch?"
"That's my father's. He sold it to me when he was dying."

A general, who was an anti-Semite, was sharing a train compartment with a Jewish man. To insult the Jewish man, the general played with his dog: "Moishe, get up! Moishe, lie down! Moishe, come here!"

After watching the general and his dog for some time, the Jewish man said, "Too bad your dog is a Jew. He could have become a general."

Q: What's the difference between a Jew and an Englishman?

A: An Englishman leaves without saying 'good-bye'. A Jew

says 'good-bye' without leaving.

"Do you know how that trial ended between the two Jewish businessmen?"

"Yes I do. The prosecutor got ten years hard labor."

Two men are having an argument.

"But black is a color," one says.

"No, it isn't!" the other protests.

"I'm telling you, black is a color!"

"No, black is not a color!"

"Well, let's ask our rabbi."

"Yes, black is a color," says the rabbi.

"See, I told you," the first man says. "Black *is* a color."

"Okay, black is a color. But white is not."

"You know nothing. White is a color too."

"No, it isn't."

"Why don't we ask our rabbi again."

"You, again?" the rabbi chortles. "Yes, white is a color."

"I told you," the first man says. "Black and white *are* colors. See! That means I did sell you a *color* TV."

In the woods near the Soviet-Polish border, a Jewish man was caught crossing the border illegally. "What are you doing here?" a guard questioned him. "Are you trying to escape in order to discredit the USSR?"

"Not at all, officer," the man explained, pointing to something on the ground. "I just couldn't find a washroom…".

"Then why does it look like dog shit?" the guard asks.

"Well, officer, and what about our life here?"

"Do you know who Rasputin was?"

"No."

"And who Moshe Dayan was?"

"No."

"See, you don't know. But I do. And that's because every

evening I take classes or go to the museum."

"Well, let me ask you. Do you know who Sergei Ivanov is?"

"No. Who is he?"

"Okay, smart guy. He's the guy who visits your wife every evening while you are taking a class or visiting the museum."

"May I talk to Rabinovich?"

"Which one, junior or senior?"

"Senior."

"They're both dead."

"Why is it that the Jews always answer a question with a question?"

"Who told you that?"

"The whole world admires our punctuality," a German proclaims.

"The whole world admires our big-heartedness," a Russian boasts.

"The whole world admires our salt pork," a Ukrainian exclaims.

"Right!" a Jewish man says. "Then we are pleased to be unpunctual, heartless vegetarians!"

Rabinovich surprised his friends when they learned that he was attending anti-Semitic gatherings.

"Well, you see," explained Rabinovich. "There, I rule the world. I control the governments. I am the richest man on earth. And who am I here? Just another salesman trying to make ends meet."

Q: Why do so many people think that the Jews are very rich?

A: Because, throughout history, they've had to pay for so many things.

UKRAINIANS

Jokes about Ukrainians tend to portray a picture of a thrifty, freedom-seeking, and tenacious nation.

When one reflects upon objective reality, one simply cannot ask too much from a joke. In the end, jokes are one genre that depend on grotesque situations and exaggeration for their impact. In much the same way that Russians are laughed at for their excessive fondness of vodka, a fair share of the jokes that are told about Ukrainians derive their punch lines from the Ukrainians' love for *salo*—the famous Ukrainian cured pork.

Q: How is a Ukrainian different from a Russian?

A: Like Hegel is different from Feuerbach. For a Ukrainian meal, *salo* (salt pork) in particular, is primary, while vodka is secondary. For a Russian, however, vodka is primary, and the meal is secondary.

"**S**alt pork for breakfast?" the wife says to her husband. "Don't you know you can get sick with arteriosclerosis?"

"I think I'm sick already," the husband replies. "Whenever I eat salt pork for breakfast, I forget about my lunch altogether."

A few days before the upcoming Ukrainian election, a couple get into an argument. "Now, so you know," she says to him, "I am going to vote for a different party than you…".

Passing by his neighbor's house, a man sees the following picture:

His neighbor Petro sits leisurely in a rocker, holding a newspaper in one hand and a cup of coffee in the other. Comfort is written all over his face. His peace is broken from time to time by the sound of a hammer.

"Petro, shame on you," the passerby yells out. "How come you're sitting in that chair doing nothing, when your wife is up there fixing the roof all by herself?"

Petro slowly puts his cup down, lifts his eyes from his paper, and replies: "Well, what if tomorrow there is war, and I'm not well rested?"

Thanks to a generous gesture on the part of the ruler, three pioneers—an Englishman, a Frenchman, and a Ukrainian— are granted as much land as they can cover on horseback in one day's ride. The Englishman stops after a five-hour ride, thinking to himself, "That is enough land for me and my family."

The Frenchman rides his horse until it becomes very tired. He then stops, saying to himself, "I will have enough land here for my family and my ancestors."

The Ukrainian, in his turn, rides all day, until his horse falls dead. Then he runs. And after he has no strength left in his feet, he takes off his hat, and throws it forward. "There," he gasps, "just a little bit more for my garden!"

A store customer back in the Soviet Ukraine asks a saleswoman, "Comrade, do you have any razor blades?"

"No, we don't," the saleswoman answers bluntly.

When the customer leaves, another saleswoman asks, "Why did you tell him that? We have tons of razor blades."

"If he calls me 'comrade', I say let him shave himself with a sickle!"

An elderly Ukrainian is dying. He calls his son and asks

"Let me cut it for you."
"Yeah, right here!"

him to invite the local party leader. "I want to join the Communist party," he explains.

"How come, father?" his son says. "You've spent all your life fighting against them, and now…".

"I am still against them. That's why when I die as a Communist, our land will have one fewer of them."

A tourist in hell sees two big pots filled with the damned, boiling miserably in smoking tar. One pot is guarded by a group of devils armed with tridents; the other pot isn't guarded at all. The tourist asks why only one pot is being guarded.

"You see," the devil replies, "we must guard this pot because we boil the Jews in it. If one of them gets out, he'll help out the rest of them. But in that pot we boil the Ukrainians. If one of them wants to get out, the rest won't let her or him do it. Why? Because that person just wants to be different from the rest."

"Why do you regularly receive parcels from Israel?" a KGB officer questions a man.

"I hid a Jewish man during the war."

"How could you, a citizen of the Soviet Ukraine, receive those parcels? Have you ever thought about your future?"

"Yes I have, officer. I'm hiding a Chinese man now."

An elderly Ukrainian nationalist once caught the magical Golden Fish. The Golden Fish promised to grant the man three wishes in exchange for her freedom.

"My first wish is for the Chinese to attack the Germans," he said. "My second wish is for the Germans to attack the Chinese. And my third wish is for the Chinese to attack the Germans again."

"Okay, old man, I will grant your wishes," the Golden Fish said. "But tell me, what's in it for you?"

"For me, nothing. But can you imagine where the Russians will be after all of this?"

"Attention please! Today is the first day of the Ukrainian

language as our only official language. Therefore, all requests for help, voiced in any language other than the official, will not be accepted."

—Heard at a Black Sea beach

"Have you heard about Ivan's new scarecrow?"
"What about it?"
"Apparently, it's so scary, the crows have brought back last year's crop."

Two friends are relaxing on the beach. "This is boring. How about a couple of drinks, Mykola?" one offers.
"You're buying?" asks the other.
A long pause ensues.
"Well, Mykola," the first says, "since you're not interested, let's think of something else."

A hard-line supporter of Ukraine's independence from Russia comes home from a meeting. Upon entering his apartment building he is shocked by what he sees:
The hall is brightly lit; the elevator is working; the building, finally, has power. At home, his wife is cooking dinner at the gas range, which, due to the frequent gas shortages lately, had become a useless piece of kitchen furniture.
Bewildered, the man grasps his head in his hands and mutters in horror, "Oh no, the occupants are back!"

"Mykola, have you ever seen the Spanish *corrida*?"
"Sure I have. That's when a bull stamps all over a Russian."
"No, no, I mean the Spanish corrida. How did you manage to fit a Russian in here?"
"Well, who else would charge a bull with a red flag?"

Somewhere in a hick village, a local party leader passes by. He sees a peasant burying a jar in his backyard. "What are you doing there, Petro?" he asks.

"I'm burying my money," the man answers.

"Well, don't you remember from my lectures that, under Communism, money will be useless? Nobody will need it, nobody will have it."

"Okay, okay, I know that. But isn't it something? I'll be the *only* one who has money!"

A dialogue in a Chernobyl village:

"Mykola, how do you manage to grow your watermelons on the bushes?"

"They're not watermelons, they're gooseberries."

"Look, your plums are ready to pick."

"Those are cherries, not plums."

"Can you hear that nightingale singing? Strange, it's already July."

"You're wrong again. That's my Geiger counter."

Three government officials—an American, a Russian, and a Ukrainian—are discussing the tax policies of their respective governments.

"An average American makes $35,000 per year," the American official says. "He or she pays $10,000 in taxes. How this person manages to live on $25,000 these days is a puzzle to me!"

"An average Russian makes $15,000 annually," the Russian official says. "The government takes $10,000 in taxes. How this person can manage to live on $5,000 is beyond my comprehension!"

"Well," the Ukrainian official says, "an average Ukrainian makes $5,000 per year. We take $6,000 in taxes. Where does he or she get $1,000 to pay those extra taxes? That's a *real* puzzle to me!"

While visiting Chernobyl, don't be to hasty about using a phrase like: 'Is that a gun, or are you just happy to see me'? It could simply be a Geiger counter.

A foreigner in downtown Kiev asks some local men how to get to the main street in that city. "Could you please tell me how to get to Khreshchatyk Street?" she says in English.

"*Sho*?" the men ask (that's Ukrainian for 'what?').

The tourist repeats the same phrase in German.

"Sho?"

The tourist repeats the same phrase in French.

"Sho?" the men ask as they look at each other.

Realizing that this approach isn't going to work, the woman simply leaves. As soon as she's gone one man says to the other, "Did you see that, Petro? She knows so many languages, but what good did it do?"

In the middle of winter, a man is visiting his friend in a village. The visitor walks into the house and sees his slightly boozed-up friend sitting on the clay furnace and playing an accordion. Meanwhile, his wife is outside in the cold, cutting logs into firewood.

"Hey, Mykola," the visitor asks, "how come you're playing accordion here in the warmth while your wife is out working on her own in that bitter cold?"

"Well," Mykola explains, "it's not my fault that she can't play accordion."

A KGB officer was conducting interrogations in the Western Ukraine during the 1939 occupation of the country by the Soviets. He pointed to the Ukrainian national blue-yellow flag, flying over a house, and then said to a man, "So, tell me, who put up that nationalistic flag?"

"How would I know?" the man answered. "When I went to bed last night it was the red flag. When I woke up this morning it was ours."

"Petro, how much sugar would you like in your tea?"

"Ten spoonfuls. But please don't stir. I don't like it too sweet."

A Ukrainian and a Jewish man are stranded in a desert. The former has a bag of salt pork, the latter has a bag of gold. Nothing more.

After two days without any food, meanwhile watching the Ukrainian eat his salt pork, the Jewish man decides that, in order to survive, he must break the religious law. And so he says, "Ivan, please, give me some pork."

"Oh no, Abram!" the Ukrainian says. "You have gold, I have pork. Why don't we trade, like civilized people?"

"Okay," Abram replies. "How much is one slice of your salt pork?"

"For you, Abram, just one bag of gold!"

"Why so expensive, Ivan?"

"Well, Abram, if you don't like the price, you can go shop around!"

"I just learned that, because it was in my 'sign' at the time I was born, Neptune may affect my health."

"And my health is affected by Uranium."

"What is your sign?"

"Never mind my sign. I used to work at Chernobyl."

"Petro, do your cows smoke?" one farmer asks another.

"No, why?"

"Then I think your stable is on fire."

A farmer steps onto a half-empty bus in a big city. When he sees a group of African men, he picks up his bags and asks them excitedly, "Are we on fire?"

Q: What country used to be the largest country in the world?

A: The Soviet Ukraine. Its borders were in the Carpathian mountains. Its capital was in Moscow. Its prisons were in Siberia. And its churches were in Canada.

THE DOCTOR'S OFFICE

A young woman visits a gynecologist. But she appears to be very embarrassed and reluctant to undergo an examination.

"Haven't you been examined like this before?" the doctor asks.

"Oh, many times," she giggles, "but never by a doctor."

An elderly man goes to see his doctor:

"Doctor," he says, "I'm not able to do anything in bed lately."

"How old are you, sir?"

"I'm 85."

"Well, what could you expect?"

"But my friend, who's 90, says he's still…".

"And you can say so too…".

The doctor studies his patient's test results. "How old are you, sir?" he asks.

"I'm going to be fifty this year," the patient replies.

The doctor shakes his head disapprovingly, and then he says, "No, I'm afraid you won't…".

"Doctor, this aching tooth bothers me so much I can't sleep at night!"

"Then why don't you find yourself a night job?"

"Doctor, please be frank with me…".

"Yes, of course, madam. After all you are the patient's wife."

"Then please tell me…will my husband be able to wash the dishes if he recovers?"

One surgeon asks another, "How did that appendectomy go?"

"Appendectomy??" the other shrieks. "I thought it was an autopsy!"

"I can't stand it anymore!" the patient says to his psychiatrist. "My wife asks me a question, answers it herself, and then spends an hour explaining to me why I was wrong…".

"Doctor, I always talk to myself."

"Does it bother your family members?"

"No, I live alone."

"Then why does it bother you?

"I'm so boring, doctor…".

"Your cough is much better today."

"I've been practicing all night, doctor."

"Where are you taking me?" the patient, lying in a hospital bed, asks the nurses who are pushing his bed down the hallway.

"To the morgue."

"But I'm not dead yet!"

"We haven't arrived there yet either…".

"Doctor, you have to help me. I'm working like a horse, eating like a pig, and I'm tired as a dog!"

"I'm afraid I can't help—I'm not a veterinarian."

"Do you have any problems with your sleep?"

"Yes I do, doctor. I always fall asleep early at night, wake up late in the morning, and I can't fall asleep after lunch."

A shy young man visits his doctor. In a low, trembling voice he says, "Doctor, one of my friends suspects that he has some sort of venereal disease…".

"Okay," the doctor interrupts him, "take off your clothes and show me your friend."

"Doctor, my wife has lost her voice…".

"Try coming home late tonight."

A writer visits his doctor:

"Doctor," he says, "whenever I stay up late writing at night, I can't get any sleep that night."

"Why don't you try reading what you've written?" the doctor replies.

A man explains his problems to a doctor. When he's finished, the doctor says, "You need to stop smoking and drinking, spend less time at work…".

"I get it, doctor," the patient interjects, "and the rest I hear every night from my wife…".

A man walks into a doctor's office and starts to undress himself. He takes his time, carefully folding all of his clothes, including his underwear and socks, then placing them neatly on a chair.

He then turns to the doctor and says, "Look here, doctor. Don't you think one of my testicles is lower than the other?"

"That is quite normal," the doctor explains. "Why does it concern you?"

"Well, doctor, don't you think it looks somewhat untidy?"

During his daily patient check-up at the hospital, the doctor remarks to one of his patients, "Well, it looks like next week Dr. Ivanov will have to see you."

"Is he my new doctor?"

"No, he's our pathology-anatomist…".

Says the doctor: "I can't come up with any diagnosis today; it could be alcoholism…".

Replies the patient: "I can come back tomorrow, doctor, when you're sober."

One doctor says to another, "One of my patients died yesterday. I've been treating him for an ulcer for two years, but the autopsy shows that he died from stomach cancer."

"Well, I had a patient I was treating for jaundice for ten years, but his autopsy showed that he was Chinese."

"Doctor," the patient says, "I'm very sick. I feel pain everywhere I touch myself. I feel pain here, here…everywhere!"

"Could I see your hand, please?" says the doctor, and he examines the patient's fingers.

"Just as I thought," the doctor exclaims. "You have a broken finger!"

"Tell me, doctor," the woman asks her gynecologist, "am I your first woman?"

"How many cigarettes per day do you smoke?"
"It depends on how many people I know that I run into."

"Doctor!" a woman cries into the phone. "My husband was just run over by a road roller at a construction site! What should I do?"
"Fax him over to my office immediately!"

The doctor examines a woman and tells her, "Unfortunately, you have high blood pressure, high cholesterol, and diabetes. I'm sorry; how old did you say you are, madam?"
"I'm twenty-eight, doctor."
"And you also have some serious memory loss…".

A man complains, "Doctor, I'm losing my hair!"
"That's because you worry too much," the doctor says.
"Maybe I do, but that's because I'm losing my hair…".

"Doctor, I have amnesia!"
"When did you notice it first?"
"Notice what?"

"How is your appetite, madam?"
"Well, doctor, sometimes I have it, sometimes not."
"When don't you have it?"
"After a meal."

A man tells his doctor, "My wife talks in her sleep."
"And what does she talk about?"
"The same phrase every night: 'No, Ivan, no'…".
"Well, it's nothing serious."

"But my name is Sergei."

"Still nothing to worry about; as long as she's saying 'no'…".

"Do you sleep well every night?"

"Very well, doctor."

"And what is your occupation?"

"I'm a night guard."

DOCTOR: "What is your problem, madam?"

PATIENT: "Well, that's what I thought I'd hear from you, doctor."

"Doctor, when I get up in the morning, I feel dizzy for an hour."

"Get up sixty minutes later."

"Doctor, how long can a man live without a brain?"

"How old are you?"

A man complains to his doctor about having constant headaches. "Do you drink alcoholic beverages?" the doctor asks him.

"No, never," he answers.

"Do you smoke?"

"No, doctor."

"What about sex?"

"I don't even think about it!"

"Sir, you're a saint, and I guess your halo is a bit too tight"

"Doctor, I have pain in my back."

"Bend over like this," the doctor says. "A little more… yes."

"I can still feel it."

"Bend a little more… more. What about now?"

"Much better, doctor!"

"Perfect! You can go now, just keep that posture."

A man visits a psychiatrist and says, "Doctor, I need your help. I think I'm a horse."

"Well, I can help you, sir," the doctor says. "But it will cost you some money."

"Money is no object, doctor," the man replies. "I just took first place in the third heat!"

"Doctor, it rings in my ear."

"Don't answer!"

"Doctor, my hearing is so bad," the elderly lady complains, "I can't even hear myself when I'm coughing."

"Here are some pills, madam. Take them three times a day…".

"Will I hear better?"

"No, but you'll cough louder…".

A woman consults an ear specialist. The doctor checks her questionnaire, and then he asks, "You have ten children?"

"Yes, because of my poor hearing."

"I'm sorry, madam, but I don't see any connection…".

"You see, doctor, when we watch TV at night, and my husband asks me, 'Are we going to keep on watching or what?', I always have to ask him again 'what?'. That's why I have ten children!"

"Doctor, I'm weak and I'm not altogether right sexually," the well-endowed young woman complains to her doctor.

"In which way, madam?"

"You see, doctor, I cannot refuse any man!"

"Doctor, what can I do to make my breasts stay perpendicular to my body?"

"Crawling may help, madam."

A man visits the dentist with his wife:

"Doctor," he says, "we're in a real hurry. Can you skip the freezing and do this tooth extraction without it?"

"Well, yes, I can do that, sir. In the end, of course, it's you who'll be in pain, not me, " the doctor replies. "Okay, let me see that tooth, please."

The man then turns to his wife and says, "Sara, open your mouth, honey, and show that tooth to the doctor."

They performed an autopsy on him and concluded that the cause of death was the autopsy.

A woman asks her seriously ill husband's doctor, "Is there any hope, doctor?"

"It depends on what you hope for, madam."

The surgery went very well. Too bad the patient will never know about it!

"And remember, madam," the doctor says, "besides the medicine, your husband needs absolute peace and quite!"

"That's what I've been telling him day and night, doctor!"

A man visits his doctor and explains his health problems. The doctor examines him and then says confidently, "Sir, you have nothing to worry about—you're as healthy as a bull!"

The same man returns to see the same doctor again the next year, complaining that he feels even worse. The doctor examines him again and says, "Sir, you're as healthy as a bull!"

The man returns again one year later, and then one year later again, each time feeling worse and worse, only to hear that he's "as healthy as a bull."

Finally, five years after the man's first visit, his wife walks into the doctor's office. "Doctor, my husband is dead," she sobs. "For the last five years you've been telling him he was healthy as a bull…".

"Well, madam," the doctor explains, "what can you expect? Bulls live for five years tops!"

"What is the patient's temperature?"
"It's normal, doctor, the room temperature."

"A glass of wine may help," the doctor tells his patient who has insomnia. "And if that doesn't help, you can have another glass of wine; then, later, one more."

"Doctor, what if even that won't help?"

"In that case, have one more and you wouldn't care whether you sleep or not anymore."

"Your blood pressure is normal, sir."

"Could you check my right arm, doctor? This one is a prosthesis."

"Doctor, can you help me to cure my snoring?"
"If it bothers you that much, we can correct it surgically."
"No, not at all!"
"Oh, I suppose it bothers your wife then?"
"No, I'm not married."
"Your neighbors?"
"No, I live in my own house."
"Then why do you want to cure it?"

"Well, doctor, I've lost my job five times already…".

They finally found a cure for apathy. The only problem is that patients don't care to take it.

"Do you really think you're suffering from indecisiveness?"
"Yes and no, doctor."

"Doctor, my wife complains that she needs three men with my potency to satisfy her in bed."
"Thanks to the latest advances in modern medical science, we're able to help people like you, sir. Here's your prescription."
"Is it for improving my potency, doctor?"
"No, it's for your cloning."

"Thank you, doctor, my back pain is gone now," the man says as he breathes a deep sigh of relief. "Was it a slipped disk?"
"No, your suspenders got twisted."

"Doctor, will I live?"
"Well, you will… but don't ask me how long…".

She says, "Honey, the doctor recommended that I go to the Caribbean or Hawaii. Where should we go?"
He says, "To another doctor!"

An elderly lady goes to see a busy doctor:
"I have a strange disease, doctor," she says. "Whenever I sit down I tend to sit, and sit, and sit. Whenever I lie down I tend to lie, and lie, and lie…".
"Excuse me, ma'am," the doctor interjects, "do you see that door?"

"Yes, why?"
"Well, why don't you get up and just go, and go, and go…".

"Do you drink, sir?" the doctor asks his patient.
"I wouldn't mind!" the patient replies.

"Doctor, I cannot get pregnant."
"Well, this could be a genetic disorder…".

"How do I take these pills, doctor?"
"Take two before going to bed tonight. Tomorrow, if you wake up, take two more."

An elderly man visits a young doctor:
"Doctor," he says, "I can climb one, and I can climb two, but for the third one I don't have any strength left…".
"Well, sir," the doctor says, "I could be your grandson, and I can't climb three of them in a row. What are you complaining about?"
"What do you mean, doctor?"
"I mean women!"
"And I mean steps…".

"Doctor, my wife stutters."
"Always?"
"No, only when she speaks!"

A doctor advises her patient: "To lessen the stomach pain, you should drink a glass of warm water every morning."
"Doctor, I've been doing that for the last twenty years. That's what my wife calls the morning coffee…".

A psychiatrist tells his friend, "I have a new patient, and he thinks that he's a car."

"So how are you going to treat him?"

"Why treat him? I can drive him home."

The doctor finishes his examination and says to his patient, "Sir, I can see that you're bothered by an old disease, one that has been spoiling your life for many years…".

"Doctor," whispers the patient, "could you please speak in a lower voice—she's sitting behind that door…".

A man walks into a doctor's office and the doctor says to him, "Sir, I can see you need a good pair of glasses."

"How do you know that, doctor? I just walked in!"

"I'm a gynecologist."

Q: What is the first thing that a doctor making a house call should know about his or her patient?

A: The address.

"Doctor, I have memory lapses."

"How often do they happen?"

"What?"

"The memory lapses."

"What lapses?"

A man sees his friend walking down the street with a swollen cheek. He asks him, "Ivan, what happened to you?"

"Well, I got two teeth extracted today."

"I thought you told me this morning that you had just one bad tooth…".

"Yes, but the dentist didn't have any change…".

A prostitute consults a doctor:

"I can see you have some problems, madam," the doctor says after examining her. "Do you lose a lot during your period?"

She thinks for a moment and then replies: "At least a couple of thousand, doc."

"Time cures all ailments!"

"Now I know why we have to wait for so long at doctors' offices!"

"Doctor, should I quit smoking?"

"Unfortunately, it doesn't matter anymore."

A group of doctors gather for a council. The chairman opens the discussion: "Well, dear colleagues, are we going to treat this patient? Or should we just let him live?"

The psychiatrist's patient says, "Doctor, I hear dogs coughing in my bedroom every night."

"That's not my specialization, sir. You need to see a veterinarian. Next, please!"

"Doctor, I need your help. I'm tired of having these dreams. Every night I have the same dream—rats playing soccer."

"Here's a prescription for some pills that will help you."

"Can I start taking them one month from now?"

"Yes, but why?"

"Well, they start their play-offs tomorrow!"

"Doctor," a nurse says to the young surgeon, "this is the third operating table you've destroyed this month. Don't cut so deep!"

"Doctor, my head is splitting from pain and my foot is swollen," the patient says.

The doctor takes a pill and breaks it in half. Handing both halves to the patient he says, "Here. Take this one for your headache, and this one for your foot."

One doctor asks another, "Has it ever happened to you that a patient's autopsy shows a completely different cause of death than the condition for which you were treating that patient?"

"No, never," the other replies. "My patients always die from the conditions for which I treat them."

"Doctor, I need your help. Every day when I come home from work my wife is in bed with another man. And when I start to say something to her, she sends me to the kitchen to have a cup of tea."

"Well, how can *I* help you, sir?"

"I just wanted to know whether I might be drinking too much tea…".

One doctor says to another, "So, how is my former patient?"

"Unfortunately, she's passed away."

"Finally, she's learned her mistake about getting a second opinion…".

The doctor looks up, sees a skeleton walking into his office, and says, "Waited a bit too long, haven't we?!"

"I don't think you have any medicine to help my disease, doctor."

"Don't worry. I have so many medicines that some of them can cure diseases that don't even exist yet."

"Doctor, please help me. I can see the future."
"When did that start?"
"Next Monday!"

"Doctor, I have a very strange form of Daltonism: I cannot see one color."
"What color is it?"
"How do I know? I've never seen it!"

"Wow!" says the gynecologist.
"Wow!" replies the echo.

He was taking such good care of his health that when he died he still didn't use it even once.

"Doctor, is it true that you can improve your eyesight by eating carrots?"
"Yes it is. Have you ever seen a rabbit wearing glasses?"

After examining his patient and failing to come up with a diagnosis, the doctor asks him, "Do you smoke?"
"No I don't, doctor."
"That's too bad; otherwise, I could have advised you to quit, and you would definitely get better!"

"Why don't you take the prescribed medicine?"
"Because it tastes awful, doctor."
"Well, if you imagine that you're drinking your favorite beer, it will be much easier."
"What if I drink my favorite beer thinking that it's the medicine, doctor?"

"Doctor, you asked me to stick out my tongue ten minutes ago," the woman says to her doctor. "But you haven't even taken a look at it!"

"I'm sorry, madam," the doctor says, "but this is the only way I can check your medical history without interruption."

"Doctor, my right leg is constantly in pain."

"Unfortunately, that's from age, madam."

"Yes, but my left leg is as old as my right, and I never have any problem with it!"

"You have nothing to worry about, madam," the doctor says. "You'll live until you're at least ninety!"

"But I'm already ninety, doctor!"

"See, I was right!"

The man says to his doctor, "Doctor, whenever I have few drinks and then make love, I cannot finish."

"Have you ever tried it without having any alcohol?"

"Yes I have, but then I can't start…".

A woman reports to her doctor for an examination. He tells her to undress and lie down.

"But will you marry me?" she asks.

The friend of an alternative medicine practitioner asks him skeptically, "Do you really think these herbs help?"

"Of course they do! I just bought a new house!"

AT THE RESTAURANT

"Waiter, there's a dead cockroach in my coffee!"
"So what do you want now, a funeral?"

The waiter says to his client, "How did you find our steak, sir?"
"It was under the fries."

"Waiter, can I have a toothpick?"
"I'm sorry, sir, but you'll have to wait—someone else just borrowed it."

A restaurant customer complains, "Waiter, why does my stake smell so strongly of vodka?"
The waiter takes a step backward and replies, "What about now, sir?"

"What would you like, sir?" the shapely waitress asks a patron.
"You know what I'd like!" he says. "But I'll eat first."

A client calls the waitress over and says, "I've always gotten two pieces of meat in my soup! What happened today?"

"I'm sorry, sir. I guess, the chef forgot to cut it."

A drunken client shouts, "Waiter! Bring me the door—I'm leaving!"

If you don't like your 'favorite' restaurant anymore, find a new girlfriend!

Q: What's the difference between an English restaurant and a Russian restaurant?

A: In an English restaurant, you can see how people eat and hear how they speak. In a Russian restaurant, you can see how people speak and hear how they eat.

A tall, strong man walks into a restaurant. He takes a seat and says to the waiter, "Bring me your biggest pitcher of vodka!"

The slightly surprised waiter asks, "Will you be ordering something to eat, sir?"

"I just ordered a pitcher of vodka—that's what I'm going to eat!"

A client asks the waitress, "Why are there no prices listed in your menu?"

"We don't want to spoil your appetite, sir!" the waitress explains.

"Why do they hire midgets as waiters here?"

"Waiter! Why are your napkins so greasy?"

"Those aren't napkins, sir. They are the blintzes
you ordered earlier."

"To make the dishes look bigger."

"Waiter, I ordered soup and roasted fish. Why did you bring me the fish first?"

"Our chef said this fish couldn't wait anymore."

"Waiter, there's a fly in my soup."

"You hoped to find a chicken for that price?"

A customer checks out her bill and says to the waiter, "By the way, the coffee was almost cold!"

"Thanks for reminding me, madam. Chilled coffee is one ruble more."

"Where is my waiter?" a rich client demands of another waiter in an upscale restaurant.

"He lost you to me in a card game last night, sir," is the waiter's reply.

"Do you think I'll eat this?!" a customer complains to the waiter. "Call over your manager!"

"No need for that, sir," says the waiter. "I don't think he'll eat it either."

"Waiter, why is there a dead cockroach in my soup?"

"Boiling water always kills them, madam."

A man checks out the menu in a restaurant and says to the waiter, "I'd like to order your *borscht* (beet soup)."

"We don't have borscht, sir," the waiter replies. "Would

you like some salad instead?"

"No, I'd like some borscht!"

"Sir, our salad is very good. Why don't you try it?"

"I'd like to see the maitre d'!"

The maitre d' then asks the client, "What happened here?"

"I'm asking for borscht, but your waiter insists on the salad!"

"But why don't you want to try our salad, sir?" asks the maitre d'.

"I want to see your manager!" the client shrieks.

The manager comes over to the table and asks, "What is going on?"

"He doesn't want our salad!" the waiter and maitre d' reply.

"I want your borscht, not the salad!" the customer insists.

"Call the bouncers over here," the manager directs the waiter. "This man came here to argue, not eat!"

"**W**aiter, why did you bring me a wet bowl?"

"That's your soup, sir!"

"**A**nd no alcohol tonight, please; I'm driving," the diner says to his waiter.

Fifteen minutes later, the waiter brings a large pitcher of vodka. "You can drink now, sir," he says. "Your car was just stolen."

Mellow from numerous drinks, a diner finishes his main course. The waiter then brings him his dessert. The diner stares at the waiter for some time. Finally, he says, "Your face looks familiar. Have we met before?"

"I don't think so, sir," the waiter replies.

"1985… St. Petersburg. You used to work at a place called…".

"No, sir, I've never been to St. Petersburg."

"1991… You worked in Kiev at a place called…".

"No, sir, I've never been to Kiev either."

"Did you ever work at a bar a few blocks from here?"

"Sir, I think you mistake me for someone else!"

"Oh, I remember now!" the client exclaims as the waiter is leaving. "You brought me the soup!"

"Waiter, there's a cockroach in my borscht!"

"Go ahead, you can eat it; we have more."

"I would like this sandwich," the client says, pointing to the menu, "and eleven bottles of this beer."

"Would you like to order the whole case of beer, sir?" the waiter suggests. "It'll cost you…".

"No! What, do I look like an elephant?"

"What a place! No veal, no chicken, no seafood…" the customer complains to the waiter. "Bring me my coat!"

"I'm sorry, sir, but we don't have your coat either…" says the waiter after searching the coat room.

A client calls the waitress over and says, "If this is a tea, I need sugar. If this is a soup, bring me some salt."

"Waitress, there's a fly swimming in my tea!"

"And what would you do in its place, sir, drown yourself?"

"Waiter, I'd like another plate of your *perogies*!"

"Sir, are you still hungry, or did you just like them?"

"Waiter, this is not a soup, it's just some warm water!"
"Not just some warm water, madam—it's boiled water!"

Studying the menu, a patron asks the waitress, "How come one hard-boiled egg costs as much as the three-egg omelet?"
"Because nobody counts the eggs in an omelet…".

"Waiter, how much is your vodka?"
"All you can drink for one hundred rubles."
"Okay, bring me enough for two hundred!"

A client calls over the waitress and says, "There's a fly in my vodka!"
"Well, it's a little fly," says the waitress. "How much can it drink?"
"Whatever amount it can, I want you to take it off my bill!"

A couple is sitting in a posh restaurant. As they order their food, the woman spots their neighbors, sitting a few tables away. She whispers to her husband, "Ivan, order something very expensive in a loud voice so they can hear you!"
"Give me some fries on three hundred rubles!" Ivan shouts.

An elderly couple walk into a restaurant and order dinner. When it's served, the husband begins to eat hungrily; meanwhile, his wife looks on and doesn't touch her food.
"Is anything wrong, madam?" the waiter asks her.
"No, I'm just waiting for my husband to finish," she replies.
"But your dinner is getting cold."

"Well, I can't eat without our teeth!"

A client who has had a bit too much alcohol calls over the waiter and says, "I guess I had too much of this vodka. Do you have something that will sober me up?"

"I can bring you your bill, sir."

"**Y**ou call this coffee strong?" the customer complains to the waitress.

"Yes, sir," the waitress replies. "Look how exited you got after just one sip!"

A man walks into a bar and says to the bartender, "How much do you charge for one drop of vodka?"

"Well..." the bartender says, confused, "I can give it to you for free."

"Then drip me a glassful!"

A restaurant patron tells the waitress, "I'm so hungry, I could eat a dead rat!"

"Then you've come to the right place, sir."

"**W**hat is that...floating in my soup?" the diner demands of his waitress.

"How would I know?" she replies. "I'm a waitress, not an entomologist."

A client asks the waitress, "Is your vodka fresh tonight?

"What do you mean 'fresh', sir?"

"Well, last week I had three bottles here and I was sick the whole day next day...".

RUSSIAN ROADS AND TRANSPORTATION

Two foreigners are having a conversation:

"I heard you visited Russia recently," one says. "Is it true that their roads are awful?"

"Frankly," says the other, "I didn't see any roads at all. But you can get around there just fine in a sport utility vehicle."

A woman on an overcrowded bus, says to a man, "Sir, can't you see? You're on top of me!"

"Don't worry, madam," he replies. "I'm not going to do anything to you!"

"In that case, you'd better get off!"

One day a donkey meets a *Lada* (a make of Russian car):

"Who are you?" the donkey asks.

"I'm a car," the Lada replies.

"Yeah," the donkey grins, "and in that case, I'm a horse!"

A conductor is checking the tickets aboard a train:

"May I see your ticket, please?" he asks a passenger.

"My ticket?"

"Yes. Please show it to me."

"Why don't you get your own?"

"Are you sick?"

"Are you a doctor?"

"No, I'm a conductor."

"And I am a plumber."

A man steps onto an overcrowded bus and says, "Could somebody give his or her seat to an HIV positive man, please?"

A moment later he says, "I just asked for one seat, not the whole bus…".

Q: Why don't Lada owners buy Goodyear tires?

A: Because the tires will last three times longer than the car.

A naked woman climbs into a taxi. When she notices the driver is staring at her in the rearview mirror, she asks, "Why are you staring at me all the time? Haven't you ever seen a naked woman?"

"Oh, I've seen many, ma'am," the driver replies. "I'm just trying to figure out where you're keeping your money."

A tractor-trailer driver asks a passerby to guide him while he backs up on a narrow street. The passerby agrees to help.

"Yeah, okay, okay, okay… Stop!" yells the helper. "Now get out of your truck and look at what you just did!"

A man was once driving a car along a side street in a small town when a woman driving in the opposite direction rolled down her window and yelled at him: "Ass!"

The man was outraged. He quickly rolled down his window and screamed at the woman from the bottom of his lungs: "You're an ass yourself, bitch!"

The next moment, around a sharp turn in the road, the man hit a donkey in the middle of the road.

"I just left a Mercedes 600 in the dust," the owner of a new Lada boasted to his friends.

"Really," one friend said. "Did you see the driver's face?"

"Oh yeah, a huge shock was written all over it. The guy even dropped the fueling nozzle...".

A man chases an overcrowded streetcar as it slowly speeds up. He yells through the half-open door, bulging with the bodies of the lucky passengers who made it, "Please! Can't you make a little more space—just enough for my foot?"

"What's your size?" someone from among the passengers yells back.

"Could you please tell me how many bicycles you sold today?" the morgue employee asks a motorcycle dealership's salesperson over the phone.

"Nine. Why?" the salesperson asks.

"Well, okay, that means two more to go."

"Cheer up, people, cheer up!" a drunk says loudly as he

steps up onto a bus.

Nobody pays any attention to him.

"Why are you so gloomy, people? It's spring outside!" he continues. "Hey, *anybody*—let's talk!"

But there's still no response from the passengers. Some cast scornful looks, others simply turn their backs to the drunk.

"Well," the drunk says, after a short pause, "since there's nobody on this bus, I guess I can take a little pee…".

"Dad, have you ever seen a wrinkled dollar bill?"

"Yes, son."

"How about a one-hundred-dollar bill?"

"Sure."

"And how about a wrinkled ten-thousand-dollar bill?"

"No. Why?"

"Well, look in the driveway if you want to see that."

Two women, whose car is stuck in the snow, ask a man passing by to help them push their car. But the man politely refuses, saying, "I'm sorry, but I know nothing about cars."

A young woman on an overcrowded bus says to a man, "Sir, that's the tenth time you've tightly pressed your body against mine!"

"Well, what can I do?" the man replies.

"If you're a gentleman," the woman says, "you'd do *something!*"

"When I heard those strange noises coming from somewhere underneath the car, I stopped, picked up everything that had fallen off the car, put it all in the trunk, and immediately drove here," the woman explains to a mechanic.

"Let me see…" the mechanic says, and he checks in the trunk of the customer's car. "Okay, this has to be replaced; this we can fix; and this, madam" he says, pointing to a sewer manhole cover, "you'll need to take back."

"Can a Lada go 55 miles per hour?"

"Yes, it can."

"How about 100 miles per hour?"

"Sure."

"How about 150 miles per hour?"

"No, it can't do that. I don't think we have a mountain high enough…".

"I can drive so fast in my BMW," one New Russian boasts to another, "that the telegraph poles along the road look like a solid fence."

"So what?" replies the other. "I can turn so sharply in my Mercedes I can see my rear license plate!"

After getting stuck in a deep pothole along an unpaved side road, the motorist is happy to see a tractor approaching him. He asks the tractor driver for some help, and gets it.

"So, how much I owe you?" he asks the tractor driver, after being pulled back onto the road.

"One hundred rubles," the tractor driver replies.

"Well, I really appreciate your help, sir, but don't you think that's a bit too much?"

"Not really, if you consider the effort I make to keep this pothole in proper condition."

"How much would you charge to get from here to Tverskaya Street?"

"Twenty rubles, sir."

"What about if I take my wife with me?"

"It's the same—twenty rubles."

"I told you, honey! You're worth nothing."

Two dandies are having a conversation while riding in a taxi cab. Says one, "Can you imagine? Yesterday, during dinner, I took my wine glass with my left hand! What a shame!"

"And I," says the other, "I ate my lobster with a fish fork!"

At these words the cab driver turns to the men and says, "Gentlemen, I hope you don't mind my facing you with my back…".

A shapely woman is hitchhiking on the side of the road in a small village, trying to get a lift to the next town. She has a large plastic can standing beside her. Finally, a small truck pulls over and the driver agrees to take her.

"What's in the can?" the man asks, thinking that this woman might share some of the moonshine that she's taking to town for sale.

"Gasoline," she replies.

"Gasoline? What for?"

"I know you bastards all too well. You all say you run out of gas just as soon as you reach the first woods…".

"Why is your car painted this way?" one cab driver asks another. "One side is yellow, the other is blue!"

"You'll know when you listen to the witnesses' testimonies the next time I'm in an accident."

"Can you fix my car?" the owner of a wreck asks the mechanic.

"Yeah."

"What would you do?"

"I'd take the bumpers off, then change everything that's in between, and put them back on again."

A cop stops a car:

"You were going well over the speed limit, sir," he says.

"I don't think so, officer," the motorist replies. "I'm sure I was doing thirty-five…".

"Honey," the motorist's wife interjects, "he's right. I saw it myself. You were doing at least fifty."

"Also, your brake lights don't work," the policeman continues.

"I just learned that from you this second, officer," the driver replies.

"I told you about that three weeks ago," his wife reminds him.

"Why are you not wearing your seatbelt, sir?" the cop asks.

"I just now took it off," the driver replies.

"You never wear it!" his wife cuts in.

"Would you shut up, please?!" the driver yells at his wife.

"Is he always like that, madam?" the cop asks the woman. "Oh no, officer," she replies, "only when he's drunk…".

Q: Why aren't Ladas available in black?

A: So they won't be confused with Mercedes.

Back in the old good days, a man once rented a hackney carriage in an unfamiliar town. But after barely three minutes of riding, the hackman told him to get out.

"What for?" the passenger asked.

"You have to help me push the carriage," the hackman explained. "I'm afraid my horse may not be able to climb up this hill."

No sooner had they reached the top of the hill and the passenger had climbed back into the carriage, the hackman once again told his passenger to get out.

"Now why?" the passenger protested.

"You have to help me hold the carriage back. It's a steep downhill slope, and I'm afraid my horse may not be able to walk it down safely."

Once they had gotten down the hill and the passenger had climbed back into the carriage, the hackman once more told his passenger to get out.

"Not again!" the passenger complained. "I don't see any more hills!"

"That's your address, mister," the hackman replied.

So the passenger paid his fare, climbed out of the carriage, and then said to the hackman, "Tell me something, good man. I know why I hired you—I needed to get here. I know why you picked me up—you wanted to earn the money. But tell me, what did we need the horse for?!"

"Can you make my horn sound louder?" a customer asks his mechanic.

"Why would you want to do that?"

"Well, I figured it'll be cheaper than fixing my brakes."

"**W**ho lost one hundred rubles?" a man shouts in an over-crowded bus.

No reply…

"Who lost one hundred rubles?" the man shouts again.

"That must be me," a student pipes up.

The man walks over to the student and says, "Then why are you sitting here? Go look for it!"

"**W**hy don't you just lie down on me completely?" the woman on an overcrowded bus complains to the man leaning against her.

"Stop drooling, lady," replies the man.

A shapely woman on an overcrowded bus says to the man behind her, "Excuse me, sir, when are you going to stop pushing my behind with your 'thing'?"

"I'm sorry, madam," the man explains, "But that's not the 'thing' you think it is. It's my wallet."

"Then you must be a very good employee," she replies, "considering your salary has raised three times already in the last half hour!"

OUR 'LITTLE BROTHERS'

Two hungry street dogs run into one another:

"So, how do you like your new life here in America?" one asks.

"Well, not so good," the other dog sighs. "Here I'm just a street dog. Back in Russia I used to be a bull terrier…".

Two cats, a Siamese and a plain street cat, share their recent dating experiences with each other:

"I met a street tomcat, last night," the street cat says. "He took me to all the garbage sites around the city, and he made love to me at the every one of them. What a romantic night that was!"

"And I met a pure-bred Siberian tomcat the other night," the Siamese cat says. "We spent the night at the best restaurants in the city. But all he did was talk about how cold it is in Siberia and how he froze his balls there."

One rooster says to another, "Let's go to the supermarket!"

"What for?" asks the second.

"We can look at naked chicks!"

Three flies—one fat, one fit, and one skinny—meet on a crumb:

The fat one says, "I dine at a posh restaurant. All I have to do is to hit any dish on a plate. The waiter takes the plate out, and all the food is mine."

The fit fly says in its turn, "I eat at a fast-food restaurant in a poor neighborhood. When I hit the soup, the client takes a spoon and throws me out. But at least the whole spoonful of food is mine."

"And me," says the skinny one, "I get my food at a student cafeteria. As soon as I land on some food, these creatures grab me by my wings, lick me all over till there's no food left on me, and then they set me free…".

A woman was walking through a poorly lit park one night, when suddenly she heard: "Stay!" She stood.

"Lie down!" commanded the same voice. She lied down.

"Crawl!" She did just that.

"Are you okay, madam?" the voice then said, coming from above. "If you need any help, let me know. I'm working with my dog here!"

Running across a desert, a dog thinks to himself, "If I don't find a tree, I'm going to die!"

Two dogs are talking:

"I saw the neighbors' poodle all wet yesterday!" says one.

"So what?"

"You should see her body!"

A man walks with a big bear along the rows of merchants at a farmers' market. Someone asks him, "Why did you bring a bear here?"

"Well," the man replies, "I'm looking for the fellow who sold me this bear as a hamster last year!"

A man once had a parrot who liked booze. Every time the man opened up a bottle, the parrot would descend onto the

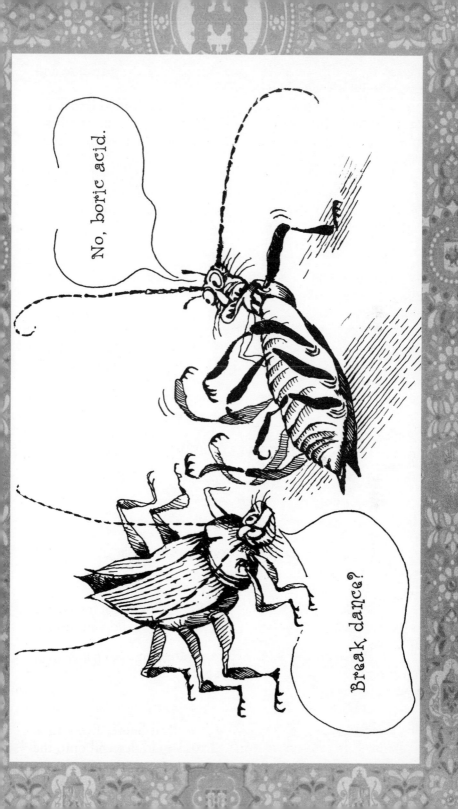

man's shoulder, demanding a drink for himself.

One day the man had had enough. "No, I'm not going to give you any today. This is my last bottle of my favorite vodka," said he.

"I swear I won't ask you again," the parrot pleaded.

"Okay, I'll give you some, but on one condition," the man said. "If you ask me again, I'll pluck all your feathers from you! Agreed?"

"Okay, agreed!" replied the parrot.

The next evening, as the man was having a drink, the parrot began nervously pacing from one corner of the room to another, his wings spread behind his back. Finally, the man got tired watching the bird flickering around, so he said, "Why are you doing this?"

"Well, I'm thinking, master…why do I need these feathers anyway?"

Two dog owners are bragging about their pets:

"My dog is so smart she does my laundry and cooking!" says one.

"And my dog brings me newspapers and magazines," says the other.

"Well, mine can do that too."

"But I don't subscribe to any of them!"

"Ivan, what was that in front of your entrance? I couldn't see it very well."

"That was our watchdog!"

"Really?! I wiped my feet off on him…".

"Madam, can you keep your dog away from me?" the man complains to a dog owner in a park. "I can feel fleas running all over me already!"

"Bobby, keep off the man," the owner commands her dog. "He has fleas!"

Q: Can a dog get a heart attack?
A: Yes, if it lives in human conditions.

Two dogs are standing in front of a butcher shop:
"Let's go inside!" says one.
"Don't you see that sign up there, the one that says 'no dogs allowed'?" asks the other.
"Come on! How do they know we can read?"

Two women are walking their dogs. One woman says, "I can see that you live in a very small apartment."
"Yes, but how did you know?"
"Your dog is wagging its tail vertically."

A woman talks to a parrot in a pet store:
"Hey, little fool, can you talk?"
"Sure I can," the parrot replies. "But can you fly, you old cow?"

A man who stutters badly, walks into a parrot shop:
"D-d-o-o y-y-o-u h-a-v-e y-y-e-l-l-o-w p-p-p-a-a-r-r-o-o-t-t-s?"
"Yes we do," replies the owner, and he walks the customer over to a row of cages with yellow parrots.
"W-w-w-h-a-t a-a-b-o-u-t g-g-r-r-e-e-n p-p-a-a-r-r-o-t-s?"
"Yes, they're over here."
"A-a-n-d w-w-h-a-t a-b-o-u-t...".
"Sir," the owner cuts in, "why don't you just buy a bird and leave the store as soon as you can? I can't let you ruin all of my merchandise!"

A parrot is painfully watching his owner stuff a goose for a holiday dinner. Finally, the parrot shrieks, "Would you stop torturing that poor bird?!"

"**W**here did I come from?" a little donkey asks his father.

"When I was young," the donkey's father says, "I was traveling mountain roads a lot. And there, one day, I met your donkey mother. After some time, *you* were born."

The little donkey then asks the same question of his donkey mother.

"When I was young," the donkey's mother says, "I was running along the mountain roads. And one day I met a handsome young deer. Then *you* were born."

"What about my father?" asks the little donkey.

"Well, your father? He's been such an ass for all of his life!"

A rabbit was once running in the woods when he spotted a lion lying on the ground. To avoid becoming lunch, the rabbit quietly turned his way back in the other direction. But the lion had spotted the rabbit too, and he cried, "Hey rabbit, help me! My paw is caught in a trap. I promise, I won't do you any harm."

The rabbit slowly approached the lion and said, "Is it really that bad?"

"Yeah," the lion roared, "I can't even move!"

At these words, the rabbit sneaked a little closer, hit the lion in the face, and shouted, "You deserve that, yellow cat!" Then he turned around and ran away.

A few minutes later the rabbit decided to return. He wanted to hit the lion again. And so he did. And later he did it once again.

"One more time," the rabbit thought to himself, circling back. "I'll show that king of animals what I think of him!"

But when he arrived this time, all he found was an empty trap. The rabbit was about to take off in a hurry, when he felt a large paw on his shoulder.

"So, what would you say now?" the lion asked him.

"Well, you probably wouldn't believe me, lion," the rabbit said in a trembling voice, "but I came back to say that I'm really sorry…".

An ant wakes up under a tractor. He looks up and says, "Yeah, looks like we had a corking party last night! But what did I bring this thing home for?"

A goat arrives at the cattle pasture, where a bull asks her, "Hey, Goat, why did you come here?"

"The farmer told me to," replies the goat. "He figured, since I give as much milk as a cow, I should be with you, the cattle."

"Well, why don't you go back and tell him that I'm not going to kneel down for you!"

Two fleas are walking down the street. It's cold and it's raining. One flea says to the other, "Such weather, and we have to walk!"

"Just a few more months, honey," replies the other, "and we'll have enough money to buy a dog!"

A crow hits a tree while flying and falls down to the ground. "I'm lucky I don't have any brains," he says. "Otherwise, I could have had a concussion!"

A fox catches a little chick for dinner. The chick offers the fox a deal:

"Look, fox," he says, "I'm so small you'll still be hungry after you eat me. Why don't you let me go, and in exchange, I'll bring you my parents."

The fox thinks about this offer for a moment and says, "Okay, it's a deal!"

The happily freed chick immediately jumps up into a tree and laughs at the fox from the top: "One little detail, Fox; I forgot to tell you that I was born in an incubator!"

A crocodile wakes up at night in cold sweat. "I'm so sorry... I'm so sorry... Why did I do that?!"

"I told you not to eat intelligentsia before you go to bed," his crocodile buddy says.

Two chickens, one American and the other Russian, lie beside each other in a supermarket fridge:

"Look at you!" the American chicken says, "You are so ugly! Your skin is blue, your body is undernourished and all bruised up. I can't look at you without feeling disgusted!"

"Well, beauty, you have nothing to brag about," the Russian chicken replies. "You grew up in a cage, pumped up with all kinds of hormones. You lived only a third of my life before they killed you, still young. And I simply passed away from old age…".

An ostrich egg was found one day at a chicken farm. A local rooster brought it over to show to the chickens. Said he, in a critical voice, "Ladies, just look what they can do abroad!"

A drunken crow walks out of a bar. She spreads her wings, looks up, and tries to lift off. It doesn't work. "Well," sighs the crow, "looks like I have to walk!"

A fly is flying over a pond in the middle of duck-hunting season. Suddenly, a bullet whistles by in front of the fly. "Hey you, down there!" buzzes the fly, "Do I look like a duck to you?"

A camel asks an ostrich, "Why do ostriches bury their heads in the sand whenever they feel danger?"

"I can't speak for all of us," the ostrich replies, "but, personally, I'm looking for oil."

A bat flies over two rats. Says one rat to the other, "Look up—an angel!"

A rooster complains to a donkey:

"You know, Donkey, I've lost all interest in my chickens. They're boring; all they ever talk about is chicks, eggs, and grains…".

"That sounds really boring," agrees the donkey. "I guess I'd lose interest in chickens too."

"Well, why would you care for chickens in the first place? You don't live with them," remarks the rooster.

"Because if I lose interest in donkeys, I'll get a kick in the head," replies the donkey. "That's why I'd be better off losing interest in chickens."

A lion runs into a sleeping knight. He sniffs the knight over and roars, obviously disappointed: "Canned food again!"

A bull once found a glove and asked his cows, "Ladies, who lost the bra?"

*T*wo camels walk across a desert. Finally, three weeks later, one says to the other, "I don't care what people say about us—I'm really thirsty!"

A little camel asks his mother, "Mom, what do we have these huge webbed feet for?"

"Because they're better suited for plodding through the desert sand, dear," the mother camel explains.

"And why do we have these huge humps on our backs?"

"Well, they help us to go longer without water, which is scarce in the desert."

"But do we need all this in a zoo?!"

*T*rembling from cold, a polar bear cub asks his mother, "Mother, do you know if there were any black bears in our family?"

"No, I don't think so," answers the mother bear.

"What about Himalayan?"
"No."
"Then why am I so cold?"

Two termites are happily eating some wood:
"Tastes like wood to me—nothing special," says one. "So why are people so excited about this Stradivari business?!"

Two crocodiles are swimming down the river. One spots a monkey on the shore, and says to the other, "You wanna have some fun, Crocy? I'll ask this monkey if she's married. If she says she is, we'll say 'who could possibly marry that ugly monkey?'; if she says she's not, we'll say 'who would marry that ugly monkey?'"

"That should be fun!" agrees the other crocodile.

They approach the monkey and ask her, "Are you married?"

"I wish I was," the monkey sighs, "but all you ever see around here are ugly old crocodiles!"

Q: Why does a bedbug have a flat body?
A: It's easier to sleep on it.

"**I** put a beautiful young lady into bed yesterday," says one. "You should have seen her!"

"You're lucky," replies the other. "All I get are old ladies!"
And the two flu viruses move on.

Two flowers are talking:
"Do you love me?" asks one.
"Yes, I do," the other replies. "What about you?"
"I love you too!"
"Where are those bees?!"

"**H**ow misleading nature can be!" said a porcupine philosophically, climbing down a cactus.

SCIENTISTS
AND PROGRAMMERS

When the physiologist Pavlov was a boy he was bitten by a dog. Professor Pavlov remembered that for the rest of his life.

"**H**oney," the professor says to his wife, "this is the best thing I've ever done for you in my life! My latest discovery—a new virus—and I named it after you!"

After completing his lecture before a group of factory workers, a renowned Soviet scientist asks his audience, "Any questions, comrades?"

One man raises his hand. "Professor, can you pass over that glass on the lectern if you're not using it?"

Two professors are having conversation:
"Excuse me, colleague, do you know the time?"
"Yes I do."
"Thank you."
"You're welcome."

An absent-minded professor has just moved to a new house. Knowing her husband's poor memory for ordinary things, the professor's wife writes a note for him, giving their new address.

During a lecture, the professor uses the note as scrap paper for his calculations. When he comes 'home,' he finds strange people in his apartment, and then he remembers that they've moved to a new place.

The professor walks downstairs, and there he sees a girl sitting on a bench in the foyer, reading a book. "Excuse me," begins the professor, "do you remember me? I used to live here, for many years, and I have a daughter about your age?... Maybe you know where we've moved to...".

"Mother was right," replies the girl, "when she said that you would forget the address anyway, Dad."

"See? You can't say that I forgot my briefcase at work today!" the professor proudly tells his wife. "Here it is!"

"Well then," she says, "whose briefcase is this—the one you left at home this morning?"

"Professor," the maid says, "there's a beggar at your door. He's asking for something."

"Okay," replies the professor. "Here, give him these two geometry problems."

"Did you hear the news, Moshe? Einstein himself is coming to Odessa!"

"Who's Einstein? Is he that famous doctor...".

"No. He's a famous scientist."

"What is he famous for?"

"He invented the theories of relativity."

"And what's that supposed to mean?"

"Well, I'll try to explain it to you. Say we take three hairs. If they're on your head, is that too much or too little?"

"I'll bet you, it's nothing."

"Now suppose those same three hairs are in your soup. Is that too much or too little?"

"And he's coming here with that old joke?!"

See those men? They respond to this light.
Every time the light goes on, they bring food.

Upon studying a request for additional funds from the dean of the faculty of the physics department, the university rector (president) complained, "How come the physicists are always asking for funds for their equipment? Take, for instance, mathematicians. All they ever ask for is money for paper, pencils and erasers. And philosophers get by with even less than that; they don't need erasers…".

Q: What's the difference between a donkey and an ass?
A: 'Donkey' is a scientific degree and 'ass' is an academic position.

A professor gets a bit carried away, misses the bell at the end of his class, and continues delivering his lecture for another half an hour. Then all of a sudden, he comes back to earth and says to his patient students, "I'm sorry, I don't have a watch. I think, my time is over…".

"What do you need a watch for, professor?" a voice from the back row asks. "You have a calendar right behind you…".

A beaming professor calls his wife into his den and announces, "Dear, look what I've just invented!" He points to something in his hand.

"Yes, and what is it?" she asks.

"Uhh… gosh… I guess I've forgotten…".

"I'm lucky it's only half, only half, only half…" the injured physicist murmurs from his hospital bed, still in shock after the accident.

"What's only half?" a nurse asks.

"Kinetic energy! I'm lucky. It's only half of the product of mass and speed squared."

A professor boards a bus, pays double the fare required, and asks for two transfers.

"Sir, why do you need two transfers?" the bus driver asks

him.

"In case I lose one," the professor answers.

"Well then, what are you going to do if you lose both transfers?"

"Well, in that case, I have a pass."

"What do you do, professor?"

"I'm a mathematician and I'm studying Fredholm equation of the first kind."

"Do you have a hobby?"

"I do. It's Fredholm equation of the second kind."

"I see you have Internet access now."

"Yes...how did you know?"

"I can tell by your eyes."

"They look smarter?"

"No, they look red."

Q: What's the difference between a rookie programmer and a pro?

A: The rookie programmer believes that one kilobyte has 1,000 bytes. The pro believes that one kilometer has 1,024 meters.

"How could you do that? What a shame!" the mother reprimands her daughter.

"He told me he'd become a registered user..." cries the young programmer.

After a sleepless night, sulking, beaten-up software developer shows up in his kitchen early the next morning to get something to eat:

"What happened?" his wife asks him. "Your program doesn't work?"

"It did," the programmer answers gravely.

"Does it work well?"

"It did."

"Why are you saying it 'did'?"

"Well, I took a nap on the backspace key…".

Q: Why don't programmers use 95 octane gasoline?

A: They fear their car will freeze up.

"**H**ello? Is this the help line?"

"Yes, sir. How can I help you?"

"I'm not able to connect to the net."

"Could you describe the problem, please?"

"Yes, I don't have a computer."

The programmer needs the 12th floor. He enters the elevator, pushes 1, then he pushes 2, and then he begins to frantically search for the 'Enter' button.

A computer professional keeps two glasses at his bedside table. One is filled with water, in case he gets thirsty. The other is empty, in case he doesn't.

Q: What's the difference between Windows 95 and a woman?

A: Nothing. They both dump megabytes of useless information on you and then ask you to confirm the obvious at least three times.

"**T**hey say that twenty years from now it'll be possible to have sex with a computer," the programmer tells his wife.

"Well," she says, "I don't imagine that would change anything for you."

"**D**ad, I've heard they'll be raising the price for Internet connection. I guess that means you'll surf less on the net."

"No, son, that means you'll eat less…".

SKYDIVING

Never argue with the man who packs your parachute.

The jumpmaster is instructing his parachutists. "If you don't want to combine two jumps in one, follow my instructions strictly!"

"But how is it possible to combine two jumps in one?" someone asked.

"Oh, that's pretty simple," the jumpmaster explains. "It's called the first one and the last one."

A jumpmaster explains the rules to a group of first-timers:

"…Don't worry. Just exit, count to five, then pull the cord. This will deploy your canopy, and a little later you'll safely land. Then a bus will pick all of you up at the drop zone."

The parachutists leave the plane as planned, but one jumper's main canopy doesn't open. He tries to deploy the auxiliary—alas, without any luck.

As the jumper is falling he thinks to himself, "Well, the guy wasn't right about the parachute. I hope he's right about the bus!"

After letting all his parachutists exit the plane, the jumpmaster is ready to jump himself. Just before taking his dive, he has another quick look around the fuselage—and he's surprised to find one parachutist still sitting in the corner.

"What are you doing here?" asks the jumpmaster.

"Well," the parachutist replies, "my canopy didn't open, so I had to come back!"

"Where do you work?"

"I pack parachutes."

"Well, that must be hard work. Have you had any problems?"

"Not really…nobody has ever complained yet."

The paratrooper is very nervous before his first jump. He asks his jumpmaster a lot of questions, and he keeps asking them over and over again. "What if my canopy doesn't open?" he asks.

The tired jumpmaster replies, "Then you wave your arms…".

Once the last trooper jumps, the plane makes a wide turn and starts its descent toward the runway. Hoping to use this moment to finally get some rest, the jumpmaster hears someone knocking on the window. He looks out, and there he sees the nervous paratrooper, who asks: "What do I do after my arms get tired?"

Once a rabbi was asked by a Jewish parachutist, "Can I jump during Sabbath?"

"Yes you can," the rabbi replied. "But you're not allowed

to open your parachute."

A Chukchi once invented a new type of parachute: It deploys upon impact.

A man is going for his first jump. His wife and son are watching. He lands, but then his wife sends her son to check to see why her husband is still lying on the ground. She says to the boy, "Go see if your father is okay, whether he's still breathing. I'll go get some help!"

The boy returns soon enough and says, "Yes, he's okay, he's breathing. But it's impossible to breathe anywhere near him...".

Two paratrooper recruits aboard a plane:
"Are you crazy? You can't jump without a chute."
"Is it mandatory to wear it?"
"Sure. Can't you see it's raining outside!"

How To Pack Your Parachute Right
Second, Revised Edition

A man buys his first parachute. He asks the sales clerk, "And what if my parachute won't open?"
"Just bring it back and we'll replace it."

Parachute for sale, used only once, never opened.

FISHING, HUNTING, AND SPORT

"Ivan, come with us! We're going fishing."
"But I know nothing about fishing…".
"What is there to know? Just pour and drink!"

Early one morning, heavily equipped with fishing tackle, a man knocks on the door of his friend's house. A woman opens the door:
"Where is Ivan? Is he ready?"
"Ivan passed away last week," the woman says.
"So is he going fishing or not?"

A fisherman's peace and quiet is broken by a noisy on-looker, who is asking one question after another:
"Did you catch any yet?" he asks the fisherman for the tenth time.
"Just one," the fisherman replies curtly.
"Where is it? Can I see?"
"I threw him in the water."
"Because he was too small?"

"No, actually, he was about your size."

A young man has just spent three hours fishing on a lake without a single bite. Meanwhile, an elderly fellow fishing next to him had been pulling in one fish after another.

Running out of patience, the young man finally leaves, but not before making note of the bait the experienced fisherman had been using.

The next day the young man comes back to the same spot. This time, he spends four hours trying to catch *anything*. He's using the old man's favorite bait, but he's still not having any luck. Just as he is about to leave, the old man shows up. Sure enough, within fifteen minutes, he catches two fish.

The young man watches the old fellow closely. He notices that he's using a different bait than he'd been using the day before. He decides it's time to ask the old pro how he chooses his bait.

"Well, son," the old fisherman begins, "all I do is look at my manhood in the morning when I wake up. If it points to the left, I go for worms. If it points to the right, I use minnows."

"And what do you use if it points straight up?" the young man asks, slightly confused.

"If it could ever point straight up again, son, you wouldn't see me wasting my time here…".

On a cold January morning, a man leaves his house to go ice-fishing with his friends. Once he gets to their favorite spot, he finds nobody there, and so he decides to go back home.

It's still too early to be up on a Sunday morning by the time he arrives back home, so he decides to catch up on some sleep.

"Is it very cold outside?" his wife asks without looking at him as he quietly gets back into bed.

"You're gonna freeze to death here! Where's your hat?"

"To hell with it. Last time I had it on I couldn't hear when they called me for a drink...".

"Very!" he answers.

"And my fool went fishing...".

A drunken man comes home from a hunting trip and announces to his wife, "You won't need to buy meat this month, honey!"

"Did you get a moose?"

"No, I spent all of my paycheck on booze!"

Two convicts, sharing the same cell, are having a chat:

"So, what did they put you in here for?" one asks.

"Illegal fishing," the other answers.

"How long?"

"Fifteen years."

"Fifteen years?! I thought five was the maximum for that kind of an offence."

"Well, I was dynamite fishing. I threw a charge in the lake and I got two fish and three divers...".

A man goes ice-fishing. He picks himself a good spot, takes out his augur, and starts to drill a hole.

All of a sudden, he hears a voice, coming from nowhere: "Sir, there are no fish here!"

The man looks around, but he sees no one. So he moves to a different spot, a few yards away, and then he resumes his drilling.

"Sir, there are no fish here!" the same voice announces again.

The man looks around, but he finds no one to whom this voice might belong.

And so he moves one more time and begins to bore a new

hole.

"Sir, how many times do I have to tell you?" the voice rings again. "There are no fish here!"

"Who is it? Who's talking?" the man asks impatiently.

"I'm the guard of this skating rink!" the voice replies.

A baby worm asks his mother, "Where's daddy?"

"He went fishing with some dude."

After a Soviet hammer thrower set a new record at the Olympics, a Western newspaper correspondent asked the hero, "How difficult was it for you to hurl that hammer so far?"

"It wasn't difficult at all. In fact, if they let me throw it together with a sickle, I could sling that thing twice as far…".

"Let me tell you about my last hunting trip to the desert," one hunter tells another. "I was walking through the sand when I spotted a huge hungry lion approaching me…".

"So, what did you do?"

"In a flash I climbed a tree!"

"A tree? In the desert? What was it doing there?"

"Well, you know, in those kinds of situations, you don't tend to think much—you just jump!"

"Yesterday I caught a huge sturgeon," one fisherman brags to another. "It was so big I had to put it on my shoulder to take it to my car."

"It sounds like that fish was over the limit."

"I'll bet you it was!"

"So what did you do with it?"

"Well, unfortunately, I ran into a fishery officer…".

"And?"

"I hid the fish in my pocket."

At a hunting resort, a group of men has decided to vary their everyday fishing and hunting routine by playing some cards. They play the entire night and then, after having a few more drinks, they head out for some hunting early the next morning. During the hunt, one of the men shoots another.

"Why did you shoot him?" his friends ask while waiting for a doctor. "We heard him yelling 'I'm not the game'!"

"Well, guys, you know him," the shooter replies, his voice trembling from shock. "I thought he was bluffing, as usual…".

A man approaches a fisherman along the shore and asks, "Any bites?"

"Sure. I've taken twenty-five big ones like this already," the fisherman answers, indicating with his hands the size of the fish.

"Do you know who I am, sir?" the man asks as he pulls out a badge showing him to be a fishery officer.

"And do you know who I am, officer?"

"No!"

"I'm a big liar!"

Coming home from a fishing trip, the man quietly enters his house. "Is the cat home?" he whispers to his wife.

"Don't be afraid, come in!" she says in a normal voice. "I've bought him some fish already…".

The coach comforts his athlete, who is obviously losing his boxing match:

"You really scared your opponent at the end of this round!"

"How's that?"

"Well, he thought he might have killed you."

Says she: "Honey, I think you love soccer more than me!"

Says he: "Well, uh, dear, but I love you more than hockey!"

Suffering from insomnia, a boxer is seeing his doctor:

"All you have to do," the doctor says, "is make yourself comfortable in bed and then count: one, two, three… until you fall asleep."

"That won't work, doctor," the sportsman replies. "I tend to get right back up on the count of nine."

"Ivan, why don't you exercise?"

"Well, it's hard before a meal and it's not advisable after!"

A man comes home unexpectedly, and his wife barely manages to hide her lover behind a wide-screen TV. The husband rushes into the living room and turns the TV on to watch a hockey game.

"Ivan, come here!" his wife yells from the kitchen, in an attempt to distract her husband's attention long enough to free up her lover. "You have to see this!"

"No, you come here, you have to see this first!" the man replies. "They just gave a penalty to a Canadian, and now he's walking naked right through our living room!"

A hockey game is underway:

"The first period has ended. The score is one to nothing in favor of Dynamo. The only goal was made in his own goal, scored by Lieutenant Ivanov of the Central Army Club. He will be playing the second period in the rank of sergeant…".

"Honey," he says, getting comfortable in his favorite chair, "do you have anything to tell me before the hockey season starts?"

A woman accidentally touches the groin of a man standing next to her on the subway. "I'm sorry!" she blurts, her face blushing.

"Oh, no, ma'am!" the man replies. "I'm a chess player, and as we always say—if you touch it, you play it!"

THE SOVIET PAST

Excuse me, Comrade, is this Communism or will it be even worse?

A Soviet judge walks out of the courtroom, barely managing to suppress his wild laughter.

A colleague asks, "What is it you're laughing about?"

"Well, I just heard a great joke," the judge says.

"A joke? Tell me!"

"Are you crazy? I just sentenced a man to five years for that joke!"

"You don't have meat?"

"No. We don't have fish."

"What about meat?"

"Meat is not available in our meat department."

Shortly before the 1980 Olympic games in Moscow, in order to avoid embarrassment before the international community, Moscow's store managers were instructed not to say 'no' to customers. Instead, they were to politely talk their customers into buying something else, or politely talk them out of the store.

One woman walked into a half-empty store and asked for a pair of gloves.

"Would you like the leather ones?" the salesperson asked her.

"Yes, please!"

"With or without a warm lining?"

"With a warm lining, please."

"Black or brown?"

"It doesn't matter."

"Well, you'll want to match your gloves to your leather overcoat," the salesperson said. "Why don't you bring it here, so we can make a good match?"

The woman left the store without making her purchase. Outside, she ran into her friend and told her about what had just happened.

"Don't bother bringing your coat here," her friend said. "Last week I wanted to buy some toilet paper. They made me bring my toilet bowl. I even had to show them my behind three times, but they still couldn't find the right toilet paper for me."

Q: What's the shortest joke?

A: Communism.

Q: What's the longest joke?

A: A Khrushchev speech.

Brezhnev asks the Pope, "Why do people believe in your paradise in heaven but refuse to believe in our Communist paradise on earth?"

"Because we never show ours," replies the Pope.

Q: Which countries does the USSR border?

A: Any country it wants to border.

During his visit to the USSR, Nixon was intrigued by a new telephone with a direct line to hell. He spoke briefly with the devil, and the call cost him 25 cents.

"I've heard about changes for the better in the USSR."

"Yeah!...They made my chain one yard longer, but they put my plate two yards further out!"

When he returned home, he found out that this same service was now available in the US too. He tried it again, but this time he received a bill for $1,000.

"How come? The same call cost me only 25 cents in the USSR," Nixon complained.

"Well," explained the operator, "over there it's a local call."

A teacher once asked a first-grade boy, "Who is your father?"

"Comrade Stalin!" the boy shouted the well-instructed phrase.

"Good. And who is your mother?"

"Our Soviet motherland!"

"Very well. And what do you want to be?"

"An orphan…".

Chernenko is dying. At the last moment, the spirit of Brezhnev appears in front of him and says:

"Your term on earth has expired. You'll soon be transferred to another world. I have some advice for you: Take a spoon and fork with you."

"Is there a shortage of such things in that world?" asks Chernenko.

"No," answers Brezhnev, "Not normally. However, whenever Hitler takes charge of the cafeteria there, he removes all the utensils and forces everyone to eat with a sickle and hammer."

A woman asks the clerk in a Soviet shoe store, "Do you sell ladies' footwear?"

"No we don't."

"What about men's footwear?"

"No, we don't sell that either."

"What about children's footwear?

"Why are you asking me all these questions, madam? You're in a shoe store, not an information booth."

RUSSIAN: The Soviet Constitution guarantees freedom of speech.

AMERICAN: Okay, but does it guarantee freedom after the speech?

During one of the *Politburo* (the chief political and executive committee of the Communist party) meetings, Brezhnev stands up to have a word: "I make a motion to award a medal to comrade Brezhnev, postmortem."

"But, comrade Brezhnev, you're still alive!"

"Well, I just thought I could start wearing it now."

Brezhnev complains to his aide that he can't get used to summer and winter time changes. "It's simple," replies the aide, "Just move the hands on your clock one hour ahead in spring, and then move them one hour back in autumn."

"Well," answers Brezhnev, "that sounds really simple. But when I sent a telegram of condolences to Egypt regarding Anwar Sadat's assassination last summer, it arrived one hour before his death."

Brezhnev and Reagan once decided to swap secretaries. Soon the American secretary wrote home from the Soviet Union: "Things are fine, except my skirt is getting longer and longer!"

At the same time, the Soviet secretary was writing from the States: "Everything is great, except my skirt is getting shorter and shorter, and I fear that soon people will spot my hairy manhood and the holster."

Q: What was Brezhnev's greatest nightmare?

A: Czechs sitting in Red Square, eating matzo with chopsticks.

Brezhnev rebukes his speechwriter:

"I asked you for a fifteen minute speech, but you made it one hour."

"No, comrade Brezhnev, it was written to be exactly for fifteen minutes; you just read all four copies."

Brezhnev gives his TV address to the Russian people:

"Comrades! I have two important announcements for you, one good and one bad. The bad news is that during the next five years we'll eat nothing but shit. The good news is that there will be no shortages of it."

A woman walking down the street is carrying a bag full of rolls of bathroom tissue. "Excuse me," a passerby asks her, "where did you buy the bathroom tissue?"

"Well, I don't think you can find it nowadays; I'm bringing mine back from the cleaners."

Q: What's the difference between a Communist and an anti-Communist?

A: A Communist has read Marx and Lenin. An anti-Communist has understood them.

"Yesterday, an American submarine was lost within the Bermuda triangle. There were no losses on the Soviet side."
                —From a Soviet news agency announcement

Karl Marx rose from the dead and asked the Soviet government to allow him to address the Soviet people on radio.

"Well, you understand, great teacher," Brezhnev said, "the times have changed. We live in a different world now."

"All I'm asking for is a chance to say one sentence!" Marx begged.

"Okay, but remember, only one."

So Marx took the microphone and yelled at the top of his lungs: "Workers of all countries, forgive me!"

Under Lenin, life was like living in a tunnel: everywhere there was darkness, but light was ahead.

Under Stalin, life was like riding a bus off-a-road: only one was driving, and the rest were shaking.

Under Khrushchev, life was like living in a circus: only one was speaking, and the rest were laughing.

Under Brezhnev, life was like watching a bad movie: everyone was waiting for the end so they could leave.

Brezhnev and his grandson visit Lenin's mausoleum:

"Grandpa," the boy asks, "after you die, will you live here too?"

"Yes, of course, son," Brezhnev replies.

At these words, Lenin raises up and screams, "This is not a hotel!"

A boy once asked his parents for a small amount of money to help his school in a campaign to help the starving people of an African country.

"They don't need our money," his father said, declining the boy's request. "They have perfect climate, their soil is fertile. They should work and they'll have everything they want."

The boy came home from school the next day and said, "The teacher says this campaign is to help the Communist party in that African country."

"Well, that's different," the father replied. "Here's some money. If they have a Communist party, they certainly have starving people down there."

Q: Why did Ilyin, Brezhnev's failed assassin, miss his target?

A: Because too many people around him were fighting one another over who should shoot first.

Permitted and Prohibited—Some National Differences:

In England, what is permitted is permitted, and what is prohibited is prohibited.

In America, everything is permitted except for what is prohibited.

In Germany, everything is prohibited except for what is permitted.

In France, everything is permitted, even what is prohibited.

In the USSR, everything was prohibited, even what was permitted.

Q: Why did the Soviet postal service have to recall the stamp that featured Brezhnev's portrait?

A: Because one half of the Russians spat on the wrong side, and the other half licked the wrong side.

Six paradoxes of Soviet life:

1. Nobody worked, but the *plan* (Five-Year Economic Plan) was always fulfilled.
2. The plan was fulfilled, but the stores' shelves were empty.
3. The shelves were empty, but nobody starved.
4. Nobody starved, but everybody was unhappy.
5. Everybody was unhappy, but nobody complained.
6. Nobody complained, but the jails were full.

A *kolhoz* (a collective farm) once received some help from

Moscow: a pair of boots. The kolhoz's chairman then gathered the workers together for a meeting.

"Comrades," he said, "I have made a motion to assign this pair of boots to me. All in support of the motion, please raise your hands."

After counting the hands, the chairman continued: "Now, all against the Soviets, raise your hands."

"Is it true that they're going to give Brezhnev the rank of Generalissimo?"

"Yes it is. Moreover, they'll give him a medal too, if he can pronounce the word."

Brezhnev is reading his opening speech for the 1980 Moscow Olympics, "Oh! Oh! Oh! Oh! Oh!"

His writer whispers behind him, "Comrade Brezhnev, those are the Olympic rings; your speech begins on the next page."

When Brezhnev's mother was visiting her son at one of his posh mansions, she burst into tears and said, "Son, I just recalled 1917 with horror. What if the Reds come back again?"

Q: What was Brezhnev's worst fear?

A: That the Chinese would learn to fight like the Israelis, and that the Israelis would learn to multiply like the Chinese.

"Could you please tell us about your hobby, Comrade Brezhnev?"

"I collect jokes about myself."

"How many do you have?"

"As of today, two prison camps."

People in the Kremlin, puzzled by the growing popularity of dissidents, decided to bring one in and find out for themselves. So they brought a dissident in from a jail, invited him to share a Kremlin dinner with them, and asked, "What would you say if we gave you a three bedroom apartment in Moscow?"

"That would be nice."

"How would you like a nice salary of one thousand rubles?"

"I would like that very much."

"Would you like to have dinner like this every day?"

"Oh yes, of course I would. But let me eat first. You can tell me your jokes later."

Q: Who's the best magician in the world?

A: Khrushchev. He sowed wheat in Kazakhstan and reaped it in Canada.

Two skeletons meet, and one asks the other, "Did you die before or after the government announced the next program to end food shortages?"

"Actually, I'm still alive."

Q: Why did Lenin used to wear shoes, while Stalin wore boots?

A: Under Lenin, Russia wasn't as deep in shit yet.

Stalin is resurrected two decades after his death. He's disappointed to see the country in great disorder, and its people caring more about themselves than about building Communism. So he goes to the Kremlin and straight into the room where the Politburo is holding one of its endless meetings. All the Politburo members rise in awe before Stalin.

"Dear Comrades," Stalin says as he takes the stand at the podium, "I have two motions: The first is to shoot all the deputies of the Supreme Soviet (the legislature of the Soviet Union). The second is to paint Lenin's tomb yellow."

"Comrade Stalin, why yellow?" someone asks timidly.

"I knew there would be no objections to the first motion," Stalin says.

GRANDDAUGHTER: Was Lenin a good man?
GRANDMA: Yes, he was a good man.
GRANDDAUGHTER: And Stalin was a bad man, right?
GRANDMA: Yes, he was a bad man.
GRANDDAUGHTER: What about Khrushchev? Is he a good man or bad?
GRANDMA: We'll know after he dies, dear.

Q: Can you wrap a bus in a newspaper?
A: Yes you can. If you use the newspaper with one of Khrushchev's speeches.

"Comrades, Communism is already at the horizon!" a propaganda lecturer says.

"Can you explain to us what a 'horizon' is?" one worker asks him.

"A horizon is an imaginary line that divides the earth and the sky, and which always moves away from you as you approach it."

"Is it true that under Communism it will be possible to order free food over the phone?"

"Yes it is. But it'll be delivered via TV."

In 1968, a few months after the Soviet troops invaded Czechoslovakia, two Soviet officials were having a friendly chat:

"Why are our troops staying so long in Czechoslovakia?"

asked one.

"They're searching for the man who invited them," replied the other.

Q: Is Communism a science?
A: No, because, if it was, they'd test it on dogs first.

Q: What's the difference between mathematics and Communism?
A: In math, something is given and something has to be proved. In Communism, nothing is given but everything is proved.

Q: What nationality were Adam and Eve?
A: They were Russians. Who else could live naked and barefooted, have only one apple for food, and claim that they live in paradise?

When Stalin arrived in hell, the devil took him to Marx and said, "Here is the dividend, earned by your *Capital.*"

AN AMERICAN: They found one of the world's oldest civilizations during recent excavations in America.
A RUSSIAN: In the Soviet Union, somewhere in a coal mine, they found a fat ass, attached a pair of ears to it, and now they're going to use it as the head of our government.

"**H**ave you stocked up on soap and detergent already?"
"Why?"
"Haven't you heard? Khrushchev is going to get personally involved in our chemicals industry."

Q: Does Khrushchev believe in God?

A: Yes. Otherwise, why would he create the largest fast we've ever had in the country?

Brezhnev summons the Soviet scientists and says, "The Americans have landed on the moon. We must surpass them. Our cosmonauts will land on the sun!"

"But, Comrade Brezhnev, they will burn there."

"We're no fools here in the Politburo. They'll land at night."

"**D**id you hear Brezhnev is going for surgery?"

"No. What kind?"

"Chest enlargement—to make room for more medals."

Q: What's the name of a cheap five-star Russian brandy?

A: Brezhnev.

During his visit to one of the Asian Soviet republics, Brezhnev is greeted by the workers:

"Salam Aleikum!"

"Aleikum Salam!" Brezhnev greets them back.

"Salam Aleikum!"

"Aleikum Salam!"

"Gulag Archipelago!"

"Archipelago Gulag!"

Q: Why did Brezhnev make visits abroad, but Andropov didn't?

A: The former was running on batteries; the latter had to be plugged into an outlet.

Q: Why didn't they have a problem with unemployment

in the USSR?

A: Because one half of the population was busy building, the other half was busy demolishing.

Q: What was the main advantage of the Soviet system?

A: It was very successful in dealing with difficulties that were absent in all other systems.

Q: What were the main difficulties of collective farming?

A: Spring, summer, fall, and winter.

"**W**hat kind of crop do you expect this year?"

"Average, worse than last year's, but better than next year's."

Q: What would happen if there was Communism in the Sahara?

A: There'd be shortages of sand.

Q: What if there was Communism in Greenland?

A: Snow would become available only through rations. Later, it would be distributed only to government officials and their families.

Q: What is a Soviet duet?

A: A Soviet quartet after a performance abroad.

After removing Khrushchev, the new Soviet government offered him a position as the director of an oncology clinic. He refused, saying, "But I know nothing about oncology!"

"But you were in charge of agriculture, and you managed to make bread disappear!"

Q: What was the 'remaining difference' between Russia and America during the time of *glasnost* and *perestroika* in the early nineties?

A: In America, Gorbachev had a chance to be elected president.

Due to shortages in feed supplies, the Soviet scientists were to breed a new cow—it was a cross between a cow and a giraffe. The new breed was able to reach for feed in Europe, but it was milked in the USSR.

"Is it true that, among all countries, the United States has the largest number of automobiles?"

"Yes, but the USSR has the most parking space."

The walls of the academy proudly displayed two portraits: one of Doctor Ivanov, who invented the steam engine and the aircraft, the other of Doctor Petrov, who invented Doctor Ivanov.

Q: What's the difference between capitalism and socialism?

A: Under capitalism, one man exploits another man; under socialism, it's vice versa.

An American millionaire becomes terminally ill. He asks his only relative, who happens to live in the USSR, to visit him in the USA.

When his relative reports to OVIR (External Passport and Visa Office), the interviewing officer makes a suggestion: "Instead of going there yourself, why don't you ask your American relative, along with his money, to come to the USSR?"

"Well, officer, I said he was sick, not crazy."

Q: What was the best senior citizens home in the world?
A: The Kremlin.

During Brezhnev's visit to one of the Eastern European socialist countries, he is greeted with fireworks fired by military cannons. After the third round of fire, an elderly woman, upon hearing such loud artillery fire, asks a policeman, "What's going on? Why are they opening fire?"

"Brezhnev is in town," the officer explains.

"Do they really need to fire that many rounds just to hit him?"

In 1957, the moon asks Sputnik, "How did the Soviets let you leave the country?"

"Well, there's another Sputnik with a dog coming right behind me."

A foreign delegation is visiting a collective farm market. Guided by the farm chairman, the foreigners approach a man who's selling his cow.

"How much do you sell it for?" they ask the farmer.

"Only five rubles," the man says hesitantly, noticing the chairman behind the foreigners' backs, frantically giving him signals that indicate "lower, lower."

"It's so affordable!" the foreigners say excitedly.

At this moment, another farmer is passing by. He overhears this price, pulls out his money, and says, "Five rubles? I'll buy it."

But, the very next moment, when he spots the angry chairman giving him signals too, he changes his mind. "Well, forget it. I'd better add two rubles and buy myself a chicken."

Q: Why is the Soviet sun so happy in the morning?

A: Because it knows that before dusk it will be in the west.

Lenin is dying. He calls in his successor, Stalin, and says, "One thing worries me most, comrade Stalin. Will the people follow you?"

"They definitely will, comrade Lenin," Stalin replies confidently.

"I hope so," Lenin says. "But what if they won't follow you?"

"Then they'll follow you," answers Stalin.

Q: When was the first Soviet election?

A: When god put Eve before Adam and said to him, "Here, choose yourself a wife."

Khrushchev, surrounded by aides and bodyguards, is visiting an abstract art exhibition:

"What the hell is this yellow circle with brown dots all over?"

"This painting, comrade Khrushchev, depicts our heroic peasants in a field."

"Uh... And what is this black triangle with orange stripes?"

"This painting shows our heroic workers in a factory."

"And what is this fat ass with ears?"

"Comrade Khrushchev, this is not a painting. This is a mirror."

How often do you have these awful line-ups at your stores?" the foreigner asks a Soviet.

"Not very often," the Soviet answers. "Only when they

have something to sell."

Brezhnev receives a letter from Communist leaders in Siberia. It reads: "Please send us a few railroad tankers of vodka. We ran out of our own pre-1917 supplies, the people got sober, and now they keep asking us where the czar is."

A collective farmer is reading a government poster about new taxes. "They're gonna squeeze me to death," he mutters to himself.

Suddenly, a man in plain clothes appears from nowhere and asks the farmer, "Who did you mean when you said 'squeeze'?"

"Well, officer, I meant my shoes."

"What shoes, you're barefooted."

"That's why I don't wear them."

A group of bureaucrats from the Ministry of Agriculture were once visiting collective farms for inspection. "What do you feed to your chickens?" they asked the chairman at the first farm they visited.

"We give them the prime grain."

"What?" the bureaucrats protested. "How can you waste the prime grain on chicken feed?! You're fired!"

At the second farm, the chairman replied, "We feed them the lowest grade."

"How can you feed the lowest grade to Soviet chickens?! This is outrageous! You're fired!"

"Comrade inspectors," replied the chairman of the third collective farm, "you came up with the daily feed norm of five *kopecks* (one-hundredth of a ruble) per chicken, right?"

"That is correct," the bureaucrats nodded.

"Well, we give our chickens the money, and they buy whatever feed they want."

During the May Day labor parade at Red Square in the spring of 1949, one of the workers, an elderly man in his eighties, was carrying a large sign that read: "Thanks to comrade Stalin for my happy childhood!"

As the man with the sign was passing the Kremlin, where the top members of the USSR government, including Stalin, were gathered to greet the workers, the police pulled him from the mob and interrogated him:

"Are you out of your mind, grandpa? When you were a child, Stalin wasn't even born."

"That's why I'm very thankful to him, son."

Brezhnev was once seeing off a politician at an airport. Apparently, he was touched so deeply with this farewell that he continued waving to the departing aircraft until it turned into a tiny dot on the horizon.

"Comrade Brezhnev," his aide said, "why don't we go now? He's not worth this kind of attention; you know, he's nobody as a politician."

"As a politician, maybe," Brezhnev replied. "But how he kisses!"

Stalin loses his famous pipe. He calls the head of the Soviet secret police (the NKVD) and says, "Comrade Beria, what's going on? We have people's enemies right here in the Kremlin. They've stolen my favorite pipe!"

"Comrade Stalin, I will take care of this immediately!" Beria snaps, and he goes right to work.

One hour later Beria comes back with this report: "Comrade Stalin, we have detained the people's enemies, and we are waiting for your orders."

"Actually, I just found the pipe under my desk," Stalin answers.

"Well, comrade Stalin," Beria explains, "we already have nineteen out of the twenty accused who have admitted committing this crime against the Soviet people by stealing your pipe."

"What? One is still claiming his innocence? Continue your interrogations, comrade Beria!"

Q: Why are bedbugs capable of starting a revolution?
A: Because, in their veins, runs proletarian blood.

Stalin is dying. He calls Khrushchev to his bedside and says to him, "Comrade, the reins of the country are now in your hands. But before I go, I want to give you some advice." He produces two envelopes marked number one and number two. "Take these letters," Stalin tells Khrushchev. "Keep them safely—don't open them. Only if the country is in turmoil and things start going bad should you open the first one. That'll give you some advice about what to do. After that, if things start going really bad, then and only then should you open the second one." And with these words, Stalin kicks the bucket.

Khrushchev succeeds him, and sure enough, within a few years things start going bad: the economy deteriorates, crops fail, the people become restless. Khrushchev decides it's time to open the first letter. But all it says is: "Blame everything on me!"

So Khrushchev launches a massive de-Stalinization campaign, and blames him for all the excesses and purges and ills of the system. And in this way, he buys himself some time.

But things continue to downslide: there's the missile crisis in Cuba, the economy deteriorates even further, crops fail even more, the Politburo is unhappy with Khrushchev's leadership, and upstarts like Brezhnev and Gromyko threaten his credibility.

So, finally, after much deliberation, Nikita opens the second letter. And all it says is: "Write two letters!"

A worker is standing in line for vodka. From his pocket he pulls out a freshly minted one ruble coin with a portrait of Lenin. Says he: "My pocket is not a mausoleum…you won't stay there for long!"

"Why do you need so many portraits of our Communist leaders?" a customs officer asks the man who is leaving the Soviet Union.

"Once I'm in the States, I'll open a gun range," the man replies.

"Do you read newspapers?"

"Yes I do. Otherwise, how would I know that we live happy and prosperous lives?"

"Hoover made people quit drinking," the American says.

"Well, that's nothing; Stalin made people quit eating," the Russian replies.

Two inmates are having a chat in a Soviet jail for political prisoners:

"What did you do before they put you in here?"

"I was a plumber."

"What did they charge you with?"

"Anti-Soviet propaganda."

"What was the charge based on?"

"Well, one day I went on a call to a local Soviet's office. They had a clogged drain there. It turned out to be a very serious case. I made the mistake of saying that the whole system had to be changed. And now I am here."

Brezhnev calls in his first aide. "Have you read my latest book?"

"Yes, comrade Brezhnev, I've read it three times. All my friends have read it, and my family spend all their time reading it. This is the best book I've ever read."

"Well, maybe I should read it too?" ponders Brezhnev.

Q: Why did the Soviets never send men to the moon?
A: They were afraid those men wouldn't come back.

President Eisenhower once had a dream in which a large group of devils invaded the White House. "What do you want?" he asked them.

"Didn't you know Stalin is dead and in hell?"

"What do you want from me?"

"We're asking for political asylum, Mr. President."

Q: What was Reagan's greatest fear during his meeting with Brezhnev?
A: Brezhnev's kiss.

French president Mitterand tells Andropov, "Mr. General Secretary, in my opinion, your national insignia are not correct."

"Why do you think so, Mr. President? The hammer and sickle represent the union between workers and peasants."

"I think your national insignia should be replaced by a cupid instead."

"A cupid?!"

"Yes. You are in such a shambles you can't even afford clothes, and still you offer your help and love to everybody."

The Americans purchase Lenin's body and place it in a little display at the top of the Empire State Building. Then one day Lenin gets up, gazes down on New York, and says with a smile of a deep satisfaction, "What a beauty! Exactly as I was telling the comrades what our future would be!"

THE ARMY

The more boneheads our army has, the stronger our defense will be.

At one time one of the largest and ablest armies in the world, the Russian army is now going through a major crisis. The massive military cutbacks that followed the disintegration of the Soviet Union were severe and often demoralizing for personnel. Poor economic conditions have made them feel even tougher for thousands of conscripts and officers.

Most of the jokes in this chapter are jokes that were born in the barracks, the military schools, and officer's quarters of the Soviet army. Being a conscript army, every Soviet male citizen fit for military service faced a two- or three-year-long term of military duty. Notwithstanding some problems normally associated with the prolonged gathering of a large number of young men in isolated places, without sufficient contact with the better part of mankind, and without enough party time and alcohol, the army has been respectfully called a "true school of life for young men."

This is probably why Russians have invented so many army jokes. And they are always welcome, in any company.

During the Second World War, a lieutenant once reported to his superior, "Comrade Major, we have received American condoms by lend-lease."

"No need for that, Lieutenant," replied the major. "For thirty years I've been using a three-inch shell, and it's still good for another thirty."

A Vietnamese jet fighter pilot is flying his MiG-17 near enemy positions when he sees a Phantom appearing out of no-where and locking in on him. He pulls out his manual, quickly scans it, and then presses a yellow button. The next moment he sees a cloud of smoke and metallic rubble, the leftovers of the Phantom.

The Vietnamese pilot doesn't put back his manual away yet, when he sees two more Phantoms coming down on him, ready to attack. Following the manual once more, he presses a green button this time. Both Phantoms, hit by rockets, go down almost simultaneously and before either could open fire.

"Now it's time to relax," the pilot thinks to himself. But he has to change his thinking again in a hurry when he spots a pack of Phantoms getting into an attack formation. He once again quickly finds the solution in his manual: Press the red button. And so he does.

The Vietnamese pilot then feels a pat on his shoulder, and he hears a voice with a thick Russian accent saying, "Hey, buddy, hop over. Let me get both of us out of this mess…".

A woman is like a tumbling bullet: She strikes you in the heart, hits your pockets, and leaves you all screwed up.

"**C**omrade Colonel, this computer will double the speed of your work!"

"In that case, Lieutenant, get me one more."

"**W**hat if I run out of ammo during combat?"

"You must continue to fire in order to mislead the enemy."

"You could be a sergeant if you didn't drink, private!"
"Sergeant?! When I'm drunk, I feel like a general!"

"Private Ivanov, get a crowbar and sweep the drill square."

"Why a crowbar, comrade Sergeant? I can do it better and faster with a broom."

"You don't get it, Private, do you? I don't need better and faster, I need you to get real bored and tired."

A little boy asks his father, a colonel, "Daddy, can I become a sergeant when I grow up?"

"Yes, of course, son," the colonel replies.

"And what about a lieutenant?"

"I don't see why not!"

"Even a major?"

"Yes son, when you grow up!"

"Can I be a colonel like you?"

"Yes you can, if you serve your country well."

"And then I can become a general, right?"

"No, son. Not a general."

"Why not, dad?"

"Because generals have sons of their own."

"Sergeant, muster your men!"

"What for, Lieutenant?"

"Okay, as you were."

"Do you think I'm an idiot?"

"I don't know, comrade Sergeant. I've only been here for two months."

"Comrade Sergeant, your order is executed!"

"I think I ordered nothing, Private."

"That's exactly what I did—nothing."

A woman sees her husband off as he reports to the army

during the Second World War.

"Where should I write you, dear?" she wonders.

"Write directly to the POW camp," he replies.

A sergeant musters his men for inspection. When the inspection is almost completed, he finds a cigarette butt in the corner of the drill square.

"Whose is this?" he addresses the line, pointing to the cigarette butt. There is no response.

"I'm asking you again…whose butt is this?" the sergeant demands.

After a long pause, someone from the line pipes up, "Looks like it's no one's. Why don't you have it, comrade Sergeant?"

Not willing to go over to the cooler himself, a sergeant sends a soldier. "Here," he says giving his mug to the soldier, "bring me some water."

Not being too anxious to do this chore either, the soldier turns the mug upside down, shows it to the sergeant, and says, "I'm sorry, Sergeant, but I can't. Look, this mug doesn't have a bottom."

The sergeant gapes at the mug for a few moments, scratches his head, and says, "Yeah I see… What a useless thing—it doesn't have an opening either."

An officer at the recruiting board is attempting to lure a group of conscripts to his garrison:

"Why don't you join me, guys! We have only three months of cold weather per year."

"What about the rest of the year, comrade Lieutenant?" one of the conscripts asks after he signs up.

"The rest of the year the weather is *very* cold."

A platoon is marching near a military base, located in some secluded area. The sergeant spots a brick lying on the ground ahead of the column and calls, "Company, halt!"

He picks up the brick, turns to his men, and says, "Private Petrov, what do you think, looking at this brick?"

"It's a waste of government property, comrade Sergeant."

"Good. What about you, private Smirnov?" the sergeant says, turning to another soldier.

"It's a threat to the expedient movement of the troops."

"Okay. Private Ivanov," the sergeant says, turning to yet another soldier, "tell us what you think, looking at this brick?"

"I think about women, comrade Sergeant."

"How's that? Explain."

"Well, I'm always thinking about them."

A strategic missile unit is preparing for a visit from the Inspector General. Private Ivanov is ordered to refresh the paint on one of the missiles. Being a lazy sort of fellow, he doesn't bother going for a step ladder. Instead, in order to reach the top of the missile, he simply throws the can of paint up in the air, aiming toward the top of the missile cone. The can hits the cone and turns upside down, allowing the paint to flow down the missile's sides and leaving a nearly perfect finish.

Except for one small detail—the empty can on top of the missile cone—the job is done.

As private Ivanov stands there thinking about how to get that can down, an officer passes by the site. He sees the top of the missile, stops, and asks Ivanov, "What is that, private?"

"That is a synchro-cyclotron, comrade Lieutenant!" the private snaps in reply. He has heard the term somewhere, and he is sure it relates somehow to a nuclear missile.

"I know that, you simpleton," the lieutenant says. "I'm asking why it's not painted…".

Some soldiers ask their sergeant, "Comrade sergeant, we understand what perestroika is. It's when we're arranged in a two-line formation and then we rearrange into a four-line formation. But what is glasnost?"

"Glasnost is when you criticize me as much as you please,

and you get nothing for that."

"Nothing at all?"

"That's right. No overcoats, no warm underwear, no extra leaves...".

"**T**ell me, Lieutenant," a general says to one of his officers over a few shots of vodka, "how do you manage to spend all of your leisure time in the town's best restaurants? And especially with your pay!"

"Well, General, it's really all about budget management. What do you do with your paycheck?"

"I give it all to my wife, and she gives some of it back to me in the form of an allowance."

"There's your problem, General. You have to learn how to treat your wife! You need to gently put your hands around her, give her a hot kiss and ask for more money."

Following the lieutenant's advice as soon as he gets home, the general sneaks up on his wife from behind, puts his hands around her and gives her a hot kiss.

His wife sighs bawdily and purrs, "Don't tell me you've run out of money again, Lieutenant."

Yesterday one of our civilian cruise ships was attacked by an American warship in the Atlantic, near the Florida peninsula. After returning their fire and sinking the American warship, the Soviet liner continued her cruise at a safe depth.

—From a Soviet news agency announcement

A young fellow was once trying hard to avoid being drafted:

"Can you see these letters?" the frustrated doctor asked, reaching to the top of the chart.

"No, doctor, I can't see those either."

The doctor then called a nurse, and a shapely young woman entered the examination room. He ordered her to undress, turned to the draftee candidate, and said, "Can you see her?"

"No, sir, I can't."

The doctor immediately walked over to the young fellow, pointed below his waist, and demanded, "Then, tell me, what's this?"

"Well, doctor, apparently he has eyes of his own."

A sentry stops an officer at the gates of a military base. The officer checks his pockets for a pass, but finds nothing. "I must have left it in my other uniform," he explains, and moves forward as if he has been cleared.

"I'm sorry, comrade Major," the sentry says, stepping in front of the officer, "but I cannot let you in without a pass."

"Private Ivanov, you know me perfectly well!" the officer shouts. "Drop the formalities and let me in!"

A few minutes pass by as the sentry, adhering to regulations, refuses to let the officer pass.

When the officer starts threatening the sentry, a voice from a room shouts out, "Hey, Sergei, are you going to waste all night on him? Just shoot him as required by the regulations, and let's finish our game!"

Four heavily damaged tanks—the leftovers of a Russian armored brigade—fight their way through a small Chechen town. When two more tanks catch fire, hit by Chechen anti-tank grenades, a head pops up from one of the remaining tanks and shouts, "Cease fire! We've won the war!"

A soldier complains about his uniform, which doesn't fit him at all, and which has seen better days.

"Comrade Sergeant, look at this uniform. It looks awful!"

"What's wrong with that, Private? Don't forget, a soldier needs to instill fear into the enemy!"

"**W**hy don't you eat your oatmeal? You don't like it?"

"I had so much of it in the army I can't look into the eyes

of a horse."

Q: Why do we never see a general running?
A: Because a running general would create laughter in peacetime, panic in war.

Sergeant Talk:

I'm not asking you where you've been, Private! I'm asking, why are you late?

I can be in charge of a battalion or even a brigade—my voice allows me.

Why are you swearing like little children?

I don't know how it should be done, but you're doing it wrong.

Why are you standing with your back to me, soldier, when I'm looking straight into your eyes?

I'm not asking where you've been, Private! I'm asking you where you're coming from!

Quiet! Or I'll turn into an animal!

You say you're sick, soldier? Study the regulations—you'll get better.

If you wanna say something, soldier, just shut up and stand still!

You live here like pigs in the stable!

There are four slackers in your platoon—and you put gel on your hair!

Here in the army, you will fall asleep and wake up on my orders.

Comrade Cadets, I've been sent here from the field army. And as you know, they don't keep morons there!

Comrade Cadet, don't make that smart face! Don't forget that you're here to become an officer!

Let's say we have *m* number of tanks. No, that's not enough—let's say we have *n* number of tanks.

A drunken pilot knocks at the door of his apartment. He hears some suspicious noises behind the door. Finally he hears his wife's voice:
"Who's there?"
"I'm board fifteen, req... request landing," the pilot says.
"I'm tower," the woman voice replies. "Board fifteen, execute missed approach. Board eleven, cleared for take-off!"

GIRL: Why don't you tell me something?
MARINE: Attention!
GIRL: How about something nice?
MARINE: At ease!

PRIVATE: An ammo box fell off and hit me in the head, comrade Sergeant.
SERGEANT: What was inside?
PRIVATE: Nothing.
SERGEANT: What about in the box?

"Why aren't your boots polished, soldier!" the sergeant yells at his man.
"That's none of your business, comrade Sergeant," the

soldier replies.

"What?!" the sergeant screams, turning red. "How can you talk this way to your commanding officer? I'll send you to the guardhouse for the rest of the week! I'm asking you one more time, why are your boots are not polished?"

"The whole unit ran out of polish two weeks ago. It's been reordered, but…".

"I don't care! That's not my business!" the sergeant interjects.

"Exactly my words, Sergeant."

"**S**ergeant, check private Ivanov's file again: Every time he finishes shooting, he wipes his fingerprints off the weapon."

A major needs to pass a medical in order to be accepted to a military academy. Apparently, he is having some problems with his eyes:

"…You can't see this either?" the doctor asks as he finishes the top row of the chart. "Well, Major, let's check the left eye."

The major is quiet.

"Can you see anything, sir?"

"Well, doc," the major says, scratching his head, mental strain showing all over his stout face, "I can see them well enough…the thing is, I forgot their names."

An officer who has had a little too much to drink musters his troops for the evening formation:

"Soldiers…why are you not standing straaaight?" he stumbles.

"That's because the earth is round, comrade Lieutenant," a voice from the line jokes.

"Who said that?" the lieutenant barks.

"Galileo, Lieutenant," someone replies.

"Step forward, Galileo!" the lieutenant orders.

"He's dead," someone says.

"Sergeant!" the lieutenant shouts, visibly confused. "What's going on here? Why didn't you report a casualty?"

"Excuse me, mister, what are you doing here dressed like that?" a girl, hunting for wild mushrooms in the woods, says to an elderly man, who's dressed in camouflage clothes, a bush affixed to his hat, and an old rifle slung behind his back.

The man looks around and says, "Don't you see, girl? I'm a guerilla fighter."

"But the war ended fifty years ago."

"Really?! Damn, then whose trains have I been destroying all these years?"

A young man named Ivan doesn't want to be drafted. He makes sure nobody sees him, then sneaks into the recruiting board chairman's office at the local military commissariat.

"Comrade Colonel," he says in a low voice, "I'll give you ten thousand if you get me out of doing military service."

The colonel looks around, ponders this request for a moment, and then says, "Okay, meet me with the money at the local cemetery at midnight."

Our hero reports to the cemetery as instructed, and there he finds the following scene: The colonel, completely naked, sits on top of a tall tombstone, playing guitar and singing loudly. When he sees Ivan, the colonel climbs down, takes the money, and then says solemnly, "You will show up before the recruiting board tomorrow at ten in the morning. I'll take care of everything else."

"Congratulations, son," an officer at the recruiting board says to Ivan the next morning. "You are drafted to serve in our doughty navy. The next three years will make a real man out of you."

Ivan is stunned. He gathers himself after a few minutes and then says to the chairman, "Colonel, what does he mean I'm drafted? I gave you ten thousand last night, and now you're sending me to the navy for the whole three years?!"

"Do you know what you're talking about, young man?" the colonel asks, with a grin on his surprised face.

"Yes I do! Did you forget about the cemetery last night,

colonel?" Ivan asks in a rage. "You were singing there naked when I gave you my ten thousand…'.

"Comrade officers," the colonel says, turning to his slightly bewildered colleagues, "as you can all see, this man is not sound mentally. I would recommend that we keep him away from our armed forces for good!"

SERGEANT: What are you so sad about, soldier?
SOLDIER: I have melancholy, comrade Sergeant.
SERGEANT: Cheer up, soldier! In the army, melancholy has to be cheerful!

Radioactive rain fell yesterday over a major part of the US territory. The rain commander is commended for a medal.
—From a Soviet news agency announcement

"Do you know who I am, soldier?" an angry general demands of a soldier, who had failed to salute him in a busy shopping mall during his leave.

"Hey, guys," the soldier says to his friends, "look! This old fart doesn't know who he is!"

A navy officer says good-bye to his wife and sets out on a long sea voyage. When his ship leaves port, the mechanic reports a major engine problem, so the ship returns to port for an overhaul.

The officer returns home and knocks on the door. The door is opened by a strange, tall man with the build of a wrestler.

"Who are you?" he asks the officer.

"I'm the husband," the officer replies.

"Take a walk, buddy. Our husband is at sea," the stranger says as he shuts the door.

In the middle of fierce combat, the commanding officer

of a platoon, that has run out of ammo hands a brick to his soldier:

"Private, can you destroy an enemy aircraft with this?" he asks.

"But, Sergeant," the soldier begins to explain, "this is only a brick…".

"Are you a Communist, private?!"

The soldier puts on a brave face, breaks the brick in half against his knee, snaps to a salute, and reports, "I will destroy two enemy aircraft, comrade Sergeant!"

"What happened to your arm, private?" an officer asks a soldier, who has one arm in a cast.

"I've broken it in two places, Lieutenant."

"Next time, private, try to avoid those places."

A young navy officer was preparing for his first overseas voyage. He asked his grandfather, a retired navy officer, what he should take with him.

"Don't forget seasickness pills and condoms," the old salt said.

Following his grandfather's advice, the young officer went to the drugstore and bought a package of each. Thinking that it might not be enough, the next day he bought two more packages of seasickness pills and two more packages of condoms.

As the rookie was packing up, his grandfather saw the 'supplies' and suggested that even more of them may be needed. That meant yet another trip to the drugstore. So off he went, and the young officer ordered double the amount of items he had already purchased during his two previous visits.

As he was leaving the store, the pharmacist, an elderly man with a fatherly look on his face, snuck up behind him, looked around and, almost in whisper said, "Excuse me, sir. This is none of my business, of course, but tell me—If she makes you so sick, why do you keep sleeping with her?"

"**P**rivate, does your commanding officer know that the trenches' sides have caved in?"

"Not yet, comrade Lieutenant. We'll let him know as soon as we dig him out."

A sad bear walks through the woods. A rabbit passes by and sees him:

"Hey, Bear, what happened? Why are you so sad?"

"I've received a draft card, Rabbit, and I don't want to go to the army."

"Well, if you pop one of your eyes out, you'll still be able to see with the other eye, but you'll become unfit for military service…Get the idea?"

The next day the rabbit runs into the bear again. The bear is wearing an eye patch, and today he is even more sad.

"How did it go, Bear?" the rabbit asks.

"They didn't draft me—I have flat feet."

RECRUITING OFFICER: Where would you like to serve, young man?

DRAFTEE: At the General Staff, Comrade Major!

RECRUITING OFFICER: Are you crazy?

DRAFTEE: Is that mandatory?

A boy asks his father, a military officer, "Dad, what do they pay you money for?"

"Well, son, they pay me for my rank, my position, and my seniority."

"And what about your work?"

"And for my work, son, I get reprimands."

To commemorate Victory Day (May 9), a school invited a Second World War hero to share his memories with the students.

The elderly man, his chest heavily decorated with medals

for his feats fifty years ago, gathered his thoughts and began, in a low, weak voice, "I was in the trenches… when the sky turned dark… filled with enemy aircraft… and… I wet my pants."

"You mean you got scared, of course," a teacher took over, to prevent her students from getting the wrong idea.

"Well, I got scared then, but just now I wet my pants."

Two bears are having a conversation in the deep woods near a military base:

"Why do you smell like gasoline?" one asks.

"Well," explains the other, "I ate a technical supply officer last week."

"That's why they turned the whole place upside down," nods the first bear. "You made a bad choice. Next time go for a *political commissar* (a political officer in the Soviet army). I had two of them this year, and it doesn't look like anyone noticed they were missing."

Did you lose your arm in combat?"
"No, on my way to the draft office."

We will deliver your parcel any place in the world within one hour. Accuracy and on-time delivery is guaranteed.
—Strategic Missile Forces of the Russian Federation

A sergeant enlightens his company:

"A good example of the force of gravity would be a stone that's thrown up in the air; it always comes back down to earth."

"Sergeant," one of the soldiers asks, "what if a stone falls down in the water?"

"That is not our concern, private. For that we have the navy."

A sergeant explains the basics of ballistics to a group of

recruits:

"The bullet's path is a curve called a parabola and it looks like this…".

"Sergeant," one soldier raises his hand. "But this means that, if we hold a gun on its side, we can shoot around the corner, doesn't it?"

The sergeant is visibly puzzled by this question. He scratches his head and snaps, "It does, I suppose! But a Soviet soldier would never shoot from behind a corner!"

A happy wolf exits the draft office.

"Did they draft you?" a rabbit asks him.

"No, I have poor eyesight," the wolf answers.

"Come on, Wolf," the rabbit says skeptically, "how did you do that?"

"Okay, Rabbit. Do you see that little hill over there with the tree on top of it? Now, can you see the little caterpillar sitting on one of the leaves on the second branch from the bottom on the left?"

"Hardly."

"Well, I can't even see the tree…".

The president asks the Minister of Defense, "How could your people shoot down that civilian aircraft? You're putting me on the spot before the international community."

"Well, Mr. President, that was an accident."

"What kind of accident? How can you shoot down a plane by accident?"

"Apparently, that's the only way we can shoot down a plane."

A fishing boat is drifting, somewhere out in the Atlantic. Its captain stands at the bridge, leisurely smoking a cigar.

Suddenly, an American submarine surfaces near the boat. The submarine's captain, wearing a crisp uniform, soon shows up on the bridge and says politely, "Excuse me, sir, we're having some problems with our navigating equipment. Could you please give me directions to Russia?"

"35 degrees northeast, captain."

The sub's captain thanks the fishing boat captain and orders his crew to submerge.

Before the fishing boat captain is able to finish his cigar, he hears the sea roaring again, and this time a Russian submarine surfaces, not far from the spot where her American counterpart had submerged just a few minutes ago.

Another ten minutes pass, and then a man in a striped sailor's sweatshirt emerges onto the sub's bridge. He whistles to catch the attention of the fishing boat captain and shouts, "Hey skipper, I'm the captain of this sub. We're lost here. Can you tell me which way to America?"

"Take a course 185 degrees southwest…".

"Oh, forget that," the Russian captain interrupts him. "Can't you just point your hand?"

There's a panic on a Russian nuclear missile carrier. The captain musters his entire company onto the main deck. He dashes back and forth, yelling at his men continuously, "Who threw a shoe into the central control panel?"

But all he gets is silence in response. The captain presses on. "Who threw a shoe into the central panel?… I'm asking you one last time. Who threw a shoe into the central panel?"

With these words, the sea begins to roar and an American submarine surfaces at a minimally safe distance from the Russian ship. Seconds later, an officer climbs up onto the submarine's bridge and shouts to the Russian captain: "Sir, could you please lower your voice a bit; our sonar man is bleeding through his ears!"

"Who cares about your sonar man anymore?" the Russian captain barks in response, and then he turns back to his company: "Who threw a shoe into the central panel?"

The American officer, now joined by his colleagues, watches the Russians with some amusement for awhile. Then once again he speaks up, loudly enough to be heard by the Russians: "You certainly don't see that kind of mockery in America."

The Russian captain looks at his wristwatch and says, "Forget about your America! It does not exist as of twenty minutes ago—not after one of my boneheads threw that shoe into the central control panel…".

A soldier on kitchen duty is ordered to peel potatoes:
"I thought the army would have a machine to do this nowadays," he complains.
"It does," the sergeant replies, "and you're its latest model."

Two women are having a friendly chat:
"So, how is your husband?" one woman asks.
"He just became impotent," replies the other.
"And my fool is still a sergeant."

"Comrade Colonel, you forgot your brain."
"I don't need it anymore, Lieutenant. I was just promoted to general."

Twin brothers report to the draft board:
"They didn't draft me! I'm staying home!" one of them says, exiting the office, happiness all over his face.
"Why don't you go again for me?" his brother suggests.
The first brother agrees, takes his brother's papers and back in he goes. When he returns to the waiting area, his brother runs up to him and asks, "What did they say?"
"I'm sorry, brother, but they did draft you."

More Sergeant Talk:

The first love of a soldier must be the regulations. The second—his commanding officer.

Every soldier must be either commended or reprimanded.

The signal for the attack is three green whistles.

Top secret documents must be destroyed before they are read.

You can't start the engine? Just drive, you can fix it later.

Erect a roadblock or assign a decent sergeant.

Hey, private, if you're an idiot, just say so, and stop trifling with the gun.

Two major army rules:
#1. The commanding officer is always right.
#2. If the commanding officer is not right, see rule #1.

A recruit examines the food that's been served to him in the garrison dining room:

"Do I have any choice here?" he asks his sergeant.

"Yes, you do," the sergeant replies. "You may eat it, or not."

A soldier requests a three-day pass, as he is to become a father in the near future.

When he returns to his base, a sergeant asks, "Was it a boy or a girl?"

"I don't know yet, Sergeant. I'll let you know in about nine months."

A draftee appears before the medical board:

"So, what's your problem?" a military physician asks.

"I'm nearsighted, doctor," the draftee explains.

"That's okay with us. We'll put you in the first trenches, young man. Next please…".

A sergeant is staring out the window, and a soldier walks over to take a look for himself. Outside, he sees three shapely women walking down the street.

"Wow!" he exclaims. "You have good taste, comrade Sergeant!"

"I don't really know what you're talking about, private. But I can tell you one of them is marching out of step."

An elderly general learns that he has a new grandson. He sends his orderly to see if the newborn resembles him.

"He's your carbon copy, sir," the orderly reports when he returns. "He is bald and fat, wets his pants, and he never shuts up."

"**W**hat, soldier? You broke your leg? Then don't waste your time just lying here—do some push-ups!"

Two soldiers are late returning from their leave, and now they're standing before their sergeant:

"How could you be late for two whole hours? What if a war broke out?"

"Well, comrade Sergeant, we went to the opera and we just got carried away with the performance."

"Opera?!" the sergeant exclaims. "I can only imagine how drunk you were to end up in the opera!"

DRINKING
AND VODKA

A delayed second shot often means a wasted first one.

"Last time I came home, I was so drunk my own children didn't recognize me."

"What happened after you sobered up?"

"Well, once I was sober enough, I realized I was in the wrong house."

Someone once offered to nominate a bottle of Russian vodka for placement at the International Bureau of Weights and Measures as the official unit of work and remuneration in Russia.

After having a few drinks, two friends are talking outside a bar:

"I know an address where we can have a corking good time tonight," says one. "There are two girls. One of them is really good-looking. She's mine. The second one... well, after you get few more shots of vodka into you, you'll find her acceptable."

"Okay, let's go," agrees the other.

The friends arrive at their destination. The doors open, and there they see two young women, just waiting for them. The less fortunate friend pauses to look at the women, then turns to his friend and says, rather skeptically, "It's not going to work, buddy.

I can't drink that much!"

A drunk is standing before a telegraph pole, poking it with his keys. He's trying one key after another, unsuccessfully, when a passerby decides to make some fun of him:

"Nobody home?"

"They must be," replies the drunk. "Can't you see the lights are on upstairs?"

Russians drink in two ways: until they run out of money or until they simply cannot drink anymore. In most cases, though, it seems they never run out of money.

"**I**van, why were you so drunk at the last night party?"

"Because I had a lot to drink, but nothing to eat."

"Well, why didn't you eat something?"

"Because they kicked out all my teeth."

A man who has overly imbibed sits on a subway bench next to a well-dressed woman.

The woman turns to the man and says, "You're drunk. It's disgusting!"

Her comment goes unanswered. So, after a few minutes, the woman says to the drunk again, "You're so drunk! It's disgusting!"

But there's no reaction from the man this time either. Irritated by the drunk's ignorance, the woman tries one last time: "You're a drunken pig. It's disgusting!"

This time the man takes a good look at the woman, and then he says, "Yes I'm drunk. That's today. Tomorrow I'll be sober, but you will always have your ugly twisted legs!"

Late one night a drunk staggers along a sleepy street shouting, "People! People! People!…"

Some windows and balconies slowly start to open, exposing a few angry faces.

"What's the problem?" someone shouts down to the drunk.

"Can anybody tell me the time?" the drunk blurts out.

"It's three in the morning, you bastard!" someone else replies.

"Three in the morning, hic," says the drunk. "Then why the hell are all of you still up, and what the hell are you staring at me for anyway?"

"If I could only get back all the money I've spent on booze in my life…"

"What would you do with all that money then?"

"I could get really drunk."

A drunken man knocks at his apartment door:

"Who's there?" his wife asks.

"Mary, it's me," replies the man.

"I'm not Mary!" says the woman.

"Well… Tanya, open the door!" he insists.

"I'm not Tanya!" the woman answers, getting angry.

"Listen, honey… what's your name… let me in, and then we can play scramble inside," shouts the man.

A farmer once got into a habit of drinking. Soon enough, he found himself in a financial crunch. To make matters worse, his wife started to hide money from him.

Then one day the farmer got an idea. He went to the market and sold all his geese. As he returned home, very drunk, his wife looked out the window and then yelled in disgust, "Where are the geese, you drunk?"

"They went south. And if you continue hiding money from me, the sheep will be going too. To the mountains," replied the farmer.

Fed up with his life, a man decides to hang himself. He gets some rope, climbs up on a chair, and—Wow!—he discovers an old cache full of booze, apparently set up by his wife, on top of the cupboard.

The man decides to have a few last drinks of his favorite vodka before he dies. And so he drinks one shot after another...and soon he starts to think to himself, "Well, life is just getting back on the right track after all."

Late one night two fiends are leaving a bar. They're unhappy because they've run out of money. "Let's go to my place," says one. "I have a gut feeling we can find some vodka there."

Upon their arrival, and without turning the lights on, the host sneaks into the kitchen and returns with a bottle of vodka. His friend whispers to him, "I think there's somebody with your wife in the bedroom."

"Be quiet!" the host whispers back. "This is his bottle...".

A filthy, stinking drunk is lying on the ground near the entrance to a liquor store. Soon enough, a cop approaches him.

"What are you doing here?" the cop asks the man.

"I'm here for advertising purposes, officer," the drunk replies boldly. "Let's just say the Ministry of Public Health is having an anti-alcoholism campaign...".

Three drunks are crawling along the railroad tracks. "These steps are so steep," says one.

"These handrails are so short," says the second.

"It'll be over in a moment, guys," says the third. "I can see the elevator coming!"

Two drunks are in a car.

"Turn left after that bridge," says one.

"Wait a moment," says the other, "I thought you were driving!"

A drunken bum is slipping on a park bench. A representative of the sexual minority passes by, sees the sleeping bum, grabs him, and, helpless in the face of his temptation, drags the sleeping bum off into the bushes.

When the attacker finishes with the bum, he sticks a five-ruble banknote into the drunk's pocket and leaves.

When the bum wakes up and finds money in his pocket, he wastes no time. He runs directly to the nearest liquor store to buy a bottle of his favorite cheap port. He empties the bottle and then he goes back to sleep on the same park bench.

The next day, by chance or not, the same homosexual runs into our sleeping hero again. And once again he takes advantage of the situation; and later, the bum once again ends up enjoying his favorite drink.

A couple of days later, the homosexual decides to share his discovery with two of his friends. This time they leave the bum 20 rubles.

Surprised when he finds this amount of money, the bum rushes off to the store again. Only this time he chooses to buy a bottle of cognac instead.

"Why do you buy the cognac today?" the sales clerk asks his familiar customer. "For the same money you can buy four bottles of your favorite port!"

"No, I shouldn't buy that port anymore," the bum replies. "It hurts my behind."

*A*n intoxicated man comes home, where he is quickly confronted by his wife.

"Where did you get so much to drink?" she asks.

"Well, two of my friends and I had a reason to celebrate," explains the husband. "I bought a bottle of vodka and…".

"And you guys managed to get so drunk just from one bottle f vodka?!" the wife interjects. (This shouldn't happen if you're a Russian.)

"Well, you see, honey," he waffles, "they didn't show up!"

"What happened to your grandfather?"

"Alcohol put him in his grave."

"I don't remember him drinking that much."

"He wasn't. He was killed when his still exploded."

It's the Soviet Union of the mid-1980s, the heyday of the government anti-alcoholism campaign. The Enforcement Commission is visiting a factory. They approach Vasily, one of the factory's best workers.

"Good work, Vasily. Tell us, could you work as well for your country if you had a glass of vodka?"

"Yes I could," replies the worker, slightly confused.

The Commission is surprised, but they decide to continue the dialogue.

"What if you drink two glasses of vodka? Will you be able to do the same good job?"

"For sure," replies Vasily.

"And what if you drink three glasses of vodka?" continues the Commission.

"No problem," says Vasily.

"Okay," says one man from the Commission. "You say you can drink three glasses of vodka and do the same good job. But I bet you, you won't be able to work at all if you were to have four glasses of vodka!"

"What do you think I'm doing right now?" Vasily says, smiling.

A surgeon says to his assistant during an operation, "Alcohol... More alcohol... A pickle...".

A very drunk sailor, wearing his hat backwards (ribbons facing the front) staggers through the street. Annoyed by the ribbons, which are constantly getting into his face, he exclaims, "I wonder when I'll be past all these damn bushes?"

After visiting the club car, a passenger is now going through every car on the train and checking every compartment. He looks around, then he looks out the window, then he proceeds to the next compartment, and then to the next car…

When the conductor finally spots the passenger, he asks him if something is wrong.

"Oh, nothing," replies the drunk. "I'm just looking for my compartment."

"Don't you remember its number?" the conductor asks, trying to help.

"Nope. All I remember is that there was a nice birch forest in the window."

Two drunks are attending their friend's funeral. They stand quietly before the casket looking at their dead friend.

"He doesn't look bad at all," notices one.

"Mind you," replies the other, "he hasn't been drinking since last Wednesday."

A Hollywood cameraman visits his colleague at *Mosfilm* (Moscow's movie production center). He is shown a beautifully shot scene of a seastorm.

Upon learning that this scene was shot during a real storm at sea, the cameraman says to his Russian colleague, "I normally shoot this kind of scene in a glass of water."

"I could do the same," replies the Russian, "but the problem is, you can't keep any glasses handy around here."

A drunken homeless man and a well-dressed woman are sharing a bench on the subway. Tired of being exposed to the terrible smell of the drunk's feet, and hoping that she could shame the man into leaving his seat, she asks the drunk, "Sir, do you ever change your socks?"

The drunk shoots right back without blinking an eye: "Yes

I do! But only for vodka!"

After the implementation of the Anti-alcoholism Decree, two men are discussing its effectiveness.

"I don't understand," one man says. "They say that, after the Decree, people are drinking less. Why, then, do we still have such a high divorce rate?"

"That's simple," explains the other one. "After they quit drinking, so many men have to take a sober look at their wives!"

A man rushes into the house, pushing everyone and everything out of his way to reach the bar. He grabs a bottle of vodka, fills up a glass, and gulps it down. His wife brings him a sandwich, but he declines it. Instead, the man refills his glass and drinks it at once.

"You should eat something," his wife begs him. "It won't be so hard on your stomach." But the husband ignores her and, without saying anything, he polishes off the bottle.

A few minutes later the man turns red, gets up, and then eats the sandwich. On his way to the sofa, his feet give out and he falls to the floor.

The man then turns to his wife, and with anger in his voice, he says, "Now look what your bloody sandwich has done to me!"

"**Y**ou came home drunk again," the wife reprimands her husband.

"You're wrong, honey," protests the husband, who can barely stand on his feet. "I didn't come home, they brought me home!"

"**W**hat do you take for insomnia?"

"A glass of wine every two hours."

"Do you fall asleep after that?"

"No I don't. But at least I enjoy being awake that much better."

$\mathbf{T}$he stages of drinking:
A man sitting in a bar falls off his chair and hits the floor. The bartender approaches him, offering some help. "Can I help you get back on that chair, sir?"
"No thanks. I think I'll stand."

A man on the street tries to catch a cab. The car slows down for a moment, but after taking a better look at his potential customer, the driver speeds up.
The man then sits down in a pile of mud and says, "Take me to a motel, please."

When a very drunken man finally reaches his house, only to find his wife in bed with a stranger, he declares to himself, "This is my wife, and next to her is…me, ten years younger?"

A drunk looks at a portrait of Karl Marx and says, "I need a shave."

The drunk walks into the kitchen, looks at his wife and daughter, and says, "Where have I seen you girls?"

The earth jumps into your face.

On your way home from the bar someone steps on your tie. You see the telegraph poles crossing the street. Then the pavement stands up, and you're left with no other option but to sleep standing up.

You walk out of the bar and somebody hits you from behind. You turn around—turns out to be the pavement.

$\mathbf{T}$hree men are drinking. A UFO comes out of the blue, lands near the drinking men, and a humanoid walks out of the spacecraft. Without paying the slightest bit of attention, the men just continue drinking.

After watching them for some time, the humanoid walks closer and declares in a metallic voice, "I am a humanoid."

"Okay," says one man, without any hint of surprise. He then turns to a younger fellow who, due to his inferior drinking abilities, apparently is in charge of pouring the precious liquid. "Pour a shot for Humanoid, Ivan."

The humanoid finishes his drink and says, "I am a humanoid."

The drunks pour some more for him. He drinks a few more shots, all the while pronouncing the same phrase over and over again after each shot, "I am a humanoid."

But after the sixth round the humanoid changes his vocabulary. "I am a humanoid, people. I come from a different planet. My planet is Alfa-Sigma 00258 from constellation Pyxis."

With this, the drunks look at the humanoid. Then they look at each other. They shrug their shoulders. Finally, one man tells Ivan, "Don't give anymore to Humanoid. That's enough for him!"

The wife comes home from a business trip to find a completely empty apartment. The only remaining piece of furniture is her dead-drunk husband, lying on the floor.

"Where's everything?" she asks.

"I sold everything," he says.

"Where's the money?" she asks.

"In the bags," he says.

"What bags?" she demands. "Where are they?"

He points just below his eyes and says, "Right here!"

A very drunk man staggers through a cemetery at night. He certainly must have had a bit too much, because suddenly he runs into a huge, ugly beast, with large teeth and horns.

Unimpressed, the man shoos the beast away. "Go away, you animal. Go back to your Spielberg!"

"Do you know what the difference is between me and a camel?" asks a drunk. "A camel can work without drinking for a very long time. I, on the other hand, can drink without working for a very long time."

A drunk is circling a large wooden barrel.
"What are you doing here?" a passerby asks him.
"I'm going home," replies the drunk.
"And where is your home?"
"On the left side right after this fence!"

A few weeks after their marriage, Vasily's wife tells him that, unless he quits drinking, she's going to leave him.
"It's going to be tough on you, Vasily," notes his friend after learning about the situation.
"Yes, indeed," sighs Vasily. "I will really miss her."

"I'll bet you a bottle of vodka," Ivan tells his friends, "that if I hide you won't be able to find me."
"I'll bet you two bottles of vodka!" challenges one of Ivan's friends. "We *will* find you!"
And so they agree to go on with their bet. After an entire day of unsuccessful searches throughout their small town, the friends begin to accept their defeat.
Finally, late that night, the friends all meet in their favorite bar, where they immediately ask Ivan where he had been hiding.
"In the library" is his reply.

"You promised me last week that you would quit drinking and that you would become a 'new man'!" a woman reprimands her husband.
"Yes, I did promise you that," explains the husband. "But it turns out that the new man is a drinker too!"

"Are you going to drink anymore, you dirty pig?" the wife berates her drunken husband, slapping him on his back.

The man remains quiet.

"Are you going to drink anymore, you bastard?" the wife continues.

He makes no sound.

"I'm asking you one more time," she insists. "Are you going to drink?"

"Okay," the man says, finally. "Give me a shot of vodka!"

The husband says to his wife, "I'm going to take a nap and I want you to wake me up when I want to have a drink."

"How will I know you want a drink?"

"It's easy, honey. Just wake me up!"

In a remote village, a journalist sees an old man sitting on a bench. The old guy looks to be at least 100.

"Excuse me, sir," the journalist begins. "I was wondering if I could ask you few questions. You've lived such a long life, it must be due to your moderation."

"Oh no," the old man replies. "I have always drunk as much as I wanted."

"Well then, you must have never smoked in your life," concludes the journalist.

"You're wrong. I smoke at least two packs a day," answers the elder.

"How old are you, sir?" the journalist asks, obviously confused.

"I'm 36. Now leave me alone, buddy!"

This drunk guy walks out of an expensive restaurant, approaches a man in uniform, and says, "Hey, doorman, I need a cab."

"I'm not a doorman. I'm a navy officer," explains the man

in uniform.

"That's okay," says the drunk. "I'll settle for a cutter."

Two drunks are walking toward a mob of youngsters. "Let's beat them up," says one.

"What if *they* beat us?" asks another.

"Us? What for?" wonders the first.

With some booze on hand, two men are looking for a third partner to join them for company. It's not a big task, and after they finish their booze at a nearby dark corner of the street, the two split away from their companion.

But much to their surprise, they soon see that the third guy is following them.

"What do you want?" they ask, stopping and facing him.

"We just had a few drinks," he answers. "What about a little conversation, guys?"

"It's either beer or me!" She puts it squarely to him.

"Okay, how much beer?" he asks her to specify.

Two friends are having a conversation:

"You don't look well today, Ivan. What happened?"

"Well, I had too little too much to drink last night."

"How's that? I don't get it."

"Well, that means I drank more than I should, but less than I wanted!"

"How could you drink that much?" an elderly woman asks a young man who's wearing a taxi driver's hat (they used to wear them some years ago). "You endanger your own life as well as the lives of your passengers."

The man is surprised. "Why do you think I'm a cab driver, ma'am?"

"Because you're wearing a taxi driver hat."

The man takes off his hat, looks at it, and sighs, "Yeah, and only a couple of hours ago it was a mink hat!"

"Dad, could you explain to me what a liter is?"

"Yes, son, of course. A liter is like a meter, only in liquid form."

"You're a filthy drunkard, not a colonel!" the colonel's wife scolds.

The colonel looks in the mirror, covers his epaulets with his hands, and declares, "That's right. A filthy drunkard."

A few moments later he takes his hands off the epaulets, looks once more in the mirror, and declares, "No, on second thought, that's not right—I'm a colonel."

In Red Square, a policeman has just arrested a foreign tourist for urinating in a public place.

"Didn't you see the sign? The public washroom is just a few hundred feet away?" the cop says.

"Officer, how could I pee in a place where other gentlemen drink wine?" protested the tourist.

After a huge party, with a lot of alcohol consumed, someone who missed it asks another who didn't: "How was the party?"

"I don't know...nobody's told me about it yet."

A Russian, a German, and an American are captured by a tribe of cannibals. The chieftain announces that he will let them go, on one condition. Each of the captives is given a rifle and a bottle of vodka—he has to drink some vodka and shoot a parrot from 300 feet.

The American drinks a shot and aims at the bird—but he misses it.

The German drinks two shots and aims longer—but he misses the bird as well.

The Russian drinks the entire bottle and shoots from the hip—and he hits the bird right in the eye.

Impressed, the cannibals demand an explanation.

"That's easy," stutters the Russian. "How could you miss twelve birds when you're shooting with a six-barrelled rifle."

"My throat is my greatest asset," says the opera singer.
"Mine too," says the drunkard.

"Defendant, you were so drunk that you fell down into the orchestra pit at the theater?"

"Yes, your honor, but it's not my fault! I ended up in bad company that night. We had a bottle of vodka to share between three of us, but it turned out that I had to finish it all by myself!"

A cab pulls over and two drunk men carry out a third drunk. Apparently, this third guy has had the most to drink tonight. Every time his friends lean him against the fence, he falls down.

An elderly woman passing by sees everything, so she decides to give some free advice: "It'll be easier for you if, instead of his head, you stood him on his feet…".

"Where have you been all evening?" she asks.
"At Ivan's place. We played chess," he replies.
"Oh! You played chess, huh?" she says sarcastically. "Why do you smell of vodka, then?"
"How should I smell?" he argues, "of chess?"

"Could you tell me, please, how to get to the bus station?" a drunk staggering down the street asks a passerby.
"Two blocks straight ahead."

"Straight ahead?" stammers the drunk. "I don't think I'm going to make it then!"

"**I**f you knew that he drinks, why did you married him?"

"Actually, I didn't know about it until one night when he came home sober."

"**W**hat happened?" the doctor asks his client, who's sticking out a black tongue.

"Well, doctor, I spilled a bottle of vodka on the driveway."

A drunk comes home late one night and shouts from the doorway, "Honey, go ahead and yell at me; I can't find the bed!"

The more I drink, the more my hands tremble. The more my hands tremble, the more I spill out of my glass. The more I spill out of my glass, the less I drink. Hence, a conclusion: The more I drink, the less I drink.

A drunken man, unable to stand on his feet, is hugging a pole at the bus stop. Another drunk wandering by asks, "What are you doing here?"

"I'm waiting for my bus," replies the first.

"Mind you, they won't let you in with that thing," cautions the second drunk, nodding toward the pole.

"**I**f you quit drinking," the doctor promises his patient, "you can significantly prolong your life."

"I agree with that, doctor," replies the patient. "I didn't have a drop for a week once. And that week felt more like a year to me!"

"Excuse me, sir," the subway attendant says to the drunk, as he steps in front of him. "You're not allowed to use the subway while intoxicated."

"I know," the drunk says. "I'm not going to ride the subway. Just tell me, is it true that you have moving ladders in there?"

"Yes, it is."

"Is it true," the drunk goes on, "that the walls and the floors are laid in marble?"

"Yes it is," the attendant says. "You've never been in the subway before?"

"No, never!" the drunk replies.

"You must be from a small town," concludes the attendant.

"No I live in this city," the drunk answers.

"And you've never used the subway?" asks the attendant.

"No," sighs the drunk, "they never let me in!"

Three friends,—a chemist, a physicist, and a drunkard—get together to celebrate an event over a few bottles of vodka. For fun's sake, someone suggests a contest, the idea being to divide a bottle of vodka into three equal parts without losing any of the precious liquid. Whoever does it best wins the prize—another bottle of vodka.

The chemist starts first. He makes some complex calculations, dividing the contents into atoms and molecules, but he ends up with poor results.

The physicist in his turn does some impressive number-crunching, accompanied by sketches and diagrams. Unfortunately, his results are the same.

At last the drunk, undoubtedly the most qualified of the three contestants, tries his luck. He quickly grabs the bottle and pours its content into three glasses, dividing the liquid into three perfectly equal parts.

"How did you do that?" his astounded friends ask.

"That's simple," replies the pro. "My experience tells me that one bottle has exactly twenty-one bubbles. That means seven bubbles per glass!"

"Please, we need an ambulance!" a drunken voice cries. "A man has just swallowed a corkscrew!"

"Tell me your address, please," says the operator on the other end of the line.

Five minutes later, it's the same drunken voice: "It's me again. I called earlier about the swollen corkscrew...".

"Yes, sir, the team is on its way!"

"Don't bother anymore. We managed to open the bottle by pushing the cork inside."

A man is running along the train, crying, "Help! Does anybody have some cognac? A woman has just fainted!"

Someone gives him a bottle. The 'good Samaritan' immediately opens it up and takes a few large gulps strait from the bottle. The passengers are shocked.

"What are you doing?" someone asks.

"I don't know about you, people," the man explains, "but I always feel weak when I see someone black out."

One cold autumn day, two village drunks were sitting in a field near a row of haystacks, having few shots.

To warm himself a bit more, one of the drunks lights up a stack of hay. Shortly thereafter, the drunks see several villagers running toward them.

One of the drunks duly notes, "Look at them! None of them wanted to light it up, and now they all come running to warm themselves here!"

A woman passes by a drunken man who's sitting in the mud. As she walks away, the man shouts to her backside, "You're a pig yourself!"

"Excuse me?!" the woman says, turning around. "Did I say something?"

"No," explains the drunk, "but you sure were thinking bad about me!"

*A*n over-imbided man has lost his keys, and now he's knocking at the door of his apartment:

"Who's there?" his wife asks.

There's no response from the man.

Some time later, he knocks again.

His wife asks the same question, this time adding, "Ivan, is it you?"

Again, there is no reply.

The next morning, while leaving for work, the woman opens the door and sees her husband sleeping on the doormat. "Ivan, I asked you three times last night if that was you," she says. "Why didn't you say something?"

Still under the influence of the alcohol he had consumed that night, the man replies, "Well, I was nodding. Too bad you didn't see!"

A teenager walks into a liquor store and asks for eight bottles of vodka. Astounded, the sales clerk says, "Will you be able to carry it all by yourself?"

"Well, that's a good question," replies the teen. "I think I'd be better off knocking off a couple of them right here!"

*H*ome-brewed champagne: Husband drinks vodka, wife provides hissing and babbling.

"...*T*hen I quit drinking and left my wife, who, with her continuous complaining, killed my passion for alcohol."
—From a court confession

*I*t's early morning on the farm:

"How about a few shots before we go to the field," the father proposes to his oldest son.

"Smart thinking, father," his son approves.

You're so clear and yet you've managed to muddle my entire life!

They have a few drinks. The father then asks his son, "How about one more round?"

"Smart thinking, father," answers his son. And so they have a few more drinks.

After that round, the father stands up, puts on his jacket, and says, "Now it's time to work, son."

"It's always like that," complains the son. "Every time you get a few drinks, father, you start talking nonsense."

"This is outrageous!" she complains. "You spend all your nights at the bar, come home at two in the morning, wake me up, and after that I can't fall asleep again the rest of the night!"

"Give me more money," he suggests, "and I'll be coming back in the morning."

A drunken man quietly enters his house, sneaks into the den, grabs a book, and pretends that he's reading. A few moments later his wife walks in.

"You were drinking again," she suggests.

"No, I wasn't!" the man protests. "I've been reading this book all night."

"Okay, drunkard," she sighs. "Just put the briefcase down and go to bed!"

"I've red so much about the harm that alcohol does to your body that, from now on, I've decided to quit."

"You've decided to quit drinking?"

"No, reading!"

"Did father come in drunk last night?" mother asks her five-year-old daughter.

"I'm not sure, mommy," the girl replies. "He didn't say. He just asked for a mirror to see who he was."

A drunk walks slowly along a fence, holding on to it with both his hands. Then he sees a pig lying in the mud, and he says to the animal, "Hey, pig, shame on you! You're so dirty, so stinky…".

"I'll look at you after you reach the end of that fence," replies the pig.

"Have you heard the news?" one man asks his friend. "Ivan has quit drinking!"

"That's simply impossible!"

"But it's true! I saw his obituary in the paper this morning."

A man sits at a small bar in Paris, where he drinks one shot after another.

An older woman, sitting at a neighboring table, politely speaks up: "Excuse me, sir, they say that every third Frenchman is ill due to excessive consumption of alcohol."

To this remark the man replies simply, "That doesn't concern me—I'm Russian."

"Doctor, what should I do? There are two people inside of me! One says, 'drink.' The other says 'don't drink'."

"Why don't you ask them to share with each other?"

Only those who drink know what it's like to be sober.

Late one morning, following a long night of serious drinking and loud partying, a landowner is talking to his butler, Vasily.

"So tell me, Vasily. What happened last night?"

"Well, your excellency, you burned down the whole village."

"Was it a big village?"

"Almost six hundred families, your excellency."

"That's not a big deal. What else?"

"Also, your excellency, you had a quarrel with your neighbor and you smashed his face."

"That happens. What else?"

"Well, if I may tell you, your excellency, you swore aloud all last night."

"Jesus Maria! It's impossible! How am I going to look into the people's eyes after that?"

"How often do you drink?"

"Every day. But sometimes I go on a binge."

Objective reality is nonsense caused by a lack of alcohol in the blood.

DRUGS

𝐀 sparrow was fixing himself a joint when an eagle landed nearby and demanded one for himself.

The little sparrow had no choice but to obey the bullying eagle's request. "Here," the sparrow said, handing a joint over to the eagle. "This is a special high-altitude mix, just right for cool guys like you, Eagle. It's best enjoyed when you climb as high as you can, and then light it up."

So the eagle did just that. But when he lit the joint a few thousand feet in the air, a great explosion produced clouds of smoke, and feathers flew all over the place.

Taking a big whiff of his joint and getting comfortable on his favorite branch, the sparrow looked up in the sky and said, "Oh boy, he went up just like a Challenger!"

𝐀 sparrow smokes some weed. A frog asks him for a whiff, so the sparrow hands the joint to her. The frog inhales, suddenly feels great, breaks into a big smile, jumps away, and bumps into a crocodile.

"Why are you so happy, Frog?" the crocodile asks.

"Sparrow gave me some pot and he'll share it with you too if you ask…".

So the crocodile finds the sparrow and asks him for a whiff. The sparrow takes one look at him and says, "I think, you've had enough, Frog...".

Two druggies run into each other. One of them carries a hoe over his shoulder.

"What do you need a hoe for?" the other druggie asks.

"I want to get rid of the weed," says the first.

"What weed?"

"Well, I've planted some marijuana, but these tomato plants just won't let it have any room to grow...".

A priest is visiting an unfamiliar town, and now he's looking for a post office. He sees a young man with a joint in his mouth, but asks him for directions anyway.

The druggie opens his eyes a bit and says, "Go straight... then turn left. You'll see it on your right...".

The priest thanks the man and says, "Son, I can see that you're lost in your life, smoking this evil plant. Come to my church, and I will show you the road to heaven."

"What are you talking about, man?" the druggie replies, choking on his smoke. "What road? What heaven? You don't even know the road to the post office!"

Two junkies run into each other in a dark alley. "Hey buddy," one says, "what is that shining in the sky now—the sun or the moon?"

"I don't know," the other says, "I'm not from around here...".

To liven up the boredom of his guard duty, a frontier guard lights up a joint. Next to the soldier, a German shepherd— an army service dog—is taking a nap.

The soldier has nearly finished his smoke when he spots an intruder. "Go get him!" he orders the dog.

The dog, its eyes red and shiny, leisurely turns its head toward the intruder and says to the soldier, rather idly, "Why don't you just shoot him?"

Two addicts have gotten high and now they're having a conversation:

"Look at that…" one says.

"Where?" the other says.

"There…".

"What is there?"

"Where?"

A man sees a hunter, who has a dog but no rifle. So he asks him, "How are you going to hunt ducks without a rifle?"

"Well, all I need is my dog," the hunter says.

"How do you hunt?"

The hunter grabs his dog by the tail, spins the dog around, and throws it into a flock of ducks, which he disturbs with a whistle just before releasing his dog into the air. The dog catches a duck and falls to the ground cleanly, holding his catch in his jaws.

"Can I see that again?" the surprised man asks the hunter.

Meanwhile, not far from the place where the hunter is

demonstrating his unconventional hunting techniques, two addicts are enjoying their joints. "Did you just see a dog flying over the lake?" one of the addicts says to another.

"Yeah... I did...".

"And you were saying they sold us some cheap crap...".

CRAZY, OR
JUST WEIRD

"Doctor, should I sleep with an open window?"
"Well, only if you have nobody else to sleep with…".

A man comes home to see his fashion-obsessed wife walking naked in front of the mirror. "What is this?" he asks.
"This is my new erotic costume, honey," she replies.
"Well, I think it needs some ironing," he continues.

A man brings his TV set to a service station and says, "The sound has disappeared."
"What happened?" the repairman asks.
"Well, I was watching my favorite show the other night," the man explains, "and, as usual, I was scratching with a fork in my right ear…".
"Next time," the serviceman interjects, "don't use sandpaper to scratch your eyes, or the picture will disappear too…".

A drunken young man, bleeding from the spot where his left ear used to be, climbs up into bus. He appears to be in a good mood, as he's constantly laughing.
The passengers shake their heads, and then an elderly lady asks the young man, "What are you laughing about, son? You just

lost your ear, and unless you see a doctor, your bleeding won't stop!"

"That's nothing, one ear," the young man replies. "I'm coming from a wedding party. We had a little fight there. They tore off my ear, but I have the fiancé's manhood right here in my pocket!"

"Excuse me, sir, your child is eating the newspaper."
"That's okay. It's yesterday's."

"Let's meet tomorrow."
"Okay."
"Where?"
"Anywhere."
"When?"
"Any time."
"Agreed. But please don't be late!"

"Excuse me," a customer asks a sales clerk, an attractive woman. "Do you have any underwear?"
"No."
"What about for sale?"

"So, you're saying that the railroad running behind your backyard hasn't bothered you at all?" a prospective buyer asks the owner of the house that's for sale.
"No, no-no, no-no…" replies the owner.

A man buys a new pair of shoes. He comes home and decides to wear them around the house. He likes the fit so well, he puts them on again after his evening shower.

As the man is leaving the bathroom, his little son sees him naked and says, "What is that arrow you have hanging there, Daddy?"

"What are you doing?"
"I'm going to have some apples."
"Apples? This is a birch!"
"I have some with me...".

"Oh, this arrow points to my new shoes. Do you like them?" the father improvises.

The boy then goes to the kitchen and tells his mother everything. She chuckles and says, rather to herself, "I'd prefer that arrow were pointing to his new tie."

"Daddy, I need running shoes."
"Wear out your skates first."

Two men are running away from the train:
"Let's get off the tracks and into the woods!" one suggests to the other.
"No, it's hard enough to run on these tracks," the other says, "never mind fighting through the bushes!"

"Doctor, will I be able to play piano after my surgery?"
"Yes you will."
"Are you sure, doctor?"
"Yes, I'm positive."
"That's weird: I can't play piano now...but after the surgery I will?!"

A man on a bus takes out a newspaper, tears it into pieces, and throws them out the window.
"Excuse me, sir," a woman says to him, "why are you doing this?"
"To scare off the elephants."
"But I don't see any elephants around here."
"It's very effective, isn't it?"

DOCTOR: "Madam, you have lice!"
PATIENT: "I know."
DOCTOR: "Then, why don't you treat them?"
PATIENT: "What for? They're healthy."

A man sits in a pothole filled with mud, beside a busy sidewalk.

"Excuse me, citizen," a policemen asks him, "what are you doing here?"

"I'm not a citizen," the man replies, "I'm a snowman."

"Then why are you sitting in a pothole?"

"Can't you see, officer...I'm melting!"

Ivan visits the doctor's office:

"Doctor, I have three testes," he says.

"Okay, take off you pants, please," the doctor says, and he thoroughly checks the patient.

"Everything is normal, sir," he concludes after the examination. "You're perfectly normal. I have found only two."

"Well, I would like to get a second opinion, doctor," the man persists.

"Okay, I can ask one of my colleagues who's working here today to take a look at you as well," the doctor shrugs.

"Yes, please. I'd like to do that," the patient continues.

When the second doctor likewise finds no abnormalities, Ivan thanks them both and, satisfied with the tests results, leaves the clinic.

Outside, he runs into his friend, who asks him about the purpose of his trip to the clinic.

"Well, I had some free time," Ivan explains, "so I decided to go to the clinic to get my balls scratched!"

A man walks into a psychiatrist's office, sits down, and starts to stuff his nose with pipe tobacco. The doctor takes a long look at him and says, "I guess, you're in the right place, sir."

"Oh...you've got a light?!"

"Doctor, I have pain here, here, and here!"

"What about here?"

"No, there's no pain there."

"Nurse, could you please bring me a hammer?"

𝐀 man walks into a pharmacy and asks for one condom of the largest available size. The pharmacist reaches for the largest size they have.

"No, I need a *really* large one! I'm going to a costume party and I want to make a point about safe sex. So I want to dress up as a penis."

"You want to look like a penis, huh?" the pharmacist, a middle-aged man, says, staring at his customer for a few moments. Then he says in a fatherly voice, "Then why don't you just straighten your tie and go as you are? That should do it."

𝐀 man is sitting in a pothole alongside a sidewalk, talking to himself. "Marx died, Lenin died, Brezhnev died, now it's my turn…".

𝐀 patient in a mental institution complains to his doctor:

"Doctor, you've got to move that crazy man from my room. Every night he puts a piss-pot on his head and says that he's a night lamp!"

"Well, why does that bother you?" the doctor asks.

"I can't sleep with the lights on, doc!"

𝐀 loony shows a blank sheet of paper to his doctor and says, "Do you see a cow grazing on the grass here, doctor?"

"No, I can't see any grass."

"Well, the cow just ate it."

"Then, where's the cow?"

"Well, since there's no more grass left, the cow left."

𝐀 man visits a circus for an interview with the ringmaster:

"I'd like to perform here with my own number," he says.

"And what is your number?" the ringmaster asks.

"Well, it's very simple. All you need to do is to attach a big bag of shit up there on the ceiling. Then you announce my number and shoot the bag with your cannon. Now just imagine: The scene is covered in shit, the orchestra is covered in shit, the audience is covered in shit, everything is covered in shit... and then I appear out of nowhere, dressed in my impeccable white suit!"

A man comes home unexpectedly and finds a strange man in his bed. The man of the house casually walks over to the closet, pulls his wife out of it, and says to her, "How many times do I have to tell you—you have to hide *him*, not yourself!"

A dwarf says to a saleswoman, "I'd like to buy a half ounce of this cheese."

"Oh boy," the woman says, "I hope you won't eat it all at once."

"Stop mocking me, lady!" the dwarf says, "Or I'll ask you to slice it for me!"

A student walks into his neighbor's room in a dormitory to borrow a cigarette. He sees his neighbor sitting in his room naked except for a necktie. "Why are you naked?" he asks.

"Well, I didn't expect any visitors."

"Why are you wearing the tie?"

"Well, you never know for sure who may drop in."

Flying over two men walking in a park, a crow discharges a drop, which hits one of them. The man turns to the other man and asks, "Do you have any paper?"

"What for? The bird is gone."

A cow swims down a river. A horse, drinking from the

shore, asks her, "Where are you going, Cow?"

"To Africa," the cow replies.

"You're going the wrong way," the horse says.

"Well, it doesn't matter," says the cow. "I'm not going to make it anyway…".

*A*n elderly lady sits in a pothole alongside a sidewalk, murmuring the same phrase over and over again: "I've lost it! I've lost it!…".

A passerby stops to give her a hand. "What is it that you have lost?" he asks the lady.

"My balance," the lady answers. "I've lost my balance!"

A man goes to see a sex therapist:

"Tell me, doctor," he says, "what if there's an erection, but no ejaculation?"

"Well, that happens," the doctor replies.

"And what if there's an ejaculation, but no erection?"

"That would be very unusual," the doctor explains.

"And what if there's an erection and ejaculation?"

"That would be perfectly normal."

"Then what if there's no erection and no ejaculation?"

This time the doctor says, "Excuse me, sir, but what exactly is it that you're here for?"

"Well, I simply like the sound of these words—erection, ejaculation. What about you, doctor?"

A young writer complains to his father that he can't come up with a title for his new book. Without even bothering himself about reading his son's book the father says, "Tell me, son, do you mention any drums in your book?"

"No," the writer replies.

"How about a whistle? Are there any whistles?"

"No. There are no drums or whistles."

"Well, in that case, we have the title: Without Drums and Whistles."

𝐀 woman climbs into a taxi:

"Where are you going, madam?" the driver asks her.

"That's my business!" she rebukes.

𝐀 barber visits the patent office with what he believes is a great invention. He says to an officer, "This is a revolutionary shaving machine! All you have to do is to put your head inside and push this button. The machine has six blades, designed for a close and comfortable shave…".

"But everyone's head is different in size and shape," the officer says.

"Yes, but that's only for the first time he uses this machine!" the inventor explains.

"𝐋et me pound a nail into your head with this hammer, would you?"

"No way! What if you were to miss the nail?!"

𝐀 woman is walking in a desert. To combat the heat she takes off her clothes. Wearing only her underwear, she soon sees a man approaching her. The man is dressed in a three-piece suit and tie, and he's carrying a car door under his arm.

"Where are you going?" she asks him.

"Home," he says.

"You're not hot in that suit?"

"No, don't you see? I keep my window down."

𝐓wo o'clock in the morning; a sleepy man gets out of bed to answer the phone:

"Yes?" he murmurs.

"Is this a stadium?" a voice at the other end asks.

"No! Are you nuts?"

"No? Then why are you standing there in boxing shorts?"

A knight is riding his horse through thick woods. All of a sudden, he sees a big palace ahead of him, all covered with shit. He enters the outer gates and notices that *everything* is covered with shit. He enters the palace, looks around, and sees nothing but shit.

Then he enters a room and there he sees a princess, covered with shit from her toes to her ears. She is playing a piano, which is also covered with a thick layer of shit.

The knight introduces himself to the princess and says, "Could you please show me to the bathroom?"

A bald man is walking in the middle of a desert when, all of a sudden, someone hiding around a corner grabs his hair, pounds him against the icy ground, and then disappears into the elevator.

In an old log cabin in a hick village, a very old couple sits at their table, quietly eating porridge with traditional Russian wooden spoons.

Suddenly, the man starts shaking. He licks his spoon clean, and hits the woman on the forehead with the spoon. Says he, his voice trembling, "I still can't forgive you for the fact that you weren't a virgin…".

"**W**hat happened to you? You're so pale!"
"Well, I spent the whole day at the amusement park."
"Why the whole day?"
"They didn't have any change for my one-thousand bill."

THE PURPOSE OF LIFE
AND OTHER THOUGHTS

He would not cause much trouble while in little need.
—Another definition of a decent person

If you only could give a kick in the ass to the guy who is responsible for your problems, you would find yourself having trouble sitting down.

"**C**ould you explain to me the meaning of the word idiot?"
"Sure. An idiot is a person who cannot convey his thoughts clearly enough that people can understand him or her. Do you understand now?"
"Not really."

Q: What is life's first lie?
A: A rubber nipple.

He had no enemies. But all of his friends hated him.

Two friends are having some coffee. One of them takes a sip and says, "Life is like a cup of coffee!"
"How's that?" asks the other.
"How am I supposed to know? I am not a philosopher…".

Q: What's the difference between an optimist, a pessimist, and a realist?

A: An optimist studies English. A pessimist studies Chinese. And a realist studies the AK-47 assault rifle.

He was so smart his brain needed larger accommodation—a new skull.

Q: What is platonic love?

A: It's when you love her, but your friend Plato makes love to her.

Tomorrow will be better than the day after tomorrow!

A crow sits at the top of a tall pine tree. A rabbit runs by, sees the crow, and says, "Hey, Crow! What are you doing up there?"

The crow replies, "Nothing. I'm just sitting here."

"Can I sit down here under this tree and do nothing, just like you?"

"Sure," answers the crow.

So the rabbit sits under the tree and, soon enough, he falls asleep. A hungry fox runs by. Spotting the sleeping rabbit, he eats him…

As she's watching the fox eating the rabbit, the crow thinks to herself, "Well, I guess I forgot to tell Rabbit that only he who's at the top can sit and do nothing."

Life is a sexually transmitted lethal disease.

Q: Can you buy an honest person?

A: No. But you can sell him.

Work turns a monkey into a man, and woman into a horse.

Fight for peace is like sex for virginity.

Q: Will there be a third world war?
A: No, but the fight for peace will leave no stone unturned.

Remember: You can't have a stroke if you don't have a heart.

"I hate them all!"
"Nobody likes them *all* anyway!"

Two drunks are having few drinks in the park:
"Ivan, can you explain to me, what is logic?"
"Well, Sergei," the other says after a short pause, "you see those two men walking down the street? One of them is clean, and the other has dirty hands and face. Now, which one of them do you think is going to a *banya*?" (a Russian public bathhouse)
"I think the dirty one!" Sergei says.
"Correct! He needs a wash; therefore, he's going to a banya. This is what is called logic."
The drunks have another drink.
"Okay, Ivan," Sergei asks again. "Tell me, how would you define dialectic?"
"Well… see those two men walking down the street? One of them is clean, and the other has dirty hands and face. Now, which one of them do you think is going to a banya?"
"Logically, the dirty one."
"No, you're wrong. The very fact that he is dirty tells us that he's less likely to be seen in a banya. Therefore, the man who is going to the banya is the clean one. This is called dialectic."
After few more drinks, Sergei asks Ivan one more question.
"If you're that smart, Ivan, then tell me, what is philosophy?"
"See those two men walking down the street? One of them is clean, and the other has dirty hands and face. Which one of them do you think is going to a banya?"

"I don't know... Now I'm confused!"
"And that, my friend, is philosophy!"

He who laughs last didn't get it at first.

It's better to be laughed at than to be cried over.

A pessimist says, "It's going to get even worse!"
An optimist says, "No, it cannot get any worse than this!"

Q: What's the difference between a pessimist and an optimist?

A: A pessimist is an experienced optimist. An optimist is a well-educated pessimist.

The more he looked into the mirror the more he believed in Darwin.

"Unbelievable...look!" one pessimist says to another. "I dropped my sandwich and it fell buttered side up!"

"Let me see it," the other says. "No, sir, you just put your butter on the wrong side!"

God informs the people that they have only three days left before the next great flood.

An Orthodox priest gathers his congregation and says, "Brothers and sisters! Let's party these three days as we never have! Let's not waste a drop of our best vodka!"

A Muslim imam declares in his mosque, "Since our days are now numbered, let's taste pork!"

A Jewish rabbi calls his people into the synagogue and says, "Brothers and sisters, we have only three days to learn how to live underwater!"

He was so old that even to sin was too late for him.

A second marriage is a triumph of hope over experience.

When an overcrowded bus makes a sharp turn a young woman, who has been standing on her feet, loses her balance and plunges into the laps of an Orthodox priest sitting in front of her.

"Wow!" she exclaims, feeling a huge lump under her behind.

"That is not a 'wow', my daughter," the priest frowns. "It's the church key!"

If a bottle looks half-full, you're sober. If a bottle looks half-empty, you're drunk.

Two cars, one driven by an orthodox priest and the other by a rabbi, have collided. Both clergymen climb out only to see their cars smashed.

"God gave, God took," the priest says.

"Easy comes, easy goes," the rabbi says. And he reaches into his car and takes out a bottle of vodka. "Well," he continues, "let's have a drink to calm ourselves down."

The priest pours some vodka into a glass. Handing it to the rabbi, he says, "You drink first."

"No, no," the rabbi insists, "after you."

The priest drinks and then he pours some more vodka for the rabbi. "Thanks anyway," the rabbi says, "but I'd better wait for the police…".

A woman is giving her confession:

"I've slept with many men, father," she admits.

"How many, my daughter?" the priest asks her.

"Well, father," the woman blushes, "I thought I came here to redeem, not to brag."

If you can't live with someone you love, love someone you live with.

The priest is a passenger onboard an aircraft. As soon as the plane is in the air, he calls a stewardess over and asks her about the plane's altitude.

"Fifty-five hundred feet, father," the stewardess replies after checking with the pilot.

"Could I have some cognac, please?" the priest asks.

Half an hour later, the priest inquires about the altitude again. This time he asks, "Then may I have some wine, please?"

Another half hour goes by, and he calls the stewardess to ask about the plane's altitude once more.

"Thirty-five thousand feet, father," she reports.

"Could I have a soft drink, please?" the priest requests.

The stewardess brings the drink and asks, "No more alcohol, father?"

"No, I'm too close to the boss now!"

How low one has to fall to get high.

There once was an orthodox priest who, for some unknown reason, turned into a devotee of Bacchus.

Coming home heavily inebriated one evening, he saw his wife praying and asking God to put her husband back on the path of the righteous. The priest walked briskly up to his wife and gave her a good slap.

"What was that for?" she protested.

"Don't snitch on me to my boss!"

One hot and dry summer, a group of farmers came to their priest with a request to ask god for some rain.

But the priest just glared at them and said, "God will not help you!"

"Why not, father?" the farmers asked, surprised.

"Because you don't believe in him," the priest explained. "For if you did, you'd have come with your umbrellas!"

"Ivan, how are you?"

"Like a Tampax: Right place, wrong time."

EPILOGUE

"Do you have any new jokes?"
"Nope."
"Me neither… what a life!"

ORDER FORM

A good book is the best gift of all.

--Russian saying

Five easy ways to order *The Best of Russian Humor*:

1. On Line via our secure server at: www.russian-humor.com
2. Fill out this form and fax it to: (519)-679-9009
3. E-mail to: orders@russian-humor.com
4. Have your credit card ready and call us toll free at: 1-877-390-4008
5. Mail completed order form along with your check or money order to:
   Russian Doll Publishing P.O.Box 25384, London, Ontario N6C 6B1

First edition special:

*Order now and we'll pay for shipping and handling**

*Offer valid in the US and Canada only

❏Yes, I want_____copies of *The Best of Russian Humor* at $US 16.95 each (Canadian residents please add $US 1.19 GST per book) ~~plus $US 4.00 shipping per book.~~

International orders: please add $US 10.00 shipping per book.

Please allow 7 days (14 days international) for delivery

We also accept checks or money orders in Canadian funds. You pay only $CAD 24.95 for each book (Canadian residents please add $CAD 1.75 GST per book).

❏My check or money order for $_____is enclosed.

Please charge my ❏**Visa** ❏**MasterCard**

Name: _____

Address: _____

_____Apartment:_____

City: _____ State/Prov: _____

Country/ Zip /Postal Code: _____

Phone: _____e-mail: _____

Card number: _____

Name on card:_____

Exp. date: _____ Signature: _____

ORDER FORM

A good book is the best gift of all.
--Russian saying

Five easy ways to order *The Best of Russian Humor*:

1. On Line via our secure server at: www.russian-humor.com
2. Fill out this form and fax it to: (519)-679-9009
3. E-mail to: orders@russian-humor.com
4. Have your credit card ready and call us toll free at: 1-877-390-4008
5. Mail completed order form along with your check or money order to:
   Russian Doll Publishing P.O.Box 25384, London, Ontario N6C 6B1

> *First edition special:*
> *Order now and we'll pay for shipping and handling**
> *Offer valid in the US and Canada only

❑Yes, I want_____copies of *The Best of Russian Humor* at $US 16.95
each (Canadian residents please add $US 1.19 GST per book) ~~plus~~
~~$US 4.00 shipping per book.~~
International orders: please add $US 10.00 shipping per book.
Please allow 7 days (14 days international) for delivery

We also accept checks or money orders in Canadian funds. You pay only $CAD 24.95
for each book (Canadian residents please add $CAD 1.75 GST per book).

❑My check or money order for $_____is enclosed.
Please charge my ❑**Visa** ❑**MasterCard**

Name: _____

Address: _____

_____Apartment:_____

City: _____ State/Prov: _____

Country/ Zip /Postal Code: _____

Phone: _____e-mail: _____

Card number: _____

Name on card:_____

Exp. date: _____ Signature: _____